Managing Software
Development Projects
Formula for Success

Neal Whitten

WILEY

John Wiley & Sons, Inc.

New York • Chichester • Brisbane • Toronto • Singapore

Quote by Frederick P. Brooks, Jr., appearing on page 141, is reprinted with permission from
The Mythical Man-Month, © 1975, Addison-Wesley Publishing Co, Reading, Mass
chusetts. Quotes by Dr. Wayne Dyer, appearing on pages 36 and 39, are © Wayne Dyer, Ph
with permission of ® Listen & Learn USA! Quotes by Thomas J. Watson Jr., appearing o
pages 112 and 145, are reprinted with permission from *A Business and Its Beliefs: The Idea
that Helped Build IBM*, © 1963, McGraw-Hill Book Company, Inc. Quote by Philip
Crosby, appearing on page 103, is reprinted with permission from *Quality is Free: The A
of Making Quality Certain*, © 1979, McGraw-Hill Book Company, Inc.

Library of Congress Cataloging-in-Publication Data

Whitten, Neal.
    Managing software development projects : formula for success /
Neal Whitten.
        Includes bibliographical references.
        ISBN 0-471-51255-9
        1. Computer software--Development--Management.   I. Title
    QA76.76.D47W49   1989   89-167
    005.1'068--dc20   C

Printed in the United States of America
  91 10 9 8 7 6 5

*To
Matt and Jenny,
and Barbara*

Preface

Your software development project can be likened to a time bomb—ticking, ticking, ticking away. The race is on to see which happens first: A quality product is delivered on-time and within budget; or the time bomb goes off with cost overruns, missed delivery dates, and questionable product quality.

The roadmap that you choose to follow for your software development project depends on the decisions that you make *today*, for it is these decisions that will determine *tomorrow*. When problems are introduced early in a project and you are unable to recognize or deal with them, you risk it all. The need to succeed in a world that grows more competitive each day leaves you looking for an edge that will reduce your risks—a **Formula For Success**. This book offers that edge, and can save you money, time, and resources.

The wealth of information in *Managing Software Development Projects: Formula for Success* might very well cause you to change something about your current or next software development project. This book identifies the most common problems that plague software projects, and presents approaches to address and, in some cases, prevent these problems from taking root in your project.

Software development problems cover all corners of a project's life, from its people to its processes to its specific activities. The major problem-prone areas discussed in this book are:

- Project Discipline
- People Communications
- Schedules
- Quality
- Tracking
- Managing Priorities
- Product Objectives
- Product Specifications
- Product Ease of Use
- Informal Testing
- Project Reviews

A full chapter is dedicated to each problem-prone area. Each chapter begins with one or more revealing stories to show how the problem can be traced through a project and its people. Then a recovery or avoidance approach is recommended.

This book is for you if you are:

- Planning to start a new programming project
- Leading, or aspiring to lead, a programming project
- Reviewing or auditing a programming project
- Defining or implementing a programming process
- Just plain interested in understanding and avoiding some of the more common obstacles that result in schedule slips, low product quality, and cost overruns

This is the book I wish I could have had during the years I spent learning the hard way. Experienced software project managers, project leaders, and project personnel will quickly relate to these common, but costly, project mistakes. Those less experienced will have the opportunity to learn from the misfortunes of others and, I hope, will be able to avoid repeating history. A legion of us have learned from these errors the hard way—by making them.

Vigorous competition and accelerating technological changes continue to demand shorter software development cycles. The challenge, however, is not only to develop products and distribute them to their markets *faster*, but also to produce products of increasingly *higher quality* at *lower costs*. By applying the hard-earned experience in this book, you can help yourself meet these challenges head-on. It is my objective that your investment in acquiring this book and in learning about and using its recommendations will be rewarded many, many times over on your current or next project.

Neal Whitten

Acknowledgments

I am grateful for the opportunities that the IBM Corporation has provided me over the years. It has been a rich and fertile arena for learning and growing alongside many talented and dedicated people, both inside and outside IBM. The views and opinions expressed in this book, although influenced by my work at IBM and association with others in the software field, are mine alone and do not necessarily represent the opinions and views of IBM or any other company or person.

I am deeply appreciative of the many reviewers and supporters who helped make this a better book than it otherwise would have been. I would first like to thank the following management personnel at IBM for their understanding and support throughout the manuscript development and preparation of this book:

Neil Eastman, Judy Fleming, Bob Manente, and Phil Zeiss

I am especially grateful to the following people for their dedicated, candid, and helpful input from review drafts of the manuscript:

Judy Fleming, Randy Forlenza, Wendy Miller, and Bob Rosenman

I would also like to thank the following people for their respective comments, suggestions, and/or support as the manuscript was evolving toward the final product:

Dick Berry, Nicole Bianco, Irene Dallas, Glen Hamblin, Clark Jokl, Don Navara, Linda Nix, Barbara Odle, Mary Ann Scope, Bob Spaulding, Ron Spriggs, Mike Traynor, Bob Williams, Marie Wolfe, and Lisa Wright.

And finally I am particularly grateful to Therese Zak and the highly professional staff at John Wiley & Sons for their invaluable guidance during manuscript editing and production. I would especially like to acknowledge the special contributions of Ruth Greif, Ron Pronk, and Laura Lewin.

Comments From You

If you have suggestions, corrections, or clarifications to this text, please feel encouraged to send them to me at the following address:

Neal Whitten
P.O. Box 276282
Boca Raton, Fl, 33427-6282

I cannot promise to reply individually to all comments; however, I will personally read all comments and appreciate the opportunity to hear from you. Thank you.

* * *

Read on, and enjoy, to better ensure that your project's well-being starts, continues, and ends in the best of health.

Contents

Introduction

I have always had a special interest in learning why some software development projects and project leaders are more successful than others. It seems to me that the value of a project leader is largely a function of how well that person manages to stay in control. Over the years, I have observed that the most successful project managers, project leaders, and project members seem to do things and work with people in similar ways. Conversely, those projects that develop the most difficulties and generate the most waste, and those people who seem to demonstrate the least amount of control, also seem to exhibit common traits. As a software development manager or project leader for over fifteen years, I have had many opportunities to apply several project management techniques and to observe their effectiveness. Some techniques have proven to be effective, while others clearly should be avoided.

It has concerned me that many of the most important lessons to be learned in a software development project take *so* long to learn! And while project personnel, managers, and nonmanagers alike struggle to recognize and comprehend these lessons, a heavy tax is being paid. This tax is levied against the product's users, the company and its people. It is felt in the form of lost revenues from extended project schedules, lower product quality and ease of use, and higher product expenses. It is felt by the countless project players who, over the years, have dedicated countless *long* days, often filled with frustration and doubt, in an attempt to produce successful products and to be part of a winning team, but who often run more on enthusiasm and hope than on anything else. The ultimate cost: loss of jobs due to cancelled projects and unsuccessful products. Everybody loses!

Knowledge about project management is usually acquired through the on-the-job classroom—a miserably inefficient way to learn such high stakes lessons. Some managers, project leaders, and other project members, for a multitude of reasons, will never learn as long as this job environment continues to be defect-riddled from one project to the next.

The purpose of this book is to share with you those principles and techniques that I feel are important to know about software development projects. It is my hope that others in the software development arena can benefit from this knowledge and experience much earlier in their careers than their current situation or process would naturally allow. Once you understand the most common problems that, time and again, plague software development projects and are shown how to recover from these costly problems, you will be armed with knowledge that can save you time, resources, and money. Whether you are a manager, project leader, or a member of a project, this book has timely and useful information to help you *today* on your current project and to prepare you for *tomorrow's* projects. Read on to learn how you can immediately begin to apply this information so it will work for you.

Identify the Problem and the Solution

People cannot effectively control what they do not understand. Therefore, the first goal of this book is to identify the most common problems found in software development projects. From your own varied experiences, you might have one or more major problems that you would add to the list. However, I trust that the problems I have chosen will also strike home in your neck of the woods. Interestingly, these problems have not changed appreciably over the years, nor do I expect them to change significantly over the next few years.

You might expect many of the problems mentioned in this chapter to be quickly apparent to a project's members. However, most of these problems will slowly infect a project rather than suddenly and recognizably appear one day. Moreover, projects in trouble often appear to be under control at any given time. Therefore, being able to recognize problems is an important first step. Since readers of this book have diverse backgrounds, I have tried to define problems as broadly and generically as I can so that they will be easily recognizable to the widest possible audience.

After a problem is identified, the next step is to understand what to do to recover from the problem—and then do it. Here again, I have attempted to be as specific as possible for such a broad audience. I have defined the recovery approach at a level of detail that will allow readers to understand how to apply the "fix" to their own projects. However, I do not provide 100 percent of the detail to, say, write a product specifications document or a test plan document. Since detailed activities and processes vary widely from company to company and from project to project, I have intentionally restrained from providing the "gnat's eyelash" level of detail. To do so would presume that the very detailed level of information I present would or could be adaptable to all projects. Instead, as an aid, I have included a bibliography at the end of the book. The bibliography refers you to sources that provide an assortment of detailed approaches—should you desire additional information. Also, each reference identifies the chapter(s) with which it is associated.

I believe the greatest value of this book is that it introduces the reader to the "big ticket" project problems and recommends a recovery or avoidance approach for each problem. But it does not get bogged down in so much detail that the reader is overtaxed with reading material. *Managing Software Development Projects: Formula for Success* moves to the heart of problems in quick fashion.

Book Organization—And the Three-Legged Stool

Each major problem revealed in this book can be associated with one of three primary elements of a software development project:

- People
- Processes
- Activities

People

The first element deals primarily with interrelationships among project personnel. These relationships may be among managers, between managers and nonmanagers, or among nonmanagers. Introspection and self-assessment for the leader is also included in this category. The people aspects of software development projects often receive secondary priority, yet deserve and require primary attention.

Processes

A **process** is defined as the manner in which a software development project, or any of its many integral parts, is planned, developed, or tracked. For example, the method of logging a problem, and tracking that problem to a satisfactory closure, is defined by a process. Another process example is the manner chosen to discover and remove defects as a product is being developed.

Activities

An **activity** is a defined portion of work within a project that typically has a designated owner, entry/implementation/exit requirements, duration, and schedules. Examples of an activity are developing the product specifications document, creating the high-level design, coding, and performing the system test.

Figure I.1 illustrates the logical book layout and shows the three elements with their corresponding problem-prone areas—one major problem theme per chapter. This figure also shows the number of the chapter in which each topic is discussed. **Post-project review** is not aligned into one of the three primary elements because it spans all three.

These three elements can be likened to the legs of a three-legged stool. If any of the legs are shaky, so also is the health of the project. For this reason, I have chosen to include the most common problems from *all* these elements. Arming yourself with the knowledge to repair and strengthen only one or two legs of a three-legged stool can undermine the operating potential of the stool, or in this case the project.

The following brief sections describe the major problem that each chapter covers. As you read these chapters, you will find that they also identify numerous lesser problems that are related to the chapter's major problem theme.

Chapter 1
A Product Development Cycle Overview

To benefit fully from the knowledge contained in this book, it is helpful to understand the basic concepts and terms used. This chapter presents

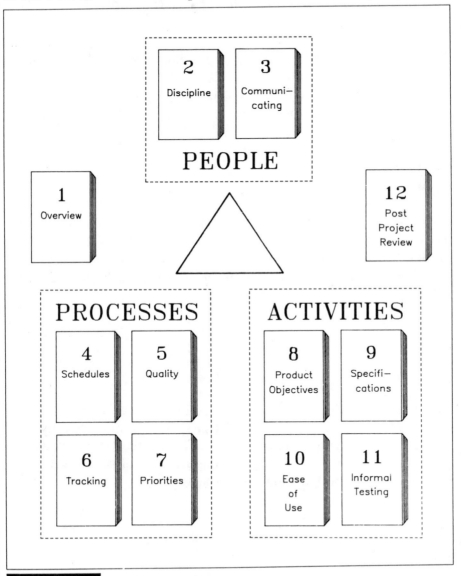

Figure I.1. The three primary elements of software development projects and the chapters that discuss their most common problems

an overview of the product development cycle and introduces you to the concepts and terms that will be referenced in subsequent chapters.

Chapter 2
Discipline: The Glue that Holds It All Together

The single greatest factor that can make or break a software development project is the degree of discipline exercised by the project leadership. This chapter discusses the need for discipline and explains how to recognize and develop a disciplined organization. It also presents the attributes of the successful leader.

Chapter 3
Communicating in Harmony

Poor communications among people within a project is one of the most common obstacles to overcome in a software development project. This chapter explains how to improve communications among project players by recognizing that the dignity and value of each individual are central to the success of an enterprise.

Chapter 4
Scheduling for Success

Creating an unachievable project schedule plan can have a domino effect that eventually topples a project, as one scheduled activity after another fails to be completed as planned. The heartbeat of a project *is* the project schedule plan. This chapter describes an effective method to follow in laying out schedules for your project.

Chapter 5
Planning for Quality

Because many people believe that the delivered quality of a product is not really definable or measurable, often too little attention is focused on the quality of a product early in the product development cycle. This chapter dispels these myths and explains how to plan early to attain the desired level of quality for your product.

Chapter 6
Project Tracking Made Easy

Tracking project status is often too little and too late to be truly effective. This chapter explains how to implement a tracking process that can identify potential problems before they happen and how to establish recovery plans before unrecoverable harm can occur.

Chapter 7
Managing Priorities Effectively

There are always problems in a software development project that are crucial to solve—but don't get the urgent attention they deserve. This chapter shows you how to identify, and stay abreast of, project priorities.

Chapter 8
Product Objectives: Providing Direction

Incomplete and unapproved product objectives can result in several major restarts for the project and an aftermath of throwaway work, slipped schedules, increased costs, poor communications across the project, and frustrated participants. This chapter defines project objectives and explains how to set the product's direction early in the product development cycle.

Chapter 9
Product Specifications: Defining the Final Product

Creeping function is the act of continually adding function enhancements to a product throughout the product development cycle. Each unplanned change in the product's function brings the project a step closer to failing. This chapter shows you what to do to describe, in detail, the total product early in the development cycle. It also explains how to define and implement an orderly process to follow when a function change must later be made to the product.

Chapter 10
Product Ease of Use

The competitive edge for many products today is the degree of user friendliness that they offer. However, this ease-of-use attribute is more often an afterthought, rather than an activity that receives early attention in the product development cycle. This chapter explains how to make ease of use a planned and basic function of a product early in the product development cycle.

Although ease of use, as a general topic, is not a single activity, I have included its discussion in the **activities** category because its implementation is spread across a specific set of activities.

Chapter 11
Informal Testing: Strengthening the Weak Link

This chapter exposes the weak link in the product development cycle, called *informal testing* (also called *unit* and *function test*). This chapter explains how to anticipate and plan for informal testing, and how you can monitor progress during this important, but elusive, period.

Chapter 12
Post-Project Review: Understanding the Past to Improve the Future

It is common to repeat the same mistakes from project to project. This chapter explains how you can learn from your past mistakes and demonstrates how to apply this knowledge to your current or next project.

Chapter Organization

Each chapter focuses on a specific major, but common, problem encountered in software development projects. Each chapter also is designed to stand on its own. This format allows you to zero-in and concentrate on the problems and, consequently, the chapters that most interest you.

Each chapter is laid out in the same manner. Figure I.2 illustrates this layout. A chapter opens with a brief summary statement of a problem. One or more scenarios then follow to illustrate how the problem can typically appear within a project. For chapters that relate to **processes** or **activities**, the scenarios also show how the problem gradually takes root within a project and can grow out of control.

The problem scenarios do not describe actual projects. They have been created as an instructional aid to help you understand and recognize the warning signals that typically accompany the intrusion of these problems into a software development project. The remainder of each chapter offers step-by-step recommendations to follow in your own project. These steps will explain how you can avoid or recover from the topic problem.

Once you have read an entire chapter, you may find it helpful to revisit the scenarios and to anticipate how each problem could be confronted through each phase of the scenario. These scenarios can also

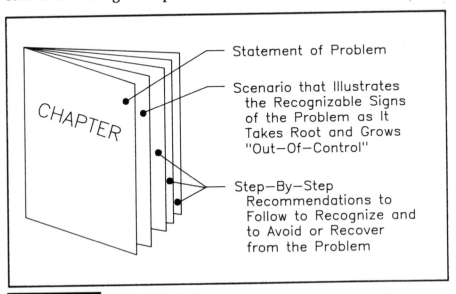

Figure I.2. Organization for each chapter

be valuable as *case studies* to be evaluated by a group of people. You may even want to add your own case studies.

Before you skip to later chapters, you might find it helpful to read Chapter 1. This overview material defines many of the concepts and terms that will be referenced in subsequent chapters. You will also find a glossary of terms at the end of the book for quick reference.

1

A Product Development Cycle

This chapter provides a brief overview of a typical software development cycle. You might find it helpful to read this material before proceeding to the chapters that follow. This overview defines many of the concepts and terms that will be referenced in subsequent chapters.

There are many ways to organize a software project. The factors, or characteristics, that influence the organizational approach include such variables as:

- Number of people involved in the project
- Experience and skill level of the participants
- Technical complexity of the product
- Degree of new technology required
- Total lines of code to be developed
- Number of products involved
- Languages used to write the code
- Availability of both product- and project-related tools
- Proximity of the people to one another
- Number of locations and companies involved
- Single or multiple customers

The organization chosen for a five-person project will be significantly different from that for a project of 500 persons. However, regardless of the size of the project and the organization chosen, there is a sequence of major activities that, if followed, can greatly reduce the problems that often plague a software project. These activities are shown in Figure 1.1. They range from providing product objectives to performing the final regression test just prior to packaging the product and delivering it to a customer. Notice that the relative relationship among the activities is shown in Figure 1.1, yet no durations are specified for any of the activities. The durations depend on the size and characteristics of the project.

The product development cycle model illustrated in Figure 1.1 is introduced here because many of the chapters to come will build upon this

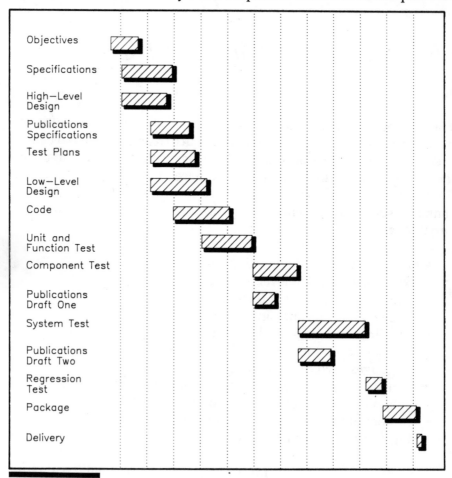

Figure 1.1. The product development cycle

model and will reinforce some of the benefits to be gained by following the model's concepts. This model was also chosen because many existing development cycle models can be mapped to it. The model should aid you in relating your personal knowledge and experiences to the concepts and ideas expressed throughout this book. However, not all project activities are shown in this model. Only the more essential activities that make up the foundation for the model are identified. Several additional activities, however, will be introduced in later chapters.

The following sections describe the primary activities of the product development cycle shown in Figure 1.1. As with any rapidly growing and changing industry, it is important to define a common terminology in order to impart knowledge and share ideas. The terminology chosen in Figure 1.1, and throughout this book, is an attempt to reach, and benefit, the broadest audience possible.

Objectives

The **product objectives** is a document that defines the requirements and operational need that must be satisfied for a new or enhanced product. This document defines a product that will satisfy a marketing opportunity and focuses on the perceived needs of the targeted customer. The product objectives document will also provide the underlying direction to be followed by the project as functional and design tradeoffs are made throughout the product development cycle. Direction for both the programming and publications pieces of the product are addressed in the product objectives. (Chapter 8 focuses on product objectives.)

Specifications

The **product specifications** describe, in detail, the **externals** of the product. That is, they describe what the product will look like to the product's user. Every function, command, screen, prompt, and so on must be documented here so that all the participants involved in the product development cycle know the product they are to build, test, document, and support. Since the product objectives provide the direction and basis for the new product, writing the product specifications should begin *after* the objectives have been started. However, the product objectives should be finalized before the product specifications are completed.

Also, the high-level design should be completed before the product specifications are finished. This helps to ensure that any high-level design considerations that could impact the externals of the product are properly reflected in the product specifications. (The product specifications is the major theme of Chapter 9.)

High-Level Design

High-level design is the level of design required to understand how the components (major pieces) of the product will technically work with one another, and with the surrounding hardware and software environment with which they must operate. This design identifies the components that make up the product, defines the functional mission for each component, and defines the interface across these components and externally to the operating environment. In some development shops, what is defined here as high-level design is called *architecture*.

The high-level design should begin shortly after the product objectives have been started. However, the high-level design should be reasonably understood before the product objectives are completed. This overlap between the development of the product objectives and the preliminary high-level design will prevent the product objectives from defining a product that could not technically be built in a satisfactory manner. There must be confidence that a high-level design supports the objectives *before* the product objectives are completed. (The relationship of the high-level design to the product objectives and to the product specifications is a topic of discussion in Chapter 9.)

Publications Specifications

The **publications specifications** may also be called a publications **content plan**. These plans describe the content and layout of each publication to be delivered with the product. Content plans include the table-of-contents for each publication and the basic content and structure of each chapter. The writing of the content plans cannot begin until the product specifications activity has been started. Otherwise, there would be too little product externals data available to plan the publications to a chapter level. Similarly, the content plans cannot be completed until *after* the product specifications have been completed.

The publications specifications document is especially important for two reasons. Both reasons center around the importance of providing information to the user in an expedient, easy-to-use, and understandable fashion. First, most products require the user to reference the publications that accompany the product. Without a good set of publications, the product will have far less chances for success.

The second reason for the importance of the publications specifications is in support of an industry direction. This direction is to provide publications-related information on-line for the product's users and to make the use of products more intuitive. On-line information—that is, the ability to access information directly from a computer workstation rather than through documents—and intuitive man-machine interfaces both require careful, advanced planning. The publications specifications document is a vehicle to help define this direction early in the product development cycle.

Test Plans

Test plans are documents that describe the *who, what, when, where,* and *how* for a designated test. A test plan is written for each test activity, such as a unit test, function test, component test, and system test. Test plans cannot be started until after the product specifications have been started. Also, the test plans cannot be finished until *after* the product specifications have been completed. Otherwise, the test plans would be incomplete, since the externals of the product would not yet be fully known and documented.

Low-Level Design

Low-level design actually represents two levels of design. The first level is the design required to understand how modules within each component will technically work with one another. (A component is typically made up of one or more modules.) This design identifies the modules that make up each component, the functional mission for each module, and the interface across these modules. (In some development shops, this level of design is called *high-level design*, not to be confused with the same term introduced earlier and used throughout this book.)

The next level of design deals with the internal design of each module of a component. This design identifies each programming decision path and may be documented by using a design language, graphic flows, and so on, or simply by writing English narratives. There is no requirement to complete all high-level design before low-level design can be started. Notice from Figure 1.1 that some overlap of low-level design activity and high-level design is typical. Once the high-level design has been completed for a component or a major portion of a component, the low-level design can begin on the modules for that portion.

Code

Coding is the act of writing instructions that are immediately computer recognizable or can be assembled or compiled to form computer-recognizable instructions. Coding can begin on those areas of components (e.g., modules) that have already been designed to a low level. Consequently, as shown in Figure 1.1, a large overlap can occur within a project between the coding activity and the low-level design activity.

Unit and Function Test

The **unit test** is the first time that the code is executed. Unit testing is usually performed by the same person who designed and coded the module to be tested. The unit test primarily refers to the isolated testing of each logic flowpath of code within each module. The **function test** is the testing of each of the product's functions through one or more modules. In both cases, artificial testing environments (called scaffolding) may be necessary since other modules of the product may not be sufficiently far enough along in their development to be included in the testing.

Since there is no requirement to finish all coding before unit testing can begin, an overlap is shown (Figure 1.1) between the coding activity and the unit and function test activity. That is, once a module has been coded, it can begin to be unit tested. Once all the modules required to test a function have been unit tested, they can begin to be function tested. The relative time period for unit and function testing shown in Figure 1.1 represents the period when testing occurs. The test cases to be used must, of course, be defined and written before this test period begins, or at least before those test cases are required. (Chapter 11 will focus upon unit and function testing.)

Component Test

The **component test** is the first test of a product in which all or some of the components are tested together. Typically, no artificial testing environment (scaffolding) is required. This independent, or *formal*, test is best performed by people other than those who developed the code. When a product is tested by an independent test group, the objectivity of the test increases. All the product's externals should be tested. The tests are developed primarily by studying the product specifications. Occasionally, the design documentation is also studied to gain more insight into areas to be tested. The component test is typically the first time that all of the product's modules are placed under **change control**. This term refers to a method designed to restrict further changes to a module. Change control is managed by a group that did not develop the code.

Figure 1.1 shows that component testing does not begin until all of the unit and function tests have been completed successfully. Some project managers may choose to integrate unit- or function-tested code into the component test in preplanned *drops*, or stages. The relative time period for component testing shown in Figure 1.1 represents the period when testing occurs. All the test cases to be exercised during component testing should be defined and written prior to the start of the component test, or at least before those test cases are required to be exercised.

Publications Draft One

Publications draft one is the first draft of the product's publications that is available for review by groups within the project. The product's publications are primarily the documentation that the user will receive with the product, and are also called *user documentation*. However, the product's publications can also include technical manuals that explain how to solve problems discovered by the user. The publications draft one should be available at, or near, the start of component testing—both for review by the project's personnel and for use by the testing organization. It should be essentially complete and accurate. Comments should be returned to the writers by the midpoint of the component test. This will help ensure that updates will be available for the final draft at the start of system testing. The duration shown in Figure 1.1 covers only the period when the first draft is distributed for review. The actual writing of the first draft can begin once the publications specifications have been completed.

System Test

The **system test** is an independent, or formal, test performed by programmers who did not develop the code. It is also performed by test subjects that represent *typical* users for the product. A system test generally tests the major functions of the product and some error situations. This testing is performed strictly by exercising the externals defined at a user level in the product specifications. Functions and interfaces internal to the product are not directly tested. These internals are only indirectly tested by exercising the externally documented functions.

During system testing, the product is also tested in a *total systems environment* with other software and hardware product combinations that are supported by the product. For example, if the product being developed is an application that must run on several different display screens and printers, then it is advisable to test the new product with all of the stated hardware. Sometimes, however, a reasonable subset may be acceptable. This applies similarly to software products. That is, if the new product must also operate in harmony with other applications, or even with different release levels of an operating system, then these product combinations would also be tested during the system test.

System testing does not begin until the component test has been completed. The product is expected to be approaching a *customer-delivery* quality level when this test begins. However, some project managers may choose to integrate component-tested code into the system test in pre-planned drops, or stages. The relative time for system testing shown in Figure 1.1 represents the period when testing occurs. All the test cases to be exercised during system testing should be defined and written prior to the start of the system test, or at least before those test cases are required for testing.

Publications Draft Two

Publications draft two is the second draft of the publications. As with the first draft, the duration shown in Figure 1.1 covers only the period when the draft is distributed for review. The activities associated with the second draft actually begin immediately after the comments are available from reviewers of the first draft, and end when the final publications are ready for the final print. For most products, the second draft will be the final draft that is distributed for review. It should be available at the beginning of the system test—both for review and for use in the final testing of the product. Comments should be returned to the writers by the midpoint of system testing so that final changes can be made before the publications are printed. The final print of the publications should not be initiated, however, until all product testing has been completed. If product testing continues, a strong possibility exists that a problem will surface, requiring a change to the publications as part of the problem resolution.

Regression Test

The **regression test** is the final test of the product. This test typically is comprised of a carefully selected set of test cases that are run against the final level of code and supported hardware. These test cases are run as a final verification that the product's code is indeed functioning as it should. Regression testing should not begin until the system test has been completed. The test cases for regression testing typically consist of selected cases from both the component and the systems tests. If a problem is found during regression testing, the problem is corrected and, with few exceptions, the entire set of regression test cases are rerun. Restarting the regression test from the beginning provides verification that the problem did indeed get fixed and that the fix did not cause a new problem.

Package

Packaging involves collecting the pieces of the product (e.g., code and publications) for delivery to a customer. Once all testing and publications changes have been completed, the code and publications are ready to be packaged in their final form. The product's programs are placed on media (e.g., diskettes or magnetic tape), and the product's publications are formally printed. Then the pieces are packaged in their final *wrap* and readied for delivery.

Delivery

Delivery is the point at which the packaged product is ready for distribution to the customer. The customer may be the product's user, a distributor, or a third party that will repackage the product in some fashion for eventual resale.

*   *   *

Now you are ready to gain maximum benefit from the chapters that follow. When new terms are introduced, they will be defined. The primary goal is to keep you in a strong posture to understand and learn. I hope you will find that this book works for you.

2

Discipline:
The Glue that Holds It All Together

All leaders want to run a *tight ship*, but not at the expense of their project personnel's creativity, sense of commitment and ownership, and willingness to take risks. If a leader is too strict or rigid, a too-high level of bureaucracy can evolve that actually has a stifling effect on employee productivity and motivation. On the other hand, if a leader is too permissive, a project can be robbed of the crucial management support and order that is so vital in maintaining a well-run, consistently productive organization. Somewhere, between these extremes of rigidity and permissiveness, is a desirable balance that offers the most in achieving and maintaining a healthy organization. Within this scale, where would you position your leadership abilities?

The single greatest factor that can *make* or *break* a software development project is the degree of *discipline* that the project leadership exercises. Briefly stated, *discipline is the act of encouraging a desired pattern of behavior*. Discipline is the glue that holds it all together. Most projects that do not meet their schedule, budget, or function fail because the level of discipline exhibited across the organization is deficient.

Discussions in this chapter include:

- The need for discipline
- How to recognize the disciplined organization
- Attributes of the successful leader

This chapter is primarily, but not exclusively, for the leaders in a project. These leaders might direct a team of two or an organization of one thousand, and can fit within a spectrum that includes technical, administrative, financial, and project leadership. Project leaders include both managers and nonmanagers. This chapter should also be of interest to those aspiring to be leaders.

The Discipline Follies

The short scenarios presented in this section illustrate situations to be avoided. They demonstrate situations where discipline is weak, misguided, or missing. Can you recognize the problems? Have you seen them before?

A new department has been created in a busy and expanding development organization. At the first department meeting, the manager, Ralph Nettle, looks over his employees and sets some ground rules for the operation of the department. Weeks later, those at the meeting recall that Nettle's most notable statement was: "Do as I say, not as I do."

In the meeting, Nettle announces that he will meet with employees individually to determine their role and degree of progress in the current project. He arranges to meet with each person for 30 minutes over the better part of two days. The first meeting takes 40 minutes; the next, one hour. At the end of two days, six employees have yet to be seen. He reschedules them for the next day, but finds time to meet with only one. He apologizes to the other five and reschedules again—and again. Two weeks later he has met with everyone. During each meeting, Nettle has committed to get personally involved with each employee on specific problem areas. He sets dates to get back with each of them. After one month has passed, only 50 percent of his commitments have been fulfilled.

* * *

This department manager, Matt Holstein, feels really in tune with what's going on in the project. He has been a manager for just under one year. However, Holstein is no newcomer to software development projects. He has held several leadership roles on past projects. He feels he has learned the "right" way to do things and wants the best possible performance from his department. To obtain this goal, he feels he must take an active role in all primary decisions and many lesser ones. He believes that no one in his department can do most tasks as well as he can. He also feels that no one seems to be as self-motivated as he believes they should be. If this department was a separate company, and he was to leave, he just knows that the company would fold. He acknowledges there are people in his department who have potential and he is determined to bring that potential to the surface.

As a manager, Holstein feels he is a natural leader and can guide his department to excellence in everything it does. To this end, he has defined himself as the focal point for all activities. He initiates and performs most planning exercises. He thoroughly reviews all his department's documents and deliverables before he will allow them to be distributed outside his department. He also, and just as thoroughly, reviews all documents generated by other departments that are for his department's review. He consolidates any comments from within his department and personally creates the response memo for his signature. He not only attends the more important meetings within his department, he runs them. Almost nothing happens within his department without his personal participation.

With all the care and attention he gives to his employees' assignments, Holstein cannot understand why everybody else seems unwilling or unable to make decisions on their own. He notices he is usually the only one working overtime. He does not look forward to being out of the office because, when he returns, he is sure there will be too much work to catch up on, and, possibly, to recover from.

*   *   *

A new project has just started. The staffing occurred almost immediately, with programmers transferred from other projects. The new project is small by some standards, with 20 programmers. The project leader, Erin Springer, sees an opportunity to achieve great things with this newly assembled talented crew, and proceeds to declare the schedules that must be met. These schedules are over a one-year period. The project members quickly recognize the difficulty in keeping such aggressive schedules. The generally held view is that aggressive schedules are good business as long as they are achievable. An attempt is made to put more realistic schedules in place but Springer holds firm. She states that the schedules have been committed to higher management and, therefore, must happen. Not much is known about Springer's past leadership experiences. In an attempt to be fair, the project members give her the benefit of the doubt and hope she has an "ace up her sleeve." A month passes and the new schedule is one week behind. The next month sees another week lost. At this rate, the project will be late by 25 percent of the schedule's length, yet Springer is unwilling to adjust the schedules. She attempts to compensate by mandating overtime and adding people to the project. Four months into the project, progress is more than one month behind schedule. Hope is rapidly fading that an ace will appear.

*   *   *

The project is four months old, with at least two years to go. The number of people involved in the project has grown rapidly. Several of the earlier people to come on board have been given the more critical lead roles. These people do not appear to be particularly experienced or gifted, but they are recognized as being loyal to June Pritchard, the project head. The project is proving to be a challenge in many ways, not the least of which are the technical complexity and sheer size of the project. As is to be expected with any project of this magnitude, daily problems arise and compete for attention. The people Pritchard has assigned to take the critical lead roles are having difficulty extinguishing fires as fast as they flare up. Small problems fester through neglect and grow into serious problems. Many decisions are made and then remade days or weeks later, causing much rework and consternation among the employees affected. Communication across the project is suffering severely. Commitments are being made without consulting the people who must carry out the commitments. The perception of many is that the people assigned to the more critical project roles are not qualified to handle these assignments. Pritchard discounts this notion. She asserts that the project leadership is as it should be. Her view is that the major problem lies in the large number of relatively inexperienced, uncommitted, and unmotivated employees throughout the organization.

* * *

Michelle Barret, a hard-working employee, feels frustrated. She graduated as class valedictorian from a prominent university and went on to earn, with honors, a masters degree in computer science and a minor in business. She has worked for one company since finishing college four years ago. At that time, it was her belief that two types of successful companies exist: those that hire their lead people from other companies, and those that grow and groom their leaders from within. She favored working for a company that placed a premium on developing its own people. She felt that this type of company would best prepare her for an executive position.

Barret's views about successful companies have not changed, but her views about her own company have. The lead people in this organization have done little to coach, counsel, or inspire her or any other of the project personnel. She actually feels the opposite happens. People are publicly reprimanded for taking on risks that fail. Those that complete their assignments on schedule and with superior quality are all but ignored. It is next to impossible to receive any personal recognition for a job well done. Barret regularly observes the project leaders that she works with reacting to people and situations without listening to the facts. Inconsistent decisions are commonplace. Advancement is significantly slower than is generally expected within companies in the same industry. Today, Barret has, with personal regret, submitted her resignation.

These scenarios depict situations that hurt the people involved, the project, and the company. Yet, there is action that can be taken to avoid replays of these stories and numerous others like them.

The remainder of this chapter offers some ways to recognize and maintain a properly disciplined organization and to understand the numerous benefits of such an organization. Also presented are the attributes that are characteristic of successful leaders—*self-disciplined* leaders. After you have read this chapter, you might find it useful to revisit the scenarios to identify their problems—and to determine how these problems could have been avoided.

The Need for Discipline

Discipline is the soul of an army. It makes small numbers formidable, procures success to the weak, and esteem to all.
                                                          George Washington

Everyone wants discipline. Everyone wants to know the acceptable pattern of behavior to follow on a given project. Everyone wants to work in an environment where people know what to expect. Again, discipline is the glue that holds a project together. It is *the* tool for managing change—and change is essential for progress. The processes and methodologies employed within a project cannot be sustained without the necessary, underlying discipline. A project needs discipline to achieve the desired level of accomplishment for each of its major parameters. These major project parameters are:

- Employee morale
- Productivity
- Quality
- Schedules
- Cost

The following sections explain the impact that discipline can have on these major project parameters.

Employee Morale

While great human achievements are not typically accomplished on morale alone, history seems to show that strong morale has added to the effectiveness of many great achievers. Obviously there is great value to a project when employee morale is high. Good morale can have a positive effect on every major project parameter. However, discipline from the project leadership is required in order to achieve high morale within an organization. For example, when project leaders exhibit discipline in insisting on an environment where the personnel:

- Know what their mission is
- Know what to expect from their leaders
- Have the desire to achieve
- Believe that project leaders make a genuine effort to understand their people and maintain good, two-way communications

than almost anything can be accomplished in such a disciplined environment. But significant accomplishment is impossible when the project management fails to exercise the necessary level of discipline that is needed to create and sustain an environment that *encourages* high employee morale.

Productivity

Employee productivity is at its best when project processes are defined, measurable, and enforced—and project members are educated about their roles. Discipline within the project is required to make these things happen. Consider an example.

In every product development cycle, the product passes through phases as it is being developed. Some typical phases are:

- Product definition
- Product design
- Code

Each of the project's phases can, in turn, be defined in more detail. For example, *product specifications* falls within the phase *product definition*. The product specifications could be divided into five activities:

- Product specifications preparation
- Product specifications review
- Product specifications update
- Product specifications approval
- Product specifications information

Each of these activities can be further defined in terms of entry, implementation and exit requirements. (See Chapter 4 for more on phases, activities, and process requirements.) The point: The best productivity is achieved when processes to be followed are crisply defined to a level at which the participants can measure their adherence to those processes. For project members to understand these processes fully, they must be properly trained and educated within the project. But one critical ingredient is still missing—enforcement. No process, methodology, or tool to enhance programmer productivity is of any value unless it is fully supported and enforced by project leaders.

In summary, discipline from the project leadership helps to sustain high employee productivity by insisting that project processes are defined, measurable, and enforced and that project members are educated about their roles.

Quality

Quality is another major project parameter that will suffer without discipline. Everyone has his or her own definition of quality. (See Chapter 5 for more on planning for quality.) Regardless of the definition used, there is always a great need to define and follow processes that will yield the desired product quality. While quality often is associated with the person in the trenches doing the designing, coding, or testing, the project leadership must first exhibit the discipline that leads to a quality-producing work environment. There is a real temptation to sacrifice quality first—whenever a project falls behind schedule. But quality actually should be the last parameter to be sacrificed, if ever. Sheer discipline from the project leadership is required to avoid the "let's lower the quality" trap. The following saying holds true for too many projects—perhaps even yours:

We never have enough time to do it right, but we always find time to do it over.

Schedules

This saying leads into the next reason for discipline—schedules. How many projects do you know about that actually finished under the same schedule they began? For those projects that changed their schedules, how much of a contributing factor was the lack of project discipline by the project leaders? Earlier it was mentioned that change is essential to progress. When a project's schedules are defined and approved early in the product development cycle, many assumptions and dependencies are identified. As time passes and some activities complete and many more begin, the project personnel who participated in the creation and approval of the schedules become more knowledgeable. For example, a certain document that was estimated to take four weeks to write might now require six weeks because the expected dependencies were late or because the effort was simply underestimated. What is happening is that *change* is being introduced into the project equation. In order to maintain the overall schedules, the discipline required to manage this ongoing change must be alive and active. Software development projects are not static. They are extremely lively and in constant need of attention. The need for discipline from project leaders is vital to maintain the overall, committed project schedules.

Cost

Cost is another major project parameter at the mercy of discipline. Budgets are affected by such factors as the number of programmers involved, the number of computer workstations available, the design of the office building, furniture, and fixtures, and so on. The list can be rather extensive. Even the timing chosen to begin moving people from one project into another can be quite costly. The opportunity to spend beyond the budget can be too tempting. *"Borrowing from Peter to pay Paul"* only defers pain into the future. It can become easy to rationalize a multitude of ways to recover costs. Of course, when recovery plans are implemented later, many turn out to have looked better on paper. Discipline by project leaders in controlling budgets is essential in containing costs.

* * *

All of the major project parameters—employee morale, productivity, quality, schedules, and cost—influence each other to some degree. For example, if morale is low, then quality and productivity will suffer. This will cause schedules to be extended which, in turn, will increase costs. But no matter which parameters are used to show this *"pinball"* effect, if any parameter "goes south," it can pull the overall project with it. Here again, it is the management of change that is critical to the success of the project. And critical to the management of change is the discipline required to hold all parameters of a project together.

Recognizing the Disciplined Organization

Have you ever noticed that some organizations seem to be more success-ful than others? That the energy level of the people involved seems to be higher? That these people generally seem to have better attitudes about themselves and the work they are doing? That more things just seem to go right? Also, have you noticed that these organizations seem to be able to attract the most interest from employees in sister organizations who desire to join?

What is so unique about these seemingly "magnetic" organizations that attracts good fortune at most turns? The general answer is that they are managed better. The specific answer is *discipline*. It is the discipline exercised by project leaders in both *what* they do and *how* they do it. Discipline comes in many flavors. But only the discipline that supports the project's mission is desirable. This is the discipline that supports the pattern of productive behavior needed in and wanted by project person-nel. This is the discipline that should be encouraged. This is called *positive discipline*. Positive discipline is what this chapter is all about.

Before venturing further into this topic, it can help to take a brief look at *negative discipline*. Remember, discipline is *the act of encouraging a desired pattern of behavior*. If the leader of a group *trains* the group's members to follow a certain pattern of behavior, and that behavior is *not* productive to achieving the group's mission, then the discipline exer-cised is negative discipline. As an example, consider an organization that needs its employees to take more risk in accepting responsibility. Now consider a leader within that organization who continually pun-ishes each risk taker that meets with failure. This leader would be displaying negative discipline since the discipline works against the project's mission. The scenarios at the beginning of this chapter provide additional examples of negative discipline.

Implementing Discipline

Now consider positive discipline once again, focusing on the discipline that project leaders demonstrate in both *what* they do and *how* they do it. Figure 2.1 shows the four essential traits that are the *what* of the well-disciplined organization. This is a good point to examine these traits closer and discuss *how* they need to be addressed.

Trait One: Set Realistic Goals

Every organization needs goals. How else can success be measured? Goals must be:

- Simply stated
- Understood by all
- Measurable

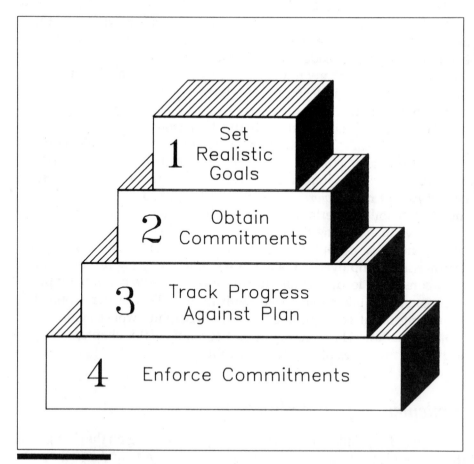

Figure 2.1. Traits of the well-disciplined organization

To "do good" is not a goal. To build a defect-free product is a goal. However, to expect a defect-free product might not be realistic. If your product will have one million lines of code, and your measure of success is to prove that it is 100 percent defect-free, then you will likely go out of business. Why? Because the tremendous cost to develop one million lines of code that is defect-free would likely extend schedules and raise the product price to a point that would significantly reduce its competitiveness. However, if your goal is to deliver this product with no more than one defect for every 1,000 lines of code, and technology is within reach to make this happen, then your goal is realistic. (In this example, assume that the customer accepts this defect rate. Also assume that the frequency and effect of the defects discovered by the customer are manageable—for instance, the defect is only encountered once during the start of leap year, and will not lead to disaster.)

How do goals (that are theoretically achievable) happen? They happen when the project leadership establishes and maintains a productive environment. The leaders must make it easy for people to do their job and must create a work environment that sets people up for success, not failure. In creating a productive environment, project leaders should strive to:

- Provide the necessary training, processes, and tools
- Offer a sense of accomplishment
- Foster teamwork
- Encourage risk-taking

Now take a closer look at these elements.

Provide training, processes, and tools   A goal is not realistic if the people expected to make it happen have not been properly trained, processes have not been defined and implemented, and the necessary tools have not been made available. The project leadership is responsible for making these things happen. In the one-million lines of code program example, project personnel will not know if they have achieved the acceptable defect rate unless a rigorous software development process has been defined and implemented to track and measure product defects carefully.

Offer a sense of accomplishment   People achieve their best when they are "stretched"—when their skills are used and their potential is tapped.

When these things happen, people sense they are valued as members of the team. Project leaders should not hold back in providing people with assignments that are challenging, but achievable. A project's goals are closer to being realistic when the project's members are happy about their work.

Foster teamwork Fostering teamwork involves encouraging the participation of *all* project members. Great human achievements are possible when people work as a team. Whether the project is to harness the great energy of the atom, to walk on the moon, or to build a large complex software program, teamwork draws on individual accomplishments. These individual accomplishments are collected in a fashion that allows greatness to be achieved at a level far beyond the abilities of any one person. Everyone has something to offer to a team. The more participation is encouraged, the greater the likelihood that the project's goals will be met.

Encourage risk-taking Taking risks is the difference between *doing* the unthinkable and only *dreaming* about it. Establishing a risk-supportive environment can allow the imagined to become reality. It may be *the* ingredient that allows the estimated one-million lines of code program to be done with 25 percent less code. Or it may simply make the difference between delivering a product on schedule—or much later. An environment that encourages risk and rewards success, but does not penalize failure is an organization to be reckoned with. The movers of tomorrow are taking risks today.

Trait Two: Obtain Commitments

The previous section, "Trait One: Set Realistic Goals," stresses that a well-disciplined organization defines realistic project goals in a manner that is simply stated, is understood by all, and is measurable. Furthermore, all project players understand their individual assignments and roles in making the bigger picture happen. A second trait of a well-disciplined organization is the obtainment of commitments from *each* person in the organization. ("Commitment of Participants," in Chapter 4, also discusses this activity.)

A committed plan does not exist until *everyone* has made a personal commitment. This means from the very top gun to the troops in the trenches, managers and nonmanagers alike. People will take more pride in their work when they have a personally committed stake, when they sense they have responsibility and accountability. There is no greater tool for motivating people to do their job than to get their personal commitment to making it happen. Giving people the opportunity to participate in developing product content, processes, and schedules is not only beneficial, it is a must.

Trait Three: Track Progress Against Plans

At this point, the organization has a realistic project plan (trait one) to which all members of the project have committed (trait two). So far, so good. The third trait is the tracking of each activity against the plan. (Techniques for tracking plans is discussed in detail in Chapter 6.)

Remember that discipline is the act of encouraging a desired pattern of behavior. Now that a plan for the project is in place, how can the project leadership be sure that the plan is continually being followed? More importantly, how will the leadership know when problems arise and where resources should be redeployed to help solve problems and protect the planned schedules? Discipline is required to track the plan on a regular and frequent basis. Tracking the plan also involves recording new problems and ensuring that current problems are being solved satisfactorily.

Consider the plight of a person walking through a desert. Without sophisticated navigation tools, it is highly improbable that this person could walk a straight line through the desert. (For this example, assume it is physically possible to track to a straight route, free of obstacles.) In this analogy, the start and end points of the person's journey represent the start and end points of a project. The straight line, which is the shortest route through the desert, is symbolic of the shortest project schedules possible. Now picture this person veering a little off course each week. For any given week, the deviation doesn't represent a major alteration of the final destination. However, as the weeks pass, these minor off-course excursions collectively could spell disaster. That is, the final destination would not be reached anywhere near the planned date. If, however, this person's direction could be reset each week, problems could be addressed close to the time they occur, so that the final destination's targeted arrival date has a much higher chance of being achieved.

The desert example is simplistic, but nevertheless provides insight into the need to track against a project plan at frequent, regular intervals. Often, just the act of tracking the plan is a form of preventive maintenance. People are more apt to meet a checkpoint if they are being regularly and frequently tracked than if they are infrequently tracked.

Trait Four: Enforce Commitments

You may want to read this section twice. The reason is simple: If everything mentioned up to now has been done—setting realistic goals, obtaining commitments, tracking progress against plans—but this final, fourth trait of the well-disciplined organization is not made to happen, then all bets are off. Enforcing commitments is an absolute must. This is not a "strong arm" tactic. Rather, the enforcement of commitments represents a statement of support from the project leadership to the project participants.

Most software development projects will encounter several severe problems along the way. (A severe problem is one that can potentially cause a delay in the final delivery of the product.) Moreover, many severe problems are not totally solvable by the specific group that is experiencing the problem. An example is the team that falls behind schedule in writing test procedures. The people are all working overtime but still may not be able to complete the activity on schedule. The person leading this team has no other resource to add to this effort. The project leadership, however, can choose to redeploy people from other areas of the project to shore up the test procedures development activity.

Therefore, one useful approach project leaders can employ to ensure that commitments are met is *management of priorities*. Priorities requiring attention will often vary from week to week. As a result, management of priorities requires discipline to ensure that the proper activities are getting the needed resource and focus. It is often more fun and easier to deal with some problems ahead of others. However, this temptation should be resisted. Instead, it is better to understand problems and take action on resolving them according to priorities that best serve the organization. (See Chapter 7 for more detail.)

Another important action to take in enforcing commitments can be called "making it happen now." This is a tightly held philosophy of leaders who have a reputation for getting things done. Whereas management of priorities ensures that resources within the organization are dynamically being diverted for the good of the total plan, "making things happen now" is the act of swiftly dealing with problems before they fester and grow out (or further out) of control. This is considered to be a strong positive act of support for the people in the organization.

Reward those who meet or beat their commitments. Whether the reward is expressed privately or publicly, stated on paper, made with money or made through some other means, it is important to provide feedback to individuals and to the organization. Let people know when their behavior contributes to the project's goals. By the same token, proceed cautiously before reprimanding failure. Be firm, but fair. Maintain a sense of justice and fair treatment. Most people don't fail intentionally. Could it be that the project leadership did not provide the proper work environment to facilitate the employee's success? If it is clear that a person is performing unsatisfactorily, don't ignore this. Help the person to develop an acceptable level of performance. If, after a reasonable energy expenditure, the person is still not showing the needed improvement, then find a job that fits this person's skills or remove him or her from the company. Do not do nothing. All eyes are on the project leadership to take proper action before the situation deteriorates further.

Attributes of the Successful Leader

Leadership is action, not position.

Donald H. McGannon
(American Broadcasting Executive)

This section is devoted to the role of the leader and contains what I believe to be the most important leadership philosophies, or tenets, that have been shared with me over the years or that I have shared with others. These leadership tenets have worked for me and I have seen them work for others. Being a leader carries a lot of responsibility, but it can also be a lonely, stressful job if you allow the role to control you rather than you taking charge of your own emotions.

Earlier sections have discussed the need for discipline within the organization and have explained how to recognize a disciplined organization. Now is a good point to focus candidly on self-discipline for the leader. First, consider what makes a person a leader. A leader:

- Is the principle player within a team
- Exhibits foresight and integrity
- Inspires, guides, and protects

- Is a continuous source of energy
- Encourages others toward a desired response
- Sets an example for others
- Is accountable

This is certainly not an exhaustive list of leadership characteristics. However, it is sufficiently complete to point out the importance of a leader in creating and nurturing a successful organization. Now, the tenets.

Don't Fear Failure or Boast Success

Life is full of paradoxes. The person who is no stranger to failure is the person who is most likely to succeed. Every failure offers a lesson and from every lesson comes strength. Fear perpetuates failure. Think of those around you who fear failure. They most likely are not leaders, are content with complacency, and seek so-called "safety" by maintaining the status quo wherever they may be. Now look at those whose failures seem to be visible, yet from each fall they rise to prepare for the next challenge. If failure means growth and opportunity, then it should never be feared. The only real failures are the experiences we don't learn from.

But what about success? It isn't all that it's cracked up to be. Our culture views success to be something permanent, something that should make one express a sigh of relief for finally arriving at some goal, something that offers instant happiness and near immortality. Instead, success is not arrived at as a permanent station in life. It is not something to be chased, but something that follows the person who continues to reach out after other goals. As Dr. Wayne Dyer, author of your *Your Erroneous Zones* and *The Sky's the Limit*, lectures: "Success is something you bring to everything that you do."

Learn to Expect and Accept Criticism

> *Criticism is something we can avoid easily—by saying nothing, doing nothing, and being nothing.*
>
> *Aristotle*

If you expect criticism, you will seldom be disappointed when you receive it. However, note that there are two types of criticism: *constructive* and *destructive*. Of course, you should welcome constructive criticism, which is well-meaning and useful feedback. Constructive criticism should leave you feeling that you have been helped. This type of feedback can help you to learn about yourself and the impact you are having as a result of your actions. It is information you can use to help make choices for yourself and to help you grow in the direction of your personal goals.

Destructive criticism is input you receive that might be maliciously rooted and offers little, if any, real value for your learning and growth. However, what may often appear to be destructive criticism might, in fact, just be an unfortunate and ineffective attempt to offer some useful information—but from a person who does not know how best to communicate the information. Be aware that some well-intended criticism might come your way awkwardly masked in destructive garb.

You will always find those who disapprove of your behavior or your decisions. Even the people you love, and who love you, will, at times, disapprove of your actions. When people criticize you, remember it is only their opinion. If you allow the absence of their approval to immobilize you, then you are allowing others to control you. You are, in effect, saying that what other people think about you is more important than what you think about yourself. Instead, you should ask yourself if there is something to be learned from the criticism. If there is, then, by all means, learn! If there is nothing to be learned, then forget the experience and go about fulfilling your dreams.

Take Risks

Great deeds are usually wrought at great risks.

Herodotus
(Greek Historian)

Risk—that simple yet mighty four-letter word. The willingness to take risks is what changed the perception of a flat world to round, gave humans wings to fly, and gives people the ability to understand their own capabilities. If you want to achieve the extraordinary, you *must* take risks. Risk-taking can occur on a small scale, such as driving a new route home from work, speaking out when you disagree with an issue, or volunteering to take on an additional assignment. If you practice becoming comfortable with going after smaller risks, you will find yourself much more prepared to recognize a larger risk and much more willing to take it on.

If you increasingly take on more risk, you will find an unexpected benefit—the recognition that your level of energy and enthusiasm grow in proportion to the risk that you pursue. Often, assignments that are the riskiest are later viewed as the assignments that were the most enjoyable, memorable, and career-building. There is nothing wrong with gradually expanding your risk-taking abilities. Only you can decide what your limitations are and what level of risk is suitable for you. The leaders of tomorrow are taking risks today.

Delegate

> *No man will make a great leader who wants to do it all himself, or to get all the credit for doing it.*
>
> *Andrew Carnegie*
> *(American Industrialist and Philanthropist)*

It is common for new leaders not to delegate. The reasons include a belief that they can do the job better or faster than another and the fear of giving others too much work. Another reason: They allow society's work ethic, being independent and self-reliant, to interfere with their duties as a leader of others. Resist these attitudes and delegate! It is good for you and good for your team members. It frees you to lead and frees them to learn. You appreciated the opportunities that others gave you to learn. Give others their chance. Everybody will win.

Be Decisive

> *Once the WHAT is decided, the HOW always follows. We must not make the HOW an excuse for not facing and accepting the WHAT.*
>
> *Pearl S. Buck*
> *(American Novelist)*

Your organization will react to your actions. When you delay in making crucial decisions, you are also delaying the time that will be needed to implement those decisions. Many organizations have the capacity to increase their productivity and effectiveness. By putting off decision-making, you are not driving your organization efficiently. If you delay your own decision making, you are also preventing the next tier of decisions from being made. This *decision queue* can build to a point where progress within the organization is seriously impacted. The result is an uncontrollable sluggishness that spreads throughout the organization, and that only the project leader can correct. The only people who make no wrong decisions are those who make no decisions.

It is better to make decisions early—when their pain and cost to the organization are relatively minor, yet when their long-term impact can have a major positive effect. Some decisions will, in hindsight, prove to be less than the best. However, if you wait until absolutely no risk remains before taking a position on a problem, then you will lose all competitiveness.

Be Persistent

Great works are performed not by strength, but by perseverance.
Dr. Samuel Johnson
(English poet, critic, essayist, and lexicographer)

Perseverance is a universal characteristic of successful leaders. This attribute can propel a so-called "common" person to achieve uncommon feats. Perseverance pushes a chemist to try that 20,000th mixture that finally succeeds, an athlete to achieve an olympic class victory, an artist to create a masterpiece, and the medical biologist to locate a crippling-causing gene. Perhaps, however, the most inspiring effect of perseverance can be seen in a person who overcomes a major physical handicap and goes on to accomplish a feat that would be difficult for even a fully functioning person to achieve.

Intellectual and physical capabilities vary widely among people. However, it is encouraging to know that we all have the innate ability to exercise perseverance and determination in achieving those goals that are important to us. Being persistent can make all the difference between dreaming and seeing the dream blossom into reality. Act like it is impossible for you to fail. You can achieve nearly anything you set out to make happen if you are persistent in following your dreams.

Be Happy

Everything you need to be totally fulfilled you already have...
Dr. Wayne Dyer
(American psychologist and author)

Be happy. Feel good about yourself. Being happy is the cornerstone of your continued effectiveness. Don't *strive* to be happy. Don't set goals and then tell yourself that once those goals are reached you will be happy. Putting off happiness until some external event occurs will guarantee that your happiness will continue to be elusive.

You have everything you need today to be fulfilled. You don't need a promotion, award, new car, vacation, retirement, or whatever, to be happy. Happiness is an attitude. It is an acceptance of what is. It is something that no one can take away from you. You can lose all your material possessions and still be happy. This does not mean you should stop working for self-improvement or improvement to your family, job, company, world, or whatever is important to you. It means that you must not allow external forces to control you to the point at which your actual happiness is no longer within your own control. However you define success for yourself, you will significantly improve your likelihood of attaining your goals if you recognize and exercise your ability to be and remain happy.

Be Serious about Humor

> *It is my belief, you cannot deal with the most serious things in the world unless you understand the most amusing.*
>
> Sir Winston Churchill

Consider this scenario: A meeting has just been called to settle a dispute between two parties. As people are assembling in the meeting room, an uncomfortable silence is felt. Everyone has arrived and the meeting is about to start. There is an instability in the air, a feeling of tension that one wrong word or action could ignite into an emotional explosion. The first words are spoken, and strike everyone in the meeting with the same response—a round of heavy uncontrollable laughter fills the room.

Can you relate to this scenario? Most of us can. That well-timed bit of humor was sorely needed. All too often we take the moment much too seriously. We fail to loosen up and find the humor in ourselves and our situation. How terribly depressing for an organization to resist expressing the lighter side of the daily problems we face. As a leader, support a healthy dose of humor in the organization. Displaying a sense of humor also helps you to remain cool under pressure and to keep problems in perspective.

Caution: Don't use sarcasm in your humor. While many people may view your comment to be amusing, it may leave an uncomfortable and unsettled feeling in others. Sarcasm can also hurt the trust you have developed with others. People appreciate benevolent humor better than sarcastic humor. If you have a hard time initiating this welcomed variety of humor, then at least show appreciation when it is advanced by others. Humor has been shown to preserve the health of people, but it also adds value to the health of the total organization.

Leave Your Ego Behind

We all have an ego. For some, the ego can cause a paralysis, inhibiting their quest for growth and opportunity. Here is another paradox: Often the person who insists on attention is the one least likely to receive the type or amount of attention desired. An overactive ego does not help win the recognition, admiration, and approval that the egotist seeks. Instead, it has a repelling effect that encourages others to want to limit their association with the egotist. Furthermore, it leads others to question the real value and substance that exist behind all the verbal arm waving.

An oversized ego can also interfere with recognizing others for their contributions. It can also bias decisions being made, favoring who is right rather than what is right. You have probably seen leaders with large egos. Having an exaggerated ego doesn't mean you will never get to be a leader. It means that fewer people will trust you or want to work for and with you. It means that you will make your job harder and less effective than it needs to be. An unbridled ego is a haunting liability. The less approval you demand from others, the more you are likely to receive.

Think Before Acting—Do Not Criticize Hastily

Resist the temptation to criticize hastily. When you suspect poor work, ask questions and listen to the answers. Once a wrong or regrettable word is spoken, it is past redemption. Give others the same courtesy that you would like for yourself. Once you understand the reason behind a problem, attack the reason, not the person. Help the person to benefit from this experience. (Chapter 3 offers additional ideas on communication skills.)

Meet Your Commitments

A chain is only as strong as its weakest link. Make no commitments lightly. Commitments should be viewed as sacred. The success of an organization depends on its ability to achieve its commitments. The project structure can quickly break when commitments are broken. Commit only to that which you believe is achievable. If your commitment is weak, so too are those commitments that depend on you. Pull your own weight and do as you say you will.

When you meet your commitments, you will be recognized as a greater value to the organization. You may also find that you will be given the option to assume greater responsibilities as well as increased opportunities. People will prefer to have you on their team or will want to be on your team. You will also find that you will be given greater freedom to manage your activities as you choose.

Coach Your Team—Be a Role Model

Teach what you have learned. Impart your knowledge and experience. Prepare others to take on more responsibility. You know what you want from your leaders, work to provide the same to your subordinates and peers, and even back up to your leaders. Work continuously to build a stronger organization this month than the one that existed last month. When you come across a problem, fix the problem—then fix the process that caused the problem. The greatest leader is the one who leads by example. Practice what you expect from others. Show you care, offer your support, be there to make it happen.

Maintain a Winning Attitude

The quality of work is affected as much by one's attitude as by one's skill.
Anonymous

Attitude is the disposition, manner, or approach that you bring to everything you do. One of the most admired traits you can have is a good attitude, or positive attitude. A positive attitude can actually bring pleasure to performance of a tedious or difficult task. A positive attitude can make a long day seem short and can even improve the productivity and quality of the work being performed. People who consistently

chapters done
1, 9

maintain positive attitudes tend to have higher energy levels than those with less lofty attitudes. These people look for something positive—and they find it—in every chore they tackle. You have probably observed a situation where two people are being considered for the same assignment and the person chosen is the one who appears to have somewhat less experience or knowledge. Yet, this person was considered the most qualified based on the importance of having someone with an obviously positive attitude in that assignment.

As a revealing anonymous quote states: "A pessimist finds difficulty in every opportunity; an optimist finds opportunity in every difficulty." People can take great liberties in choosing how to think. A glass of water can be half filled or half empty. How a person thinks does not change the fact that the glass has 50 percent of its capacity *used up* by water. But how a person chooses to think does have an affect on the efficiency with which a task is completed and on the enjoyment the person derives from accomplishing that task.

As a leader, you want the people whom you are leading to demonstrate good attitudes in every endeavor that you assign them. People who exhibit these up-beat attitudes are considerably easier to manage and more enjoyable to be around than less positive people. In order for a winning attitude to permeate your team, you must demonstrate and encourage that characteristic. As a leader, the manner in which you approach your work is also the manner most likely to be adopted by those who work under, alongside, and above you. Adopt a winning attitude in the tasks that you undertake and you will also adopt winning people and winning products in the process.

Checking the Organization's Pulse

If you follow this chapter's advice up to this point, how can you tell if it is working for you and your organization? The external signs should be quite evident. For example, the status of the project plan would be known at regular and frequent intervals, schedules should be tracking to plan, and any exceptions would have recovery plans. Problems would be logged, assigned an owner, and target dates for closure committed. But what about the internal signs? What do the individual project members really feel about their organization and how it is being run?

There are many methods managers can use to test the effectiveness of the discipline exercised across a project. Some of the more common methods are listed here:

- Random walks through work areas
- Scheduled one-on-one interviews
- Scheduled group roundtables
- Formal opinion surveys
- Quality improvement teams

Random walks through work areas have the greatest immediate payback because listening to project members' spontaneous opinions offers the best opportunity to learn. These walks can build a closer and more trusting working relationship between managers and nonmanagers. Understanding problems at the point where pain is felt the most also adds valuable insight into providing the support needed. These walks are most effective if they can take place for at least 30 to 60 minutes each day, and not less frequently than two to three times per week. Surveying the members less frequently is still, however, a valuable method for gaining insight into the way a project is running, but it will be more difficult to maintain a personal bond with project members.

Scheduling "chats" with project members for 30 to 60 minutes per person is also a useful way to get feedback. These **one-on-one interviews** can be scheduled once or twice a week with a different person from a different group each time. The person can be given up to a week's notice. The meeting should be set at a convenient time for the invited member. The actual interview should first focus on any questions or thoughts that the member wants to pursue. Then the manager might ask a few general questions of the project member.

Roundtables are a productive way to meet the most people in the least available amount of time. Roundtables typically involve a gathering of 5 to 15 people from across the organization. These sessions may occur once every one or two weeks and may last up to two hours. This is not only an informative tool for the manager, it is also a team-building technique for roundtable members.

Formal **opinion surveys** are typically administered on paper or through a computer workstation. The anonymous survey may ask a few or many questions, most of which would be answered by rating the participant's views from "very satisfied" to "very unsatisfied." This is an effective tool for medium- to longer-range planning.

Quality improvement teams are another effective way to understand the problems that can stifle parts or all of an organization. These teams are described in the "Quality Improvement Teams" section of Chapter 5. Quality improvement teams are mentioned here due to their considerable benefit in encouraging participation of project members from across the organization. These teams can candidly assess any discipline-related problems that may exist, and can offer creative recommendations that have the added benefit of being sponsored from the bottom-up rather than from top-down.

The Desire for Discipline

You must want discipline in order to make it happen. Discipline cannot and will not happen without your support. If you say you want discipline, but your actions tell another story, the entire organization will read you like a book. Vague policies and permissive attitudes convey the impression that unproductive (destructive) behavior is acceptable.

You hold the keys to building a poor, ordinary, or extraordinary organization. You are the boss. You can initiate change whenever and wherever you want. Most problems are not as large as they appear. What is large is the fear or hesitancy to deal with problems head-on—when they first appear. This is not to say that all problems are easy to solve or can be solved in a short time. Problems that compete for resources or time need to be prioritized according to the needs of the organization. Then, these priorities need to be managed with the urgency they deserve.

Discipline is an everyday thing. It is not occasional. Discipline is the glue that holds it all together. Everyone wants positive discipline. Exercising discipline has great value to each project participant, to the organization as a whole, and to the products that are developed by the organization. Everyone wins. Can you afford to have your project fail, to be less than it needs to be? Be a winner!

3

Communicating in Harmony

In software development projects, the inability of people to communicate effectively with one another represents one of the most common obstacles to the achievement of high product quality and high productivity. This obstacle might manifest itself as poor communications among employees, between management and their employees, or among management. Communication problems are common topics of complaint within most projects. Everyone knows what they do not like, but few act to really do something about perceived problems.

Lack of communication is a problem area that technology has done little to improve, an area where nature has left its mark so ingrained that the term *human nature* is often used to excuse uncommunicative behavior. It is an area that has particularly frustrated many project leaders and managers. Rapid advancements in technology have not reduced the need for people to communicate and get along. To the contrary, the need for effective communications among people is at a greater premium than ever before. The dignity and value of each individual is central to the success of an enterprise. Improving communications among project players offers substantial morale, product quality, productivity, and, therefore, cost benefits to a project. Once communications problems surface, the process to follow in bringing the problems under control is:

- Understand the cause of the problems.
- Put corrective action into place.
- Enforce an ongoing communicative work environment.

47

But the real goal should be to prevent the problems from developing. The approach lies in this simple yet powerful statement: *Respect the individual.*

Where's the Respect?

Demonstrating respect for others is the cornerstone for improving communications among people. The following collection of scenarios illustrates how poor communications are fostered and tolerated. How many of the situations portrayed in these scenarios have you encountered? Can you spot the problems? As you read through these scenarios, keep in mind the words of Harold Nicholson, British statesman and author, "We are all inclined to judge ourselves by our ideals; others by their acts."

Sophie Berger, a programmer working in the test area, has been assigned to review the drafts of the product's publications as they become available. Berger has agreed to review each chapter as it is completed by Mark Hood, the writer. This review process was requested by Hood's manager and approved by Berger's manager. It is intended to aid in obtaining an early assessment of the progress being made on the publications. The review process will also provide Hood with the opportunity to work more closely with a programmer (in this case, Berger) in those areas in which Hood requires assistance. Berger has more than five years experience in software development. Hood, on the other hand, has just completed his first year. He has been primarily drawing his information from the "final" product specifications, which, incidentally, happen to be incomplete. Hood also has, on many occasions, requested additional information from the programmers who have written the product specifications. These programmers have frequently stated that they do not have the time to brief Hood on the specifications. However, several of the chapters reviewed by Berger require major revisions in some sections because Hood made invalid assumptions. Berger seems quick to tell her peers, "The `Pubs' people don't know diddly-squat about this product. I could write these chapters faster than the time it takes to teach this writer what he needs to know." Berger has influenced her peers to the point that they agree with her whole-heartedly.

* * *

Nobody seems to know what is happening in this project, except maybe a handful of lead development programmers. These programmers seem to remain inaccessible to anyone whom they do not have any direct responsibility for or commitment to. These lead developers meet on a regular basis with their respective teams. The goals at these meetings are to exchange status, to conduct design reviews, and, in general, to plan their next one to four weeks. The peripheral groups (writers, testers, quality assurance, schedulers, tools people, and so on) have asked if they can attend or send a representative to these regularly scheduled meetings. The reply is almost always, "No, we don't have any information to share at this point." When no other groups are around, the developers chatter among themselves, saying, "The other groups sure have cushy jobs. You never see them working after hours. They just sit around and complain that things aren't just like they think they should be." The management from the development shop and the other shops have not attempted to discuss the situation.

* * *

The management in this company recognizes the value of receiving an independent assessment of the progress for products being developed. Managers also acknowledge the benefit of an independent group working closely with product development groups to help guide the developers, as efficiently as possible, through their processes. For these reasons, management declares the creation of a **quality assurance** group. Furthermore, to help maintain objectivity, no quality assurer will directly report to the project leadership of whose products he or she is assuring. To higher management, the quality assurance mission is understood and welcomed. The troops in the trenches, on the other hand, see little value being added by quality assurance. As one developer quips to another, "Nonconcurred! I spent weeks writing my section of the product specifications and one assurer nonconcurs just because of a few TBDs (to be determined) that I had in the document! I said I would complete those sections just as soon as I have some free time. Now I have to finish the sections by next week. I was hoping to do some coding first. How can I meet my commitments when I keep getting sidetracked? I thought quality assurance was here to help us, not slow us down!"

* * *

A manager, Bill Foley, has just called his department together for a meeting. These meetings occur infrequently. There are several topics to be discussed, some timely and some that have been accumulated until this meeting. Foley is known for being outspoken and saying what is on his mind. Some of the department members have been annoyed over the poor communications and working relationships that appear to be rampant on this project. The mission of Foley's department is to design and code product enhancements. The department members are currently "under the gun" and are working an average of 30 percent overtime. Someone asks Foley if the department will be hiring anyone to help with the workload. Foley replies, "The budget does not permit any additional employees on this project. What we ought to do is reduce or disband some of the test, publications, and support departments. I never see any of them here on weekends or after hours. I really can't see the value that they are adding to the project. It seems all they do is slow us down."

*   *   *

There are nearly two hundred people assigned to this software development project. Many processes have been defined and implemented to better control critical activities within the project. One such critical activity is the *library control and build* procedures. These procedures are used to ensure that all modules being developed and tested are properly identified, added to a library of modules residing on a set of computer disks, and access-controlled through a *checkout scheme* that allows orderly modifications to be made to the library modules. The build group is responsible for ensuring the smooth operation of this activity. The build group also is responsible for building **drivers** for the development and test organizations. (A driver is a collection of modules that are linked to form a workable "product" that can be tested and evaluated.)

The product being developed is considered to be complex and resides across several different types of computer systems. When new modules are ready to be added to the library, a long list of information about each module must be collected from the development organization. This data is essential to compiling and linking these modules with other modules. Whenever the development group delivers modules, it seems that some valuable information about the modules is overlooked. This missing data causes the build group to waste scores of person-hours trying to debug new drivers that must contain these modules. To correct this loss of productivity, the build group initiates a meeting with the developers to create a comprehensive checklist that can be used by development each time new modules are added to the library. The build group must rely on special knowledge and skills that the developers possess regarding the modules and the environments in which the modules must operate.

The first real use of the checklist arrives and the build group, for once, feels good about the data the developers deliver to them. Unfortunately, the build group spends two full days and several people trying to build a driver with the new modules. Frustrated, they ask the developers to participate with the debugging. The developers quickly locate the problem and blame the build team for not asking the right questions on the checklist. A member of the build team snaps, "But we had asked you to make sure that all the needed data was being requested."

A developer responds, "Do we have to do all of your work for you? We are up to our ears developing a product. The least you can do is handle the operations of the library control system!"

Later, one developer says to another, "I know ten times more about building libraries than that entire build team. I see problems with their procedures that they don't even realize exist. When are they going to get their act together?"

* * *

This project developed and issued a *quality plan*. It was approved by all. The plan defined, among other things, how the code was to be designed, coded, unit and function tested, inspected, and formally tested. The developers then issued their unit and function test plans. These plans were also approved by all. Development followed the plans to the letter. Then the developers delivered their code, on schedule, to the formal test group for additional testing.

Several of the programmers in the test area are now upset with the "low quality" of the code that the development programmers delivered to the testers. It is taking the testers longer than they had anticipated to run their "bucket" of test cases successfully. The feeling of these testers, and of other testers who have come under their influence, is that the developers must not be very proud of their work, seem to lack any real dedication, and, in general, appear not to know much about what they are doing. Although the testers are constantly grumbling, there has been no formal communication with the developers on this matter. The developers are not aware of the severity of the quality problem as perceived by the testers. The testers are not aware that the developers are beaming with pride in delivering "high-quality" complex code, following the approved process, and on a very aggressive schedule.

* * *

Every software development project member has at least one, similar, war story. And each member has added, at one time or another, his or her share to the communications problems that can plague a project. Most project members don't cause such problems on purpose. They just don't think. They have their own problems to deal with, and expect others to solve their own as well. Seldom do people make plans to anticipate and, therefore, head off communications problems before they grow out of control. The good news is that most problems can be dealt with effectively, many before they have a chance to fester. This chapter describes methods to deal with these problems directly.

Respect the Individual

If you are looking for that special phrase or set of words to carry along with you after you have read this chapter, this is it: *Respect the individual.* Similar pearls of wisdom have been uttered through history, such as this one by Confucius, "What you do not want done to yourself, do not do to others," or this one from the New Testament, "Do unto others as you would have them do unto you." Don't be blinded by the simplicity of these words. There is gold here. To help relate these words to your job and your work environment, the remainder of this chapter is divided into sections, each with a theme on which to focus. You will probably find yourself being able to identify with many of these themes. You may also find much of the guidance offered to be common sense. Don't be satisfied with merely understanding the messages within these themes. Understanding is just the first step. You must then work to break old habits and develop new habits that support the messages you wish to convey to your peers, superiors, and subordinates. Practice these guidelines and you will see, firsthand, the positive impact they can have in your daily environment. Practicing the Golden Rule is not a sacrifice, but an *investment*.

When You Are Wrong, Admit It

There will be times when you are wrong. You will know when this happens. So will the person you wronged. Being stubborn at this time only serves to build walls between people. Don't cling to the work ethic that says admitting fault or apologizing is a sign of weakness. You gain respect when you are wrong and have the courage and integrity to admit it. Immediately, tensions ease. The face of a meeting changes from *you and me* (confrontational) to *us* (cooperative). Also, the meeting begins to be productive because one or both parties are now open to learning rather than defending.

Compromise

It is not unusual for two parties to disagree on an issue. It is not only conceivable but probable that neither party has the best or "right" solution. Compromising at this point might actually result in a superior resolution. In the few cases where it might not, then at least the goodwill generated from the compromise might more than make up for the lost ground felt by one or both parties.

You might discover that compromising is not nearly as painful as you perceive it will be. In fact, you might find that the greatest pain comes from being rigid in holding to your position. It is this rigidity that can cause a major barrier to further progress. It takes a big person to take that big step to meet another person half way.

Exercise Tolerance

A typical situation calling for tolerance involves a person who is learning. It could be a new employee, an employee in a new assignment, or an employee learning something in their existing assignment. It could be a peer, a subordinate, or your boss. It could be you.

Recall a few of those times when you unintentionally "screwed up." Remember how you felt when you were met with zero tolerance for your mistake? Now recall your grateful response from an instance when tolerance was extended to you. You can have a similar, positive affect on others who are in a learning position.

Meet People

It is far easier to criticize behind someone's back rather than face to face—especially when you have never met the face! Go out of your way to meet the people on whom you are dependent or who are dependent on you. Talk to them. Invite them to your meetings, ask to attend theirs. Call them on the phone instead of sending a note. Your goal should be to initiate communication that is immediately interactive. Communicating through memos and third parties lacks a dimension of rapport that must be available in order to build a close, working relationship. Next time you call a meeting, ask yourself who else could benefit by attending. Then extend an invitation. You will find this to be an inexpensive yet productive investment, not only in building preferred relationships, but also in improving morale and productivity within a project.

Be Quick to Assist

Help others along when you can. Encourage a team atmosphere, which is more fun and more productive than working alone. However, be careful not to do the work of someone else. You have your own work by which you are being measured. If you do somebody else's work, your commitments might be missed. Also, if you do the work of others, you are encouraging them to be dependent on you. Instead, teach them self-reliance. Help them to "get going." Suggest things they can do to learn, such as looking at examples or reading a special book or article.

Regardless of the size of a group, it is typical to have one or more people whom others know will show them the way when they are in need of help. These helpers are frequently the most respected and admired members of a team. Set an example of helpfulness. Let others know what they can expect from you, and live up to that expectation.

Ask Others for Assistance

Everyone has something of value to add to a project. This fact cannot be over-emphasized. Tap into the resources available from those around you. Ask for assistance in reviewing a test plan, a publications chapter, a memo, an idea, or whatever. You might be surprised, not only when your request is accepted, but also when you receive the response that transforms your piece of good output into excellent output. Of course, the person whom you asked for assistance will also feel pretty good. People want to belong, they want to contribute. Offer them that chance and you could find yourself discovering valuable assets and friends. You cannot beat this "win-win" combination.

Use Tact—Put Your Comments in the Correct Perspective

> *Tact is the art of making a point without making an enemy.*
> Howard W. Newton
> *(American advertising executive)*

Use tact in defining the problems of others. Put yourself in the other person's shoes. Ask yourself, "How would I react if someone were to approach me in this manner about this problem?" If your answer is not positive, then search for an alternate approach. Finding problems should be viewed as a positive contribution to an organization. Only the perception of your approach to communicating the problem can turn the situation negative. Keep emotion out of the discussion. Focus on the facts at hand. Show people that you are willing to work with them where appropriate, that you are attempting to add value to the product or process.

Consider an example: If your assignment includes evaluating output from another department or organization, then, before you respond with problems or issues, carefully consider your remarks. The output you are reviewing could be a product specifications document, a test plan, or a publications draft. If you are about to dispute one or more items, find a way to state your case tactfully. Finding legitimate, serious problems is a great help. But if problems are minor, don't blow them out of proportion. If you feel you should list relatively small problems, make sure they are listed separately from major issues. Concentrate your energies on meaningful problems. Ask a friend or a peer whose opinion you value to assess both the problems you are about to catalog and the wording you have chosen. If you believe that your statements will be misunderstood or you are not sure how they will be received, then share them with the owner of the output you reviewed or call a small informal meeting to discuss them. This is professional courtesy. You might find that you had false assumptions about an issue, or you might even be able to resolve an issue immediately.

You lose the desired and rightful impact of your positions when you frequently overplay or emotionalize your response to someone. Your responses add value to a project's mission. Your responses and those of others should all be encouraged. Exercise caution: Present your positions so that their real value can be appreciated and recognized. Give others the same respect as you would wish them to give you in similar circumstances.

Keep Others Informed—Do Not Surprise

Most people like to be surprised—at a surprise party or some other situation where the surprise is affectionately intended. However, most people do not like to be surprised in their work environment, especially bosses. Why? Surprising others represents a way of broadcasting that they are not in control or that something they are doing is not acceptable to you. The reference here is to bad news, which is what most surprises are all about. If you are surprising someone with good news, there is little chance of harm—either to you or that person. But surprise someone with bad news and that person may remember the stunt for what can seem like an eternity.

Bad news does happen. But *how* bad news is delivered can make all the difference. Avoid revealing bad news to the principal party in a public setting. You should disclose such news in as private a setting as possible. Put yourself in this person's shoes and decide how you would want to receive the news. A concerned, sensitive approach to revealing bad news can even leave the recipient with a greater respect for your kindness and judgment. You might also find that you will receive more support and less criticism when the news is made public.

If you have surprising news, it is usually beneficial to reveal the news as early as possible. Delaying bad news will usually only amplify the negative reaction of others when the news is finally revealed. The goal is to put the bad news behind you quickly, learn from the experience, and channel your energies toward making further progress. Surprises do not always have to have an unhappy ending. Remember, with a thoughtful approach, not only are you saving face for others, *your* face will look better, too.

Show Appreciation

By appreciation, we make excellence in others our own property.

Voltaire

"Thank you." These two short words go a long way. When people do something for you, show your appreciation. It will give them a more gratified feeling of acceptance. They will probably also be more willing to help you again. If you can give praise where others can also hear, the sincerity and benefit of your appreciation grows geometrically by the size of the gathering. The more ears that hear, the stronger the echo of appreciation will sound. Remember those times when you did something kind or unusual, whether it was for someone in particular or just an outcome of your assignment. Then remember how you felt when the expected "thank you" did not materialize. And remember how you felt when a "thank you" eventually *was* expressed, especially if that "thank you" was not anticipated. Share that feeling with others.

Be a Good Listener

Communication is a two-way process. To be an effective communicator, you must be able to send *and* receive information. Listening is the fundamental act of receiving information. Listening requires a certain level of concentration. A person who sends information (a speaker) rarely has a problem concentrating. This person is often deeply immersed in thought. However, the person receiving, or listening, can be distracted by other, pressing thoughts. The listener could be focusing on what was said two minutes earlier and is mentally structuring a response, or the listener could be counting the seconds until he or she can escape, or the listener could simply be daydreaming. Whatever the distraction, two-way communication will not be effective unless the listener provides total attention to the speaker.

Many useful techniques are available to help a listener concentrate and retain information. One of the more popular techniques is to ask the speaker questions about the subject matter being related. Another frequently used technique is to restate the message to the speaker. Both of these approaches flatter the speaker by demonstrating an attentive listener. But the person who listens gains much more than the speaker's approval. The listener gains knowledge. It is from this knowledge that a listener can learn, grow, and add value to a project. The next time someone has something to say to you, give it your undivided attention and witness the results for yourself.

Greet People—Remember Their Names

Remember when you were passing a senior manager in a hallway and you were greeted not only with, "Good morning!" but you also were acknowledged by name? It helped to perk up your day, and made you feel appreciated, important, and accepted. All this from a five- to ten-second greeting.

Now, recall how you felt on another, similar occasion, with a different senior manager who passed you and not only said nothing, but ignored you altogether. To make matters worse, you and the manager ride in an elevator, in silence, for a full 30 seconds.

These two simple, but common, examples demonstrate the power of acknowledging another person. The positive effect of a greeting is magnified when you address the person by name. You do not have to be a senior manager in order to brighten someone up. That someone can be a peer, a subordinate, or even someone who is in a higher job position. We *all* like the feeling of being recognized, of being accepted, no matter how low or high our job status. We also tend to work a little harder, do a little more, for someone who is friendly to us.

Ask Questions—Do Not Assume

Don't assume or force others to assume. If you have information that others need to do their jobs effectively, then make that information readily and clearly available. Whether the information is in your desk, in your head, or in your intentions, share it as soon as you can. Can you remember a time when someone gave you an assignment without also providing you with all that you needed to know? You went off and did what you thought was expected—you made assumptions. Remember how you felt when you learned that some of your assumptions were invalid? Remember also how much time and energy you wasted? Assumptions and waste share a common ancestry; however, they are likened more to sisters than distant cousins.

Everyone makes assumptions. Sometimes this is the right thing to do or even the only option available. But most times it is the absolutely wrong thing to do. Asking a question, clarifying a point, restating the assignment—all of these things take so little time. Yet, when you don't take the initiative, literally hours or days of misdirected time can be wasted. This time cannot be recovered. Lost time can even affect a major activity on a project. Reduce waste: Ask questions and don't assume.

Know What to Expect

Some of the most common communications problems among people, departments, or organizations are misunderstandings that arise from expectations about the responsibilities of others. That is, people expect certain things from those on whom they rely in some manner. Unless these expectations, or dependencies, are clearly documented, measurable, and approved, it is folly to expect that they will occur.

It is so easy to assume that other people or groups will know what you expect from them. The fallacy here is that no one can ever know what you expect unless you communicate your expectations. And you cannot know what others expect unless they offer to share it or unless you ask. When two parties agree to communicate their expectations of each other, it is important for these expectations to be documented, measurable, and approved. Documentation can reduce the chance that misunderstandings will arise later. Measurability is needed to track the execution of an agreement, to ensure it is being implemented correctly. Approval ensures that all involved parties understand the conditions of an agreement and commit to support these conditions. *Knowing what to expect is* such an important topic that some examples are provided next. Each example is divided into a *problem, scenario,* and a *solution.*

Problem Development's expectation of the role of those who have been invited to a design inspection meeting does not match the expectations of the invited. (Note: An inspection involves a group of people, typically peers, who gather to examine an activity with the goal of identifying and removing defects and problems. See Chapter 5 for more about inspections.)

Scenario When the development group is planning an inspection of its design, several groups from outside the immediate development area are invited. These groups typically include publications, test, performance analysis, product support, quality assurance, and even other development areas. The developers expect the invited groups to evaluate the design technically. What often happens, however, is that most of the design inspection period is consumed by educating invited group members in the way this portion of the product works, rather than discovering design defects. It irritates developers to get so little benefit on their investment of time spent preparing for and conducting the design review. Ill feelings are also exhibited by many of the invited guests, who see these design inspections as one of the few opportunities to acquire much-needed education about the product.

Solution There should be a small inspections-related document that not only defines the what, who, how, when, and where of the inspection process, but also states the objectives of the inspection process as they relate to *each* of the invited groups. This document should be reviewed and approved by all the attending groups *before* the first inspection occurs. Once everyone knows what to expect from one another, then the same meeting described in the scenario can actually be viewed as a successful meeting—where all groups walk away as winners.

* * *

Problem Testers are frequently asking developers to fix problems in the code, which later turn out *not* to be problems. The developers expect only valid problems to be reported to them.

Scenario Once the code has been developed and is in the hands of the formal test group, all types of problems will be reported to the developers for them to fix. Many of these problems will not be actual code defects and therefore will be rejected for one or more reasons. Some examples of invalid problems include:

- User error
- Duplication of a problem already reported
- Not reproducible
- Suggestion—function not intended in this release

Perhaps as many as one out of every two problems reported turn out not to be problems at all. For a developer who must investigate every problem reported against his or her code, this can lead to a great deal of wasted effort, not to mention be an annoyance.

Solution   A meeting should be called by the developers. The invited are the testers. The objective is to limit the number of problems that are logged and eventually rejected. Guidelines for the testers to follow should be created. An example: The telephone numbers of certain developers are made available to the testers to allow questions to be asked. This will help testers establish the validity of each problem before it is logged. Also, subsequent meetings should be called to examine the problem statistics to ensure that the number of *rejects* being logged continues to decrease. It should be agreed that the developers and testers will work together to improve their mutual productivity— should additional action be required.

* * *

Problem   The publications writers expected the product specifications to be complete for use in writing the product publications.

Scenario   The first draft of the publications is being written. These publications will become part of the final product. The writers are having a very difficult time acquiring the necessary information about the product. Most of the data was expected to be included in the product specifications. The only option remaining to obtain the necessary information is to go to the developers and ask them dozens of questions, answers to which are to be found only in their heads. This option, however, is infrequently exercised. It would not only be unbearably time consuming for the writers, but the developers would object to spending any appreciable time doing this.

The first drafts are finally made available for review. Later, the responses from reviewers show that the publications have some serious omissions and that numerous assumptions made by the writers are not correct. The writers are peeved at the developers for not providing the necessary data when it was originally required. The developers are peeved at the writers for not getting "up to speed" more quickly on the product and for consuming as much of the developers' precious time as they did.

Solution   The writers should have made their expectations known to the developers at the beginning of the product development cycle. It would have been so easy. The writers should have documented what information they expected from the product specifications. The writers should also have documented the need for occasional consulting from the developers and the nature of the consulting. The developers may want to designate one or two developers as the focal point for the writers, rather than allow all the developers to be interrupted from their assignments. These requirements should then have been approved by the development shop. Now the two parties know what to expect. If the product specifications become available and do not meet the agreement, then the publications shop must not approve them until they are updated to the agreed-upon level. The point to be made here is that, once a *document of understanding* has been agreed upon by these two groups, it is relatively easy to address and resolve any conflicts that may arise.

Management Tools

In the end, management is accountable for creating, encouraging, and enforcing a healthy communications atmosphere across a project. Of course, the efforts from nonmanagement personnel are vital, but management sets the tone. Some examples of actions that can be taken by management to foster the desired communications are:

- Catch communications problems early—don't allow them to fester.
- Ensure a level of information flow, throughout the project, that is viewed as at least adequate from a frequency, quantity, and quality basis.
- Treat everyone equally—be fair, but firm.
- Do things that are fun.

Nonmanagers look to managers to correct both intra- and interdepartment communications problems before they become serious. Most problems will be apparent to the astute manager. Some will be difficult to uncover. It is the manager's responsibility to maintain an open two-way channel of communication with employees, with peer management, and with senior management. This communications link should keep the manager aware of serious, or potentially serious, problems that occur. All eyes will be on the manager. The worst thing that could happen is for the manager to take no action. This will be viewed as condoning the problem and this can cause a decline in morale among the project players. (See "Checking the Organization's Pulse," in Chapter 2, for more ideas on how project leaders can maintain an open channel of communications within a project.)

Project members want to be kept informed. Usually, the amount of information that members expect will be more than they need to perform their assignments. Department meetings are a great way to communicate information in a fairly small and informal setting. It encourages camaraderie among the department members and stimulates the flow of good, open communications. The frequency of department meetings really depends on the type of department, but consider having one each week. At least schedule meetings for the same time each week, and if something interferes with that time slot, it is okay to skip a week now and then. It would be helpful if all departments within an organization or project reserve the same half-day for such meetings (a given department meeting duration would typically be one hour or less). This *united* approach will help to ensure the availability of this period of time each week. The department manager should keep the meeting flowing with useful, interesting, or entertaining information. If the manager allows meetings to linger past their usefulness, the participants will begin to look for ways to avoid the meetings—and rightfully so.

Area meetings, where two or more departments get together, can also be a good communications tool. However, area meetings should be held less frequently than department meetings. Area meetings should share the accomplishments of all project groups that are participating in the meeting. This is also a good place to recognize those employees who have accomplished something special or unique.

Another useful technique is to invite selected nonmanagement leaders and aspiring employees to attend management meetings where the project is tracked. This will provide insight for the nonmanagers, insight that they might be able to utilize in their assignments and share with others. It will also help make nonmanagers visible to the management team.

Management must do its best to treat all employees the same. No biases should be allowed to exist. In addition to fairness, management should develop a reputation for being firm and for acting swiftly, which will foster confidence in the management team. Employees want an action-oriented management team. Inaction will breed complacency and contempt for the organization.

Encourage hard work, but make sure that a healthy dose of fun is included. Many ideas are available to foster enjoyment. Some examples include providing unique entertainment at selected meetings, sponsoring seminars, and having picnics with softball or volleyball challenges. A particularly beneficial, creative idea is a *skills enrichment day*—a day set aside to allow project participants to listen to speakers who are experts in various technology areas and self-improvement topics.

We Are All in This Together

Coming together is a beginning,
Keeping together is progress,
Working together is success.

Anonymous

Reams of material have been written on the subject of interpersonal communication. This chapter is intended to expose you to some of the more common communications problems encountered in software development projects. You have probably recognized that many of these problems are common to any group of people, in practically any field of endeavor, who are assembled to achieve something.

You might also have recognized that the recommended way to eliminate or at least control these problems requires actions that many would view as common sense. If sense were so common, communications problems would not be so pervasive. A concerted effort is required on everyone's part to fix these problems. Management, in particular, must build and then maintain a work environment that supports effective, interpersonal communications.

Demonstrating respect for others is essential for improving communications among people. When project players understand that "we are all in this together" and that it is through harmony with one another that achievements are reached, then they have risen above providing the adequate to producing the best.

4

Scheduling for Success

The schedules created for a software development project can make or break the project, the product, and the people. The attention and forethought applied to this critical scheduling exercise can mean the difference between:

- Management in control and management in panic
- High product quality and poor product quality
- A full-function product and a limited-function product
- High employee morale and low employee morale
- High employee productivity and low employee productivity
- On-time (or early) delivery and late (or no) delivery
- Competitive product costs and uncompetitive product costs
- Successful market entry and unsuccessful market entry
- Customer satisfaction and customer dissatisfaction
- Marketing strength and marketing weakness
- Timely next release and late (if at all) next release
- Product success and product failure

Simply put, the project scheduling activity can make the difference between profit and loss. The heartbeat of the entire product development cycle *is* the project schedules. Every organization, every machine, and every person is directly affected by schedules. If the schedules are unreasonable, then the expected progress will soon become blocked. This blockage will cause project challenges to emerge, challenges that would otherwise be unnecessary, challenges that must now be met in order to deal with the obstructions. The failure of a major activity to be completed on schedule will eventually impact the schedules of subsequent project activities. This domino effect could continue until the project topples.

Three primary elements are important if a successful project schedule is to be developed. The project schedule must:

- Be well thought out
- Have the commitment of the participants
- Be aggressive but achievable

Scheduling for Failure

The following scenario illustrates how an unrealistic project schedule plan can snowball into a major mess. Doing a less than adequate job developing a project schedule plan is akin to scheduling a project for failure.

During the first month of the project, an unofficial, rough scheduling estimate allows for a 12- to 18-month product development cycle. A month later, a preliminary schedule is developed that suggests a 12-month duration. Everyone in touch with the project knows that this 12-month schedule is quite optimistic. However, no one is overly concerned since the schedule is only preliminary. A final schedule with all the necessary detail is forthcoming.

In the meantime, the product objectives are completed and all the participating groups agree on the direction the product should take. The writing of the product specifications document has begun. The high-level design is also beginning. There is an overall good feeling about the project. Staffing of people with the required skills is underway. Coming on board are programmers, for both developing and testing the product, publications writers, and support personnel.

It is understood by all that this project is extremely important to the company. It is also understood that the product must be delivered to customers as soon as possible. Two factors are offered as major reasons for supporting an early customer delivery. The first reason is to bring in revenue in the next fiscal year, which starts in one month (and, therefore, ends in 13 months). The second reason is to help ensure that several key customers choose this product over competitive products. No one doubts that the product must be delivered as soon as possible.

The project planners commit to having detailed project schedules in place within the next two weeks. One planner remarks, "The detailed schedules could really be available within just one week. This project is a lot like others that I have planned and there really isn't much to laying out the schedules." The planners decide not to include the technical people in the project scheduling activities. The rationale is, "Leave the technical people alone as much as possible so they can get some real work done."

A draft of the detailed schedules is ready in three days, when it is reviewed by a few members of the management team. Everyone agrees that the schedules are aggressive, but they also believe that this is the "right" schedule plan if the product is to hit the marketplace on time. Some minor changes are made and a final draft is produced. The planners survey the key technical leaders about the schedules. Some technical leaders express opinions that the schedules are too aggressive and could only be met "if the wind is at our backs." Also, there is concern that the projected staffing might be too aggressive to be achieved, or, if staffing levels are achieved, the skill level of the new people might be lower than required. If the project is staffed with people with a lower skill level than anticipated, more time will be necessary to bring these people "up to speed." The reply from the planning department is "Don't worry about staffing. That is our turf and we are working on it."

Some of the technical leaders feel that vacations and holidays have not been planned into the proposed schedule sufficiently, especially since some people have accrued excess vacation days from the previous aggressive project. The response is, "Overtime was not planned. Therefore, overtime acts as a buffer should it be needed. Besides, there are many months before the end of the year when major holiday and vacation periods could occur. We should be in pretty good shape by then."

Another concern is that the expected programmer productivity rate is on the high end of the range rather than in the middle or on the low side. The response from planners is that most of the technical leaders are seasoned veterans whose high skills skewed the productivity rate higher. The planners add, "If this project is to be successful, we will have to achieve the higher productivity rate." A few other concerns are raised but are essentially shrugged off. However, to address the concerns of the technical people, schedules are lengthened by two weeks. While this does not significantly satisfy the technical people, it does help to reduce some of the tension that is building. The technical leaders rationalize, "The product will be done when it's done, so why make a big deal of it now? Anyway, nearly every project seems to follow this pattern. So what's new?"

The planners grumble, "It's too bad the lead technical people don't have more business savvy and realize that, to make it big in this business, you have to take big risks. That's why the technical people don't run the business. We will just have to drive the organization to achieve this schedule."

There seems to be an unsettled feeling across the project, something of a standoff. No mutual meeting of the minds ever took place where each side could work through the concerns of the other side. (In fact, there should not be a notion of "sides." Instead, the business and technical objectives should be shared by all. A "we are in this together" spirit should be the prevailing goal.) The general conclusion is that perceived standoffs like this have never stopped forward progress before. This is "business as usual."

The product specifications are written, then reviewed. There are more review comments than expected. The reason appears to be that the specifications were not quite finished, but in the interest of maintaining project schedules, they were distributed on time. The planners are happy. The technical people are not happy, but recognize the importance of meeting schedules. The product specifications are updated to address the review comments and then redistributed for everyone's use. More comments are generated from the updated specifications. The most recent comments are all but ignored. It seems that the schedules did not allow for a second review of the product specifications. It was expected (and hoped) that the review cycle could be shortened to a single, three-week review period, rather than two, two-week review periods with a document update period in between.

Since more time is required to perform the single update of the product specifications than has been planned, the high-level design is now behind schedule. The developers are working overtime in an attempt to finish the high-level design within the planned schedule. Furthermore, one of every four design inspections is failing. The schedule had allowed for design inspections but not for recovery time for inspections that failed. Even with the overtime that people are working, the schedule is slowly and frustratingly slipping. High-level design is finally completed, yet is two weeks behind schedule. The perception is, "Not too bad," especially when the two weeks that were added to the project are taken into account.

As low-level design, coding, test plans, and publications plans are being developed, a disturbing realization takes hold. The product specifications are still not sufficiently complete. The prevailing thought is that they would have been complete if they had been through two review periods, with a document update period in between. Unfortunately, it is too late to turn the clock back. The developers do their best to refine the specifications data as they proceed with their low-level design and coding. However, there is no time for them to physically update and redistribute the product specifications to other groups within the project. Now the testers and the publications writers begin to fall behind their schedules. Many options are offered, but only one will really solve the problem: The developers must update and redistribute the product specifications. They do just that.

Several weeks pass. The product specifications have been updated and distributed throughout the project. The low-level design has been completed. The coding, unit testing and function testing, however, are further behind schedule. Also, the testers and writers discover that they are not able to recover all their lost time. The testers and writers perceive that the real, critical path lies not with them but with the developers—in getting the code ready to enter the first phase of the formal test period. It seems that, when the schedules were developed originally, no one thought to include the writing of the unit test and function test plans. In the interest of protecting schedules, the unit test is abandoned and the function test is now the focus of activity.

The project is now six weeks behind the planned schedule. If any additional slips occur, the project will not be able to bring in revenue for the next fiscal year, as planned. (The two-week buffer, plus starting one month before the fiscal year began, accounts for the six-week leeway.) In response, the code is declared ready for the first formal test phase—the component test. Plans are put in place to complete the function test in parallel with the component test.

A medium disaster develops. Two groups, the developers and the testers, are performing tests on the same code and at the same time. Many of the same **bugs** (defects) are being discovered by both groups. To make matters worse, the response time of the developers in fixing the bugs found by the testers is much longer than desirable. The reason: The developers are busy trying to complete their own function testing. To "fix" this problem, the developers are instructed to correct bugs according to priorities set by the testers. The project leadership stresses the importance of containing the duration of the component test to its original plan. However, in spite of this mandate, the component test takes four weeks longer than planned. The code that the developers delivered was just too "buggy."

The schedule is now ten weeks longer than was originally planned. The developers have been working a heavy dose of overtime for many months. People are weary, frustrated, and edgy. The major holiday and vacation period has arrived, but few are able to take any appreciable time off. The most repeated phrase is, "I don't want to go through this again!" The second most repeated phrase is, "But it will happen again. It always is the same way. We never seem to learn from our mistakes!"

If this scenario were to run its course, the project would be nearly four months late. This would cause the product cost to come in significantly higher than planned. Even though the "planned" project schedules were apparently too aggressive to begin with, the expected, and missed, delivery date promised to the project leadership, marketing, customers, and other interested groups can only cause disappointment. Disappointment, however, may be too kind a word, since the plans that outside groups have made based on the product's expected delivery date will need to undergo serious modification.

Other negative "fallout" will also be felt. Some expected customer sales will have disappeared, the next release will be available much later than planned (if at all), and a sometimes irreversible toll on the personal lives of the project team might have occurred. Whether the blame for lateness rests with the planners, the project technical people, or should be shared by both is not a point for debate here. The point is, the more a project schedule is thought out and mutually agreed to by all the key participants as being aggressive, but achievable, then the greater the likelihood that *everyone* will win.

The Successful Journey

A project's schedules should guide the project on a successful journey toward delivery of the product on time, within cost, with the expected quality, and without demoralizing the project's personnel. As stated earlier, three primary ingredients are necessary for developing a good project schedule plan. The schedule plan must:

- Be well thought out
- Have the commitment of the participants
- Be aggressive, yet achievable

Many factors contribute to the successful implementation of these primary ingredients. The remaining sections of this chapter identify the more important factors that should be considered in constructing a project schedule plan.

When to Develop the Project Schedule Plan

For a new project, broad, project-oriented schedules should be identified within weeks of the project's conception. Although these schedules will be preliminary, they will set the pace and level of expectation for the project until better schedules can be developed. A *near-term* set of schedules, however, should be available almost immediately. "Near term" is defined here as being one to six weeks in duration.

The full project schedule plan cannot be seriously developed until after the product objectives have been approved. However, the project schedule plan should be completed a short time after the high-level design and product specifications are approved. Once these activities have been completed, there should be sufficient understanding of the product to support a definition of a full set of schedules.

Cyril Northcote Parkinson, British historian and author, once wrote that "Work expands so as to fill the time available for its completion." Schedules are critical to maintaining a healthy productivity rate for the members of a project, whether for a small group of people or for a large organization. It is difficult to measure progress unless there is a plan to track against. Resist waiting until all imaginable details about the product content and the project plans are known before working the full project schedule plan. Each person has a **variable productivity potential**. Analogous to a variable resistor, a person has considerable flexibility to vary his or her productivity to match the needs of the task at hand. Aggressive, but achievable, schedules will help to harness the energies of project personnel so that an acceptable level of progress can be achieved throughout the duration of the project. Also, a "busy" person is much more content than a partially busy or idle person.

Overlapping Activities

Allowing activities that have a relationship to one another to overlap rather than be performed in series can be either good or bad, depending on the kinds of activities and the amount of overlap involved. For example, the high-level design of a product must be done before the low-level design. However, it is possible, and frequently recommended, to allow some low-level design to begin before all the product's high-level design has been completed. This is okay, providing that all of the high-level design that can impact the specific area to be low-level designed has been completed. In this example, no revisions or duplicate work loads are anticipated. It is a fairly clean example.

There are cases where overlapping two activities can be harmful. In the scenario earlier in this chapter, overlapping the function test and the component test was *not* okay, and resulted in lower productivity for both activities and a project that was certainly difficult to manage. An approach that would be acceptable, however, is to allow the component test to begin only on those functions that have already been function tested. Now two groups aren't duplicating their time by finding the same bugs. A caution to note here is that, if the same developers who must fix the bugs discovered in the component test are still function testing other code, then a productivity "impact" will occur as their time is shared across two goals.

When you examine activities that might benefit from being overlapped, it should be readily apparent whether the overlap is acceptable. The key is to look for dependencies among the activities. You should avoid scheduling two activities to overlap if one can be impacted by the other; in other words, if one has a dependency on the other. Whenever an impact occurs, someone or something must wait for someone else or something else. This cuts into productivity, which is directly related to scheduling.

Another example from an earlier scenario involves the publications writers who were waiting for the product specifications to be completed. It is not possible to write product publications at the same time the product is being defined in the product specifications. The writers require the product specifications to define the subject matter for the publications.

Consider the following negative by-product, which can result when one person is waiting for another person: Jerry Miller is waiting for Ann Smith to complete an activity. There is a tendency for Miller to try one of two things. Either Miller will further slow down Smith, by asking questions and gathering data, or Miller will make assumptions. These assumptions might not all prove correct and, consequently, revisions will be necessary later.

Overlapping activities that will not impact one another can have a positive impact on overall schedules. For instance, management should consider overlapping activities when a schedule needs to be refined to shorten its total length. However, bear in mind that the complexity involved in managing schedules increases as the total number of overlapping activities increases. Also, be certain that the people and machine resources required to implement each of the overlapping activities are not tightly shared between the activities. If you do plan to share these resources, and allow little or no room for contingency, then you are risking a situation in which one or both activities are not completed on time. If one activity falls behind schedule, the resources to complete the other activity are immediately impacted. This situation places an undesirable competition for resource attention upon both activities.

Review Cycle for Project Documents

Project documents include any document that must be delivered at some point in the product development cycle. Examples include:

- Product objectives
- Project schedule plan
- Product specifications
- Contracts with vendors
- Process and methodology documents
- Design documents
- Publications plans
- Test plans
- Publication drafts

All project documents must be reviewed for completeness, accuracy, information, and agreement. After these documents have been distributed, responses are expected to be returned to the originator.

Figure 4.1 illustrates a recommended, five-phase review cycle for most documents. The first phase is *preparation*. This is usually the longest phase and can vary anywhere from one week for very small, simple documents to many weeks for large, complex documents.

The next phase, *review*, begins when the document is distributed for examination. This phase is typically one to four weeks in duration, depending on the document type and size, and on the proximity of the reviewers. (Do they work in the same building? Same city? Same country?) Test plans might take two weeks, product specifications four weeks. You should make certain that each document is distributed to all parties that have a need to approve or review the document. This is the time to ensure that the distribution list of people is complete and that no

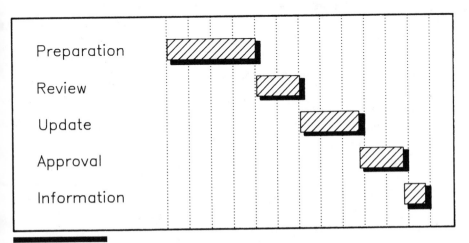

Figure 4.1. Review cycle for product documents

required people or organizations are overlooked. It is recommended that a meeting of the primary reviewers be called during the latter part of this phase. A face-to-face meeting is an excellent way to allow all participants to voice their concerns to one another and to identify and log as many problems as can be identified. You should not expect to resolve many problems in this type of meeting. In fact, the primary purpose for the meeting is to record problems, not resolve them. Spending more than one to two minutes to resolve a problem is usually detrimental to the progress of the meeting. Problems that require more time to resolve should be logged and then solved outside the meeting.

The third phase, the *update*, is used to modify a document in response to comments from reviewers. This phase sets aside time to react to comments and concerns that, once addressed, will ensure a better product or project. This phase may be from one to six weeks in duration, depending not only on the size and type of document, but also on the quantity and complexity of the problems identified and the comments made. Any updates made to a document should be highlighted in some fashion, such as the use of *change bars* in the margins. This will later allow the reviewers to locate quickly the most recent changes to the document.

The fourth phase, *approval*, is the final opportunity for responses on a document. It is expected that the majority of comments and concerns have already been received from the review phase and addressed during the update phase, so relatively few comments are expected. This phase is called approval because final agreement on the document's contents must be reached here. This phase is also typically one to four weeks in duration. As with the second phase, the review, it is recommended that the primary reviewers gather for a meeting during the latter part of the approval phase. This meeting is even more important than the review phase meeting because the final approval of the document is solicited. As in the review phase, you should expect to log some problems for resolution outside the meeting.

The last phase is *information*. This phase is used to record any changes to the document that have occurred during the approval phase. The document is then distributed for informational purposes only; no more comments are expected or solicited. This phase could be as short as one day (to issue a memo describing any agreed-upon changes) or as long as several weeks (to update changes in a large document). Again, if changes are made in the document, then some form of unique change bars should be used.

Some documents might need only the preparation, approval and information phases. These documents are usually quite brief and provide little controversy. However, to omit the review and update phases for documents that are considered primary—such as product specifications, test plans, and product publications drafts—is usually a grave mistake. Do not attempt to shorten the product development cycle in these areas.

For documents that have both a review and approval phase, you should be aware that there is a tendency for the review phase draft to receive a less thorough review than you might expect. The reason: Reviewers will attempt to manage their own time as effectively as they can and, knowing that another draft will be forthcoming during the approval phase, they will frequently put off a thorough review until a document is at its best. While this type of procrastination might make sense for reviewers, it is inefficient for the document and the project as a whole. The owner of the document has a responsibility to ensure that reviewers participate throughout the document review cycle.

Planned Buffers

A **buffer** is a designated period built into a schedule to serve as extra time or contingency to help absorb delays that might unexpectedly occur. There are three buffer categories for a product development project:

- Planned buffers
- Overtime, shifts, and temporary personnel buffers
- Holiday and vacation buffers

This section will discuss planned buffers. The remaining categories are discussed in the two sections that follow.

Every project schedule plan should have some buffer built into it. This buffer plan should not involve holidays, vacations, and overtime. If the schedule plan is built for things going "right," they won't. Ante-up the buffer now—other than holidays, vacations, and overtime—to avoid making the regrettable mistake of having to live through an "oversight" for possibly the duration of a project.

Typically, major work activities should have some buffer built into them. For example, when planning for a system test, recognize that the system test procedures must be run more than once. The first time they are run, defects in the product code or in the test procedures themselves will be found. Once corrected, the tests can advance further, but more defects will likely be discovered. There are many algorithms available for determining the duration of major activities, such as for a system test. However, any generalized algorithms are subject to debate and this is not a point of discussion here. If you believe it takes one week to run all the system test cases, assuming everything runs with no problems, and it is your belief that the system test will be an equivalent length of four such runs, then you have identified four weeks of work. Whatever algorithm you employ, however, attempt to factor in a 10 to 20 percent buffer. This holds true for most activities, including the writing of product specifications, designing the product, and coding the product.

A frequently made mistake is to place a buffer at the tail end of a project. The buffer should be proportioned throughout the activities of the project if the project schedule plan is expected to hold together. This scattered placement of a buffer significantly increases the likelihood that people will meet their intermediate project schedules. It will also help to reduce a buildup of frustration that results when a project is continually beyond reach of completing major activities as planned. This frustration not only has a negative effect on morale, but also robs the project of valuable productivity that can never be recovered. Occasionally, the "luxury" of a buffer will not be possible for some project activities. When this happens, activities that fall somewhere before and after the *no-buffer* activities must have an ample buffer to compensate.

It is useful to schedule activities to end on Fridays and start on Mondays. This paces the organization to complete an activity by Friday, but, if more time is needed, the weekend can act as a mini-buffer. If activities are scheduled to end on Mondays, there is a tendency to plan on working on the weekend. When a weekend is planned, it no longer serves as a real buffer.

Overtime, Shifts, and Temporary Personnel Buffers

Never plan for overtime. It will happen anyway. Overtime is a natural buffer to help protect imperfect project schedule plans. If overtime is planned, even more overtime will be needed—a trap to avoid. The greatest cause of "burnout" is excessive overtime. Burnout is a condition that typically results when a person works long hours across many days and takes an insufficient amount of time away from the workplace for rest and relaxation. Burnout results in a person making more mistakes, being less productive, and frequently being more irritable to co-workers. Again, excessive overtime is the greatest cause of burnout. You want to avoid both.

The advice offered in this section is generalized. There are more specific exceptions, of course. For example, if a project is only one month in duration, then perhaps all three areas—holidays, vacations, and overtime—must be factored into the schedule plan. In this case, however, the employee can be given time off immediately after the month's activities are completed. For very long projects, it should be easier to honor the goal of not planning the use of holidays, vacations, and overtime in the project schedule plan.

Assigning people to work split shifts can be an effective way to manage limited resources within a project. For example, if the project is entering a formal test phase and there are a limited number of machines available to use for testing, then people might have to work split or separate shifts. One test team can work from 8 AM to 4 PM, while another test team can work from 2 PM to 10 PM. The two-hour overlap is useful to ensure continuity between the two test teams. When projects resort to working shifts, the greatest difficulty is to ensure that all necessary personnel are also available to support the longer work day. In the example just cited, developers must be available to fix problems that testers find. Also, the people who support the machines must be available to ensure that the machines remain operable.

The use of temporary personnel can be another effective way to buffer schedules. These additional people can come from within or from outside a company. However, several pitfalls can reduce the effectiveness of this option:

- Failure to plan ahead
- Failure to plan for training time
- Addition of management and communications overhead
- Loss of skills

It is not realistic to expect that the number of people with the precise skills needed will be available for transfer to your project on short notice. You must anticipate the need for temporary personnel if you expect to obtain skilled people when they are required. Even if you find skilled people to help, they will still require some time to get "up to speed." Therefore, factor in this *training curve* when you set the start date for temporary recruits. A caution, assuming the temporary personnel are just that, temporary: Do not forget that, when the temporary personnel leave, they take with them knowledge and skills that you may need later in the project or on a subsequent project.

Finally, remember that more people, even though temporary, will require additional time to manage and lead. Communications, already a major obstacle in software development projects (see Chapter 3), will also require additional time and attention from the project leadership.

Holiday and Vacation Buffers

Do not plan to work holidays. There are two reasons for this. The first is that everyone needs some time off, whether to spend with family members, friends, or just to be alone. In the heat of trying to maintain schedules, this oasis of holiday time can be therapeutic physically, mentally, and emotionally. Having said that, the second reason for not planning to work holidays is that these days represent the very last buffer to reach for. An example is in order:

> The product being developed has already been announced to the public. The delivery date for the product also has been announced. A customer has placed a very large order and is expecting special delivery on the same day the product becomes available. For whatever reason, the project has since fallen behind schedule. A company commitment has been made to the customer. The customer has made an appreciable financial outlay in people and materials in order to be ready for the product the first day it is available.

Now what happens? Every reasonable attempt must be made to honor the commitment to the customer. Unless there is extenuating personal hardship, the employee should be asked to work a holiday. This example is an extreme case. While it is not likely to happen often, it occur. Note that this example applies to a recovery schedule plan, not to the original project schedule plan.

A project schedule plan should be developed with the preferred vacation days of each participant in mind. Hardship cases, especially, must be recognized and planned for. Once a project schedule plan begins to take shape and mismatches are being negotiated, vacations, with the approval of the vacation owner, are likely targets of movement. Most employees will be flexible with their vacation days. For example, there are times throughout a project development cycle when a given person is most busy and least busy. It is strongly preferred that a person plan his or her vacation during a least-busy period. This "vacation factor" is a useful tool when arranging schedules.

Commitment of Participants

All participants in the product development cycle must feel ownership for their piece of the total project schedule. Only then will an individual's optimal productivity be possible. It is both productive and expected that one person or a small group of people will put a preliminary, **top-down** project schedule plan together. This is an attempt at understanding the general "ballpark" for the overall schedules. However, this top-down schedule must never lock in the overall participants to committed schedules. Instead, a **bottom-up schedule** must be developed.

To create a bottom-up schedule, the owners of each work activity should be solicited for information. This information includes what activities each person owns, the duration for each activity, and the dependencies each activity has on other activities. This data is collected from each organization in the project and is merged into an overall plan. Then, mismatches in dependencies, deliverables, and schedules are negotiated with each organization. Each organization has at least one representative that interfaces with other participants within the group. Therefore, all participants are represented either directly or indirectly. This manner of developing a project schedule plan is tedious, but sensible. Not only are all participants listened-to, but problems are identified that would otherwise go undetected until it is too late to recover.

You might have observed instances where an individual did not feel ownership of the schedules for his or her activities. When the going gets tough, this individual might not put the extra effort forward. This not only hurts the individual, but hurts the project as well. Personal commitment from each participant is a must.

Project Schedule Model

A project schedule model is a method used to help understand the relationships between a project's activities and the ways these relationships impact the duration of the total project. A model is built by following these steps:

1. Identify all work activities.
2. Identify the duration of each work activity.

3. Identify the dependencies that each work activity has on other work activities.
4. Construct a single chart that demonstrates the relationships among Steps 1, 2, and 3.
5. Analyze this chart for missing data and update as necessary.

When you have completed these steps, the project schedule *model* becomes the project schedule *plan*. These steps are summarized in Figure 4.2.

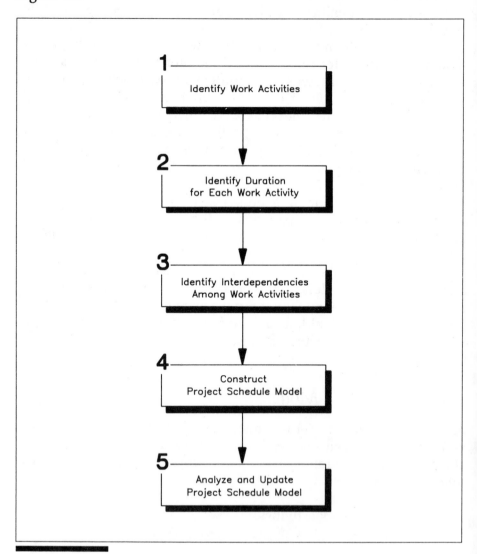

Figure 4.2. Steps in building a project schedule plan

Step 1: Identify Work Activities

Step 1 requires that all work activities for the project be identified. Examples of work activities include:

- Each project document (list phases: *preparation* through *information*)
- High-level design
- Low-level design
- Design inspections
- Coding
- Preparing a lab for product testing
- Developing test tools
- Selecting and installing a module library control system
- Each test (unit, function, component, and so on)

Figure 4.3 begins to list the activities that may comprise a product development cycle. For illustrative purposes, four categories of activities have been chosen:

- Product objectives
- Product specifications
- Component test
- Publications

All the activities listed under the column heading WORK ACTIVITY center around these four categories. Notice that Figure 4.3 has three other columns of information. The first column, NUMBER, is the number that is assigned to each activity. Although this number is arbitrary, you may find it helpful to number categories of activities with similar and/or sequential numbers. For example, note that all the publications-related activities are defined in the 200 series of numbers. This serves as an aid to quicker recognition of each activity category. Also, it is useful to choose numbers with an ample quantity of unused numbers in between, such as 10, 20, 30, 40 (rather than 1, 2, 3, 4). This will allow you to add new activities later, within their *logical* place in a category. Notice that Figure 4.3 shows new sets of activities (called groups) starting with a number divisible by 10 (such as 200, 210, 220, 230, 240), thus leaving room for five or more activities to be added later, if necessary, between any of these groups of activities.

The third column, DURATION, defines the number of work days for the activity. The fourth column, DEPENDENCY, identifies any dependencies that an activity has for another activity. More about these headings in the next sections.

For each activity that is included in developing a project schedule plan, a paragraph should be written to briefly describe the activity and its entry and exit requirements. (See Chapter 5 for a discussion on entry

NUMBER	WORK ACTIVITY	DURATION	DEPENDENCY
.	.	.	.
.	.	.	.
8	Product objectives review	15	7
9	Product objectives update	15	8
10	Product objectives approval	10	9
.	.	.	.
.	.	.	.
50	Product specifications preparation	50	8s
51	Product specifications review	20	50
52	Product specifications update	20	10,51
53	Product specifications approval	15	52
54	Product specifications information	5	53
.	.	.	.
.	.	.	.
100	Component test plan preparation	30	51s
101	Component test plan review	10	100
102	Component test plan update	10	53,101
103	Component test plan approval	10	102
104	Component test plan information	5	103
105	Component test	40	103,231s
.	.	.	.
.	.	.	.
200	Publications plan preparation	15	8s
201	Publications plan review	10	200
202	Publications plan update	5	10,201
203	Publications plan approval	5	202
204	Publications plan information	5	203
210	Publications content plan preparation	20	51s,203
211	Publications content plan review	10	210
212	Publications content plan update	5	53,211
213	Publications content plan approval	5	212
214	Publications content plan information	5	213
220	Publications test plan preparation	20	211s
221	Publications test plan review	10	220
222	Publications test plan update	5	213,221
223	Publications test plan approval	5	222
224	Publications test plan information	5	223
225	Publications test	50	223,231s
230	Publications initial draft preparation	40	213
231	Publications initial draft review	10	230
232	Publications update	20	231
233	Publications final draft review	10	232
234	Publications final update	10	233
240	Publications to production	30	234
.	.	.	.
.	.	.	.

Figure 4.3. Information used in developing a project schedule plan

and exit requirements.) This information will allow project personnel, at a general level, to understand a project's activities better. It will also identify the general dependencies that any given activity has for another activity. A detailed list of entry and exit requirements for each activity is not required until the specific plans for that activity are available for review and approval.

Step 2: Identify Duration of Each Work Activity

Step 2 is to identify the duration of each work activity. For example, if a component test plan is required, then five work activities would be identified (preparation, review, update, approval, and information activities). Each component test plan activity would then be assigned a duration. Figure 4.3 illustrates this point with activity numbers 100 through 104. Don't forget to define these durations in work days, not week days. These durations should have some historical basis behind them, such as the length of time required for each of these phases on past projects of comparable size and complexity. This is a good point to determine the people resource, called *staffing*, that will be required to perform each activity. Obviously, the number of people involved, along with their skill levels, will have a direct impact on the duration of each activity. If an activity is extensive in scope, such as the time required to design and code the product, then it is essential to develop productivity rates per person, per week or month, and to use past experiences as a guide for reasonableness.

Step 3: Identify Interdependencies Among Work Activities

Step 3 is the identification of all dependencies that each work activity has on other work activities. For example, Figure 4.3 shows that the "product specifications preparation" (activity 50) is dependent on the "product objectives review" (activity 8) being started. The "s" notation in the dependency "8s" means this activity is dependent on the "start" of the dependent activity—in this case the "product objectives review." The "product specifications review" (activity 51) is dependent on completion of the "product specifications preparation" (activity 50). And so on. Upon careful study of Figure 4.3, dependency relationships can be seen that might have otherwise been too subtle to fully understand and plan around. For example, the figure shows that the component test plan can be prepared (activity 100) after the product specifications have been prepared and made available for the start of review (activity 51s). However, the component test plan cannot be updated (activity 102) until the product specifications have been approved (activity 53) because any change that might occur during product specifications might also affect the component test plan. Therefore, product specifications must be completed and approved before the final update to the component test plan can occur.

As you continue to study Figure 4.3, it might not seem obvious, in some cases, why a certain activity is dependent on some other activity starting or finishing. That's okay. This section is not attempting to sell you on specific activities and their dependencies. Your project might have somewhat different needs as well as different identified activities. Instead, this section is intended to introduce you to a proven technique for developing a project schedule model. This technique is valid regardless of the actual names of activities or the ways their dependencies are defined.

When identifying the dependencies for an activity, you need only to specify the nearest level of dependency. That is, if A is dependent on B and B is dependent on C, it is also true that A is dependent on C. However, there is no need to specify the dependency that A has on C since the dependency that A has on B implies a dependency to C. An example of this can be demonstrated in Figure 4.3. In truth, activity 100 not only is dependent on activity 51, but also on activity 8. Since activity 51 is dependent on activity 50, and activity 50 is dependent on activity 8, then activity 100 implies (also has) a dependency on activity 8.

This is not as complex as it may appear. When you are developing a list similar to Figure 4.3, list all dependencies. When you are done, simply delete references to dependencies that are already addressed, through implication, by a closer or more immediate dependency.

Step 4: Construct Project Schedule Model

Step 4 requires that the data developed in Steps 1 through 3 now be applied in picture form so that the model can better be understood and studied. Figure 4.4 shows a simple example of how such a model can be drawn. All of the activities listed in Figure 4.3 are charted in Figure 4.4. Each box in Figure 4.4 is an activity identified by its activity number. The length of each box represents the duration of the activity. The scale at the top of Figure 4.4 depicts work days. The work days do not include weekend days or holidays. Along the left side of the figure are activity categories or, in the case of the publications category, four publications groups (plan, content plan, test, and drafts). For example, the component test category actually represents six activities, five required for the component test plan (activities 100 through 104) and one for component test (activity 105). There is nothing magical about these categories and groups. They can be redefined as you wish in order to make the picture more logical and easy to follow.

If one box directly joins another box, then the latter box depends on the preceding box. For example, the product objectives category shows three boxes, representing activities 8, 9, and 10. The placement of these boxes means that, before activity 10 can begin, activity 9 must be completed. In other words, activity 10 depends on activity 9 to be completed before activity 10 can begin. Likewise, activity 9 is dependent on activity 8.

The double dashed lines also show dependency paths. The dashed lines are used to separate boxes that happen to have one or more additional dependencies. For example, box 102, in addition to its dependence on box 101, also is dependent on box 53. Since box 102 must begin after its *latest* dependency has completed, then box 102 is shown by vertically aligning it to immediately follow box 53. An arrow with the designation "53" links box 102 to 53 to show the dependency that box 102 has on box 53.

When a box is dependent on a second box, but that second box is not close enough on the chart to allow a line to directly link the two boxes, a tag is used. For example, box 202 is dependent on box 10. However, if a line were drawn from box 10 to box 202, that line would cross over box 50. This crossover reduces the visual ease of use of the total chart. The solution is to draw a small arrow that points into box 202 with a descriptor tag of "10" to show the dependency that box 202 has on box 10. These tags help to enhance the ease with which the chart can be read and used.

There may be times when the visual ease of use of an area of the chart is improved by *offsetting* one box from another. Box 104 illustrates this offset option. Box 104 could have been drawn to abut box 103 horizontally. However, if this had been done, then the dashed lines from box 105 would have to be removed since they would connect box 104 (rather than box 103). The tag of "103" would then be added to the "231s" tag that points to the start of box 105. To see precisely how this would be drawn, see boxes 223, 224, and 225 directly below boxes 103, 104, and 105.

As each activity box is added to the chart, it is aligned with those boxes that it is dependent upon and those boxes that are dependent upon it. The result is a chart like Figure 4.4. Of course, this chart is for illustrative purposes and does not show all the activities for a full project. Have you noticed that, once you have built a list like Figure 4.3 and then converted the activities to boxes, as shown in Figure 4.4, you no longer need to know what activity a box represents? It doesn't matter (except to get a box in the right category or group). The placement of boxes is made strictly on the basis of rules that have already been

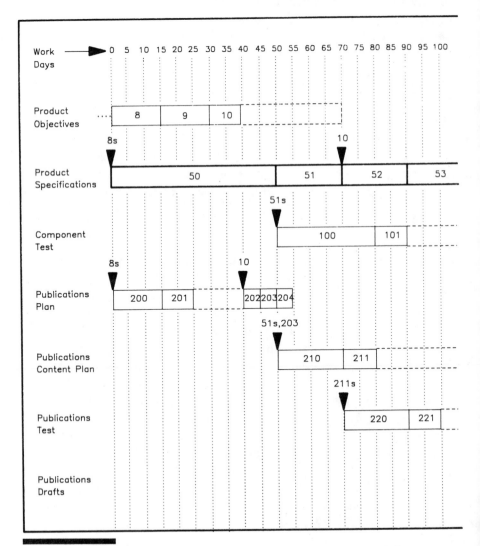

Figure 4.4. Developing a product schedule model

discussed. This greatly simplifies the building of a project schedule model.

Step 5: Analyze and Update Project Schedule Model

Once the model is initially drawn, it can be studied to determine if all work activities have been identified and all the dependency relationships have been addressed. It should also become more evident where

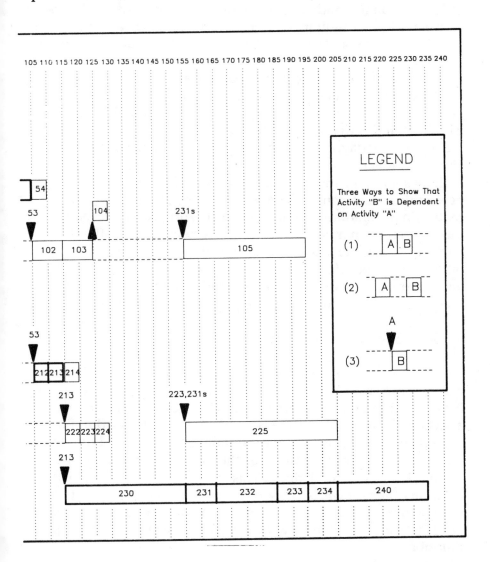

the "critical paths" are in the project development cycle. A critical path is a collection of work activities that are neck-to-neck and defines the longest duration for the project. The critical path in Figure 4.4 is shown as a darkened area beginning with box 50 and ending with box 240. This critical path is defined from the following 12 boxes:

50-51-52-53-212-213-230-231-232-233-234-240

If any of the activities represented by these 12 boxes requires more time than was planned, and none of the remaining activities on the critical path have their duration shortened, then the total duration for the project will increase. The only way to prevent the total project duration from increasing is to offset the increase by decreasing one or more of the remaining activities on the critical path by a corresponding amount.

To shorten the total project schedule, you must decrease the durations of the activities along the critical path. For example, in Figure 4.4, if each of the 12 activities on the critical path were to have their durations reduced by one day, then this critical path would be reduced by 12 days. However, it is possible to shorten the *current* critical path by 12 days without shortening the total project duration by 12 days. The reason: A new critical path could emerge that is not affected by any further reduction in duration of the activities on the original critical path. When this happens, you must now focus on the new critical path activities if you are to continue to shorten the overall project schedule. Figure 4.4 offers an example. If the combined duration of boxes 231, 232, 233, 234, and 240 was decreased to become shorter than the duration of box 225, then a new critical path would emerge. This critical path would then be:

50-51-52-53-212-213-230-225

It is useful to recognize the flexibility that you have in the placement of activities that are not in the critical path. An example can be seen with boxes 200 and 201. If you assume that box 202 will start immediately after box 10 has completed, then boxes 200 and 201 have a duration of 40 work days to be completed (total duration of boxes 8, 9, and 10 is 40 work days). The combined duration of these two boxes is 25 work days, leaving 15 days of "slack time." This means that box 200 could start 15 days later than shown, or box 201 could start 15 days later than shown, or something in between could be developed. This is an example of what boxes to *not* concentrate on when trying to shorten the total project duration.

Once, the model has been exercised to show the optimal critical path, the next step is to add real dates to each work activity. This should be easy since the duration of each activity has already been identified. Don't forget to account for holidays. (If you forget them you may find yourself and the team working through holidays.) Now you have a project schedule plan. Of course, this plan must still be reviewed by each organization participating in the project to ensure its accuracy, completeness, and commitment by all.

Steps 4 and 5 can be quite time consuming. There are CASE (Computer-Aided Software Engineering) programs on the market that will perform Step 4 automatically once Steps 1 through 3 have been input. These programs can also significantly speed up the performance of Step 5, the analysis step, by allowing "what if" variations of data (work activities, durations, staffing, and dependencies) to be entered so that the program user can immediately view the result. As an example, note that this discussion has focused primarily on building project schedules by depicting activities. When all the staffing required is also tabulated, you could find that the duration of some activities might need to be adjusted to account for a reasonably smooth "ramp-up" and "ramp-down" of people working on the project. You do not want to build a schedule that looks great on paper but does not reflect realistic staffing requirements. These CASE programs are great for identifying and making relatively easy manipulations in building the right project schedule plan for your project. Using one of these programs can save a significant amount of time and can provide insight that would otherwise be difficult to attain, particularly for very large projects with many hundreds of work activities.

These programs are also useful when changes occur within your business. This is especially true when *actual* versus *planned* dates are input to the program. Be aware that these CASE programs have varying levels of function and present pictures in radically different styles and sizes. Figure 4.4 is generic and is provided as a general example. This figure might be drawn differently by a CASE program that you choose to use.

Identifying Milestones

A project can be divided into major pieces. When one of these pieces has completed, a significant accomplishment, or milestone, for the project has been reached. Examples of milestones are:

- Product objectives approved
- Product specifications approved
- Product design completed
- Product code completed
- Unit and function test completed
- Component test completed
- System test completed
- Product delivered to customer(s)

There are two major reasons for identifying milestones in a project schedule plan. The first reason is to avoid losing sight of the big picture. A project may have several hundred distinguishable work activities. The owners of those activities are concentrating on their particular tree in the project forest. It is important to see the total picture and to put accomplishments into perspective. A particular work activity might be well behind its committed schedule. Yet, the delayed completion of this activity might have little or no real impact on the bigger picture. Of course, the opposite can also be true. A manageable way to view the total picture must be achieved so that problems and their consequences can be understood and dealt with in an effective manner.

The second major reason for identifying milestones is to report status to higher management. This is an effective way to relate progress. Higher management will usually not have the interest or time to become mired in project details. More data can always be prepared for presentation if needed.

Project milestones can also be divided into smaller milestones, called *minor milestones*. These minor milestones are sometimes used to provide further dissection of the project milestones, now called *major milestones*. This allows visibility and tracking at the next logical level of detail. For example, the minor milestones that could be defined for "product specifications approved" might be:

- Product specifications distributed for review
- Review comments and concerns received
- Product high-level design completed
- Updated product specifications distributed for approval

In this example, "product high-level design completed" is added as a minor milestone because it is difficult to completely define a product as the customer would see and use it unless a certain level of the product's design has been verified as feasible. Also, note that the next logical milestone to be added to this list would be the major milestone, "product specifications approved." This major milestone could be repeated at the end of the list to indicate that, when the list's activities have been achieved, then the major milestone that the list represents has also been achieved.

The Second Opinion

It is a beneficial exercise to have an outside person or group review the proposed project schedule plan before it becomes committed. Someone who is not emotionally attached to the project can offer insights that might otherwise be missed. This individual might also provide you with the encouragement to go in the direction you had felt, deep down, was the *right way*, but were too reluctant to mention.

The cost, in terms of time, to get a second opinion will be much less than one may expect. It is my belief that someone reviewing the project schedule plan for a week or less will discover better than 80 percent of the potential problem areas. The additional time and dollar cost for this second opinion can be insignificant compared with the potential savings of time and expense throughout the project.

A word of caution: If you don't expect to listen or react to the advice from the second opinion source, don't solicit a second opinion. More harm could result in ignoring what might prove to be good advice than in not getting any outside advice at all. The harm can come from two directions. The first is from the person(s) who was designated to provide the second opinion. A lot of work might have gone into the analysis, and that person could feel that his or her time was wasted. The second source of harm is from your subordinates, peers, and/or your project leadership. If you turn down what is viewed to be good advice, and the project later suffers for literally months, then your credibility as a decision maker could be impaired. However, if the person providing the second opinion offers poor advice, you are obviously better off by not adopting that advice.

Changing the Project Schedule Plan

It is rare for a project to be significantly ahead of schedule. It is unfortunately not so rare for a project to be significantly behind schedule—particularly if the product being built is the first of a series of products or incorporates new technology. No one wants the task of reporting bad news up the management chain. Consequently, a tendency might exist to hang on to the original, even though unachievable, schedules longer than is best for the product or the people who are building the product.

When a project has fallen behind schedule, there can be two major reasons for *not* changing the project schedule plan. The first reason focuses on people. As long as the people within the project feel a commitment to the schedules, and as long as there is a prayer's chance of recovery, then the productivity of the organization will frequently rise to the occasion. Creativity and breakthroughs often peak during these times of stretching an organization to its performance limits. There also, incidentally, is an element of art in recognizing the balance between what is achievable and what is not achievable. Years of experience can help to fine tune this art for some.

The second major reason for not changing the project schedule plan is an inability to see clearly how the schedule plan should be changed. Just because a schedule is "in the ditch" doesn't mean that arbitrarily moving the schedules one week, one month, or even six months will necessarily solve the underlying problems.

Never change a project schedule plan unless you believe the following four items to be true:

- The original schedule plan is no longer achievable.
- The problems causing the schedule slip are understood and reasonable solutions are known.
- The proposed project schedule plan change is achievable.
- The proposed project schedule plan has the commitment of the people who must make it happen.

Once you believe these four items to be true, then you must sell higher management, or whomever must be sold, that the schedule plan must change. Here is where the project technical leadership and the project management have a joint responsibility to fix a bad situation. They have a responsibility to the people on the project, to higher management, to their company, and to themselves. Some things cannot and should not be delegated.

When you contemplate major changes to a schedule plan that has a duration of one year or less, plan to make the major changes only once. Do not attempt to change a plan every two or three months. There is a cost to the overall productivity within a project each time a plan is reset.

It takes time to evaluate new schedules and, once they are adopted, to reset the project's pace to these newer schedules. There is also a cost to the long-range attitude of the project's members. There is a strong tendency for people to become accustomed to the culture and ways that they have been exposed to day after day and month after month. When project schedules are frequently readjusted, it sends a message to all that this is acceptable behavior. This, in turn, conditions the project personnel to expect a pardon when their own schedules become uncomfortably aggressive. After all, if you thought it was acceptable behavior, wouldn't you opt to move back the schedules for your own activities rather than increase your working hours each week? (Although some people would not, I believe most people would.)

For projects lasting a year or longer, you should expect some major adjustments to be required as a project evolves and progresses. Making major changes every 9 to 12 months will not be unusual. Again, avoid making major changes every two or three months.

Whenever a project schedule plan is changed, all personnel affected by that change must be informed—not just the project leaders. Everyone must be working toward the same goals. When some affected personnel do not learn of the change until well after the fact, they likely will spend valuable, unrecoverable time and effort working on the "wrong" thing. There is an even greater likelihood that personal commitment and team attitude, desirable in every project, will suffer some damage. The morale problems that often result could have been avoided. The more timely a change is communicated to the affected people, the smoother and stronger will be the transition of support from the project personnel.

Aggressive But Achievable

Some unknown wit once wrote that "The longest distance between two points is the shortcut." Defining an aggressive project schedule plan is good business. The higher the productivity of the participants, the shorter the overall project schedule and the lower the project expense. The lower the project expense, the lower the cost of the product to the customer. The lower the customer cost, the higher the volume of sales. The higher the volume of sales, the more profitable and successful the product.

Defining an aggressive but *unachievable* project schedule plan is bad business. Everyone suffers—even the customer, assuming the product is ever delivered. The customer suffers because the product's cost will likely be higher and the product's quality lower.

It is usually acceptable, although not welcomed, to make some mistakes in developing a project schedule plan. It becomes less acceptable to make the same mistakes twice. It is inexcusable to make the same mistakes project after project. The project leaders, whether managers, planners or technical leaders, are responsible for learning from past mistakes, for looking after the welfare of the project, its people, the company, and, of course, the customer. Listen to your subordinates and peers. Trust your instincts. Follow your hunches. Work together as a team to develop the right schedule plan. Not everyone's advice will be worth implementing, but listening and sorting will benefit everyone.

Building a schedule that is aggressive, but reasonable and achievable, may appear to yield a longer schedule plan than one that is too aggressive but is reset several times. It takes time to reset schedules. It takes time to address the problems that an unthoughtful schedule helped to cause. There is no better schedule than the one that is a balance of aggressiveness and achievability. If you must work through a schedule plan that is months, or even years, in length, doesn't it make sense to plan these months carefully? After all, you will be living through each one of them.

5

Planning for Quality

Quality means many things to many people. One definition:

> Quality is what you get after making a *reasonable* effort toward achieving a goal. This reasonable effort is related to the degree of difficulty of the task at hand.

Another definition is simply:

> Quality is the result of *doing your best*.

Many people believe that quality is a subjective thing and can even be viewed differently from one day to the next.

If you are serious about achieving a satisfactory level of quality for your product, you must *abandon these notions*. Otherwise, you risk a spin with quality roulette. Don't leave to chance that which can be planned and controlled.

Quality is definable, measurable, and attainable.

Quality in Name Only

The bitterness of poor quality lingers long after the sweetness of meeting schedules is forgotten.

Follow this scenario and see if you can spot the problems. These problems collectively undermine any chance of predicting whether the outcome will be a *quality* product.

The project is three months old. The product objectives are written and approved. The writing of the product specifications is underway, as is the high-level design. The project is two-thirds staffed. The schedules are defined, committed, and aggressive. In other words, the project is off to a "normal" start.

Various groups within the project—designers, developers, testers, product publications writers, and so on—have met twice now to better define the roles among the groups. The activities that each group must perform have never been clearly defined. Since most of the players have had experience from other projects, many just assume that everyone knows what to expect. Someone in this latest meeting comments to the others that, although most of the people have prior project experience, few people worked on the same project. This individual suggests that his perception of each group's role within the project might not match the perceptions of others. The conclusion offered is that perhaps the precise activities, deliverables, and expectations from each group should be listed to ensure no surprises appear later.

Another person speaks up: "On an ideal project where there is plenty of time to do what's 'right' that would be fine, but I don't have hours to spend on this."

A third person declares: "The checks and balances are obvious. For example, before the test group accepts the code for testing, it will run a set of 'acceptance test cases' to help ensure that the code meets minimum requirements for entering the test."

A developer in the room requests that she be given these test cases so she can check for those conditions as part of her own test. The test person agrees to this. The meeting rambles on a bit longer and then adjourns. There is an uncomfortable feeling by many of the participants, a haunting feeling, that something's not right. No one seems to communicate this feeling openly. (Could it be that the trusted instincts are raising a red flag?)

Two months pass. The product specifications are now completed and approved. The product's high-level design, however, has several more weeks of inspection activity. Each of the many design inspections has a different person, called a **moderator**, leading and controlling the inspection meeting. For some inspections, people from many different groups have been invited to participate, while a conspicuously few are invited to others. Someone who happened to be invited to two separate inspections observed that they were conducted very differently. Each seemed to generate a similar number of major problems, yet only one of the inspections resulted in the moderator failing the inspection and requesting rework and a reinspection.

The high-level design inspection period finally ends. It is estimated that about 70 percent of the total high-level design was actually inspected. By some, this is considered a notable achievement.

The project continues relatively on course into the low-level design activity. Overall, the project schedules have been missed by about two to three weeks, but that is considered "normal." Also considered normal is the pressure that everyone feels to not only prevent the schedules from slipping further, but to attempt to regain some of the lost schedule time.

Another month passes and the project is midway into performing low-level design inspections. There is a replay of the inconsistently moderated inspections that were "normal" during the high-level design activity. Also, not all of the low-level design is inspected, with an estimated 40 percent escaping inspection. At the start of the low-level design activity, a decision was made to forego inspections of any design developed from the more experienced programmers, as well as the design for the simpler modules of the product, regardless of the experience level of the authoring programmer. Even so, a 60 percent inspection coverage is considered acceptable by the project leadership. Project schedules slip another week, but it is perceived that the slippage would have been worse had an attempt been made to inspect all of the low-level design.

Coding is underway. A small number of programmers have requested inspections for their code. In all cases there is a less-than-expected turnout at the code inspections. Several of the programmers coding some of the more complicated areas of the product were hoping to, as one put it, "Invest some time now to prevent a lot of potential rework later." The view by these programmers is that, as they progress through the design and coding activities, many assumptions are made that relate to the interpretation of the product specifications as well as to the internal design and interfaces of other related areas of the product. These programmers were hoping to verify all assumptions during the code inspections. Unfortunately, they feel that the code inspections did not accomplish their personal objectives.

Three months later, the code is completed and the unit and function tests are now primary activities. The project is six weeks behind schedule. Many programmers, in an effort to recover some of the schedule, skip the unit testing and directly proceed to function testing. Several programmers express concern that this omission of a vital test will cause additional problems to be found during function testing and beyond. These programmers additionally explain that this test omission may further perpetuate the erosion of schedules. The reason: A problem discovered during function testing of one person's code might in turn affect the progress of many other programmers and testers since the code begins to be integrated during function testing.

After some thought, the project head decides, "This is business as usual and is the best way I know to try to recover some of the schedule slip. After all, the final product delivery date has been communicated and committed to higher management." He goes on to say, "We will just have to work harder during function testing to remove those problems that would have been found during the unit test." Testing continues.

Another three months pass. Function testing is declared completed. Two weeks have been recovered from the schedules, largely due to the omission of the unit test. The project leadership's hopes for recovering more schedule time increases. The function-tested code is delivered to the formal test group. The test group had indicated earlier in the project cycle that a set of acceptance test cases will be run. If the test cases run successfully, the code will be accepted and formal testing will officially begin. If not accepted, the code must be reworked and the acceptance test rerun. The acceptance test cases are run—and quickly fail. Someone then remembers that the developers had requested an early look at the acceptance test cases so they could be pretested. Unfortunately, the request was not part of a formal agreement or part of the exit requirements for function testing. Consequently, in the heat of trying to complete function testing, the developers felt there was no great need to exercise the tests. With "loose" requirements to start formal test, the project leadership declares victory and officially recognizes the start of formal testing.

The acceptance test cases are now run to ensure that the code is reasonably stable. The test cases require nearly two weeks of formal test time before the code begins to show signs of stability. Someone mentions aloud, "I wonder what the `quality' of the code is? Will we get through the remainder of formal testing smoothly?"

Another person counters, "Your guess is as good as any, but I wouldn't bank on it." No one seems to know what to expect.

Formal testing uncovers a rash of problems. To some, the quantity and type of problems being found seem to be in the realm of reasonableness— based on past experiences. But several others see that many of these problems could have been discovered during design and code inspections, unit testing, and even function testing. A tester mutters, "If only there had been a requirement for the function test plan to be reviewed and approved before the function test could start."

Another tester replies, "I just wish the design and code inspections had been better defined and enforced."

Midway through formal testing, an analysis of the problems that have been discovered shows that several modules in the product have a higher problem rate than others. A meeting is convened to evaluate what action, if any, should be pursued. The meeting participants represent the project leadership. The group is divided about the direction to take. One side feels that the error-prone modules should have their design and code inspected and reworked as necessary. The other side feels that most of the problems have probably already been discovered and that any rework of modules would only introduce new problems. The project head makes the final decision: "There will be no reworking of modules. We cannot afford any further delays on this project. Time is money. We have committed to senior management to announce the product next week. Along with that announcement, we will also announce when the product will be available. I don't want any more delays."

One week passes and the product is announced. Three months later, formal testing finally is completed. The product begins to be packaged—*four times*—for delivery. The product had to be recalled from packaging three times to correct newly discovered defects. The original schedule was missed by four months. The product was announced on time, but was not shipped on the announced ship date. Instead, a token few were shipped to satisfy the more outspoken customer requests. All of these token shipments had to be replaced with later, repackaged versions.

After another six months, the scenario develops into this:

During the first six months after the product was delivered to customers, an "unexpectedly" large number of problems is reported. The problems seem to be concentrated in several modules, the same modules that were earlier determined to be error-prone. Members of the team assigned to maintain the product find themselves overworked and making tradeoffs, just like those before them. The tradeoffs are balanced on the side of schedules rather than quality. After all, quality is subjective, isn't it?

The remainder of the chapter will provide you with a better understanding of what quality really is, and will explain:

- How to define quality
- How to measure quality
- How to plan for a quality product development cycle to *do it right the first time*
- How to drive toward an expected level of quality
- How to fine tune the quality process along the way
- How to recognize and encourage the achievement of quality goals

Quality Defined

The quality of our expectations determines the quality of our actions.
Andre Godin
(French social reformer)

Quality is *conformance to requirements*. Only after product requirements have been defined to the desired level of detail, and only then, can a judgment be made about the quality of the final product. Consider an example.

Two computers are operating at full capacity and installed side by side. One is a personal computer. Its approximate cost is $3000. The other computer is a mainframe with an approximate cost of $2,000,000. If both computers were developed and manufactured by the same company, and representatives of that company were asked which of these two computers is considered to be *quality*, the expected answer should be "Both." The reason is that each computer had requirements that were documented prior to its development. Then, throughout each step of the product's development cycle, each computer was measured to ensure it met its requirements. If any requirements were not being met, the defective area was reworked and then remeasured. This approach continued until all requirements were met. After each computer had demonstrated conformance to all of its respective requirements, it was rightfully labeled a quality product.

Users of products compare the *quality level* of one product to another, and are not really interested in whether the manufacturer's requirements for a given product were met. Users are more interested in whether the product matches *their own* expectations. Here is where the product developers must do their homework. Not only must they know the requirements of users, but they must also be able to measure the product throughout the product development cycle to ensure that those requirements are being met. If user requirements are not satisfied, the product will likely fail in the marketplace.

If you want your program product to be viewed as "high quality," you must define requirements in a manner that can be understood and verified by the intended users. If the product is for general distribution external to the company developing it, or, in some ways, will compete with an existing or soon-to-be released product, then the requirements must also compare favorably with other, competing program products. Then you must be able to measure the extent to which the product conforms to requirements. Consider this example of product requirements:

> Before building a word processor, you would first define precisely the word processor product to be built. You would list the product's functions—such as the ability for the user to set margins, set page numbers, move blocks of text around, merge multiple documents into a single document, and so on. You would also define the **user interface**, the performance characteristics, and so on. When you are satisfied that the product is defined exactly as it should look and perform when it is completed, you could say the product requirements are now known and defined. If the final product is developed to conform to those requirements then you can say you have built a quality product.

But there is another set of product requirements that may be less obvious than those just discussed. These are expectations that the product owner has for the product as it progresses through the many phases of the product development cycle. These requirements are more *process related* than product-function related. For example, before the product passes from the informal test phase to the formal test phase, certain exit and entry requirements must be satisfied:

- Informal test exit criteria:
    - All *major* problems have been corrected in the code.
    - All remaining problems have a committed plan to be resolved.
- Formal test entry criteria:
    - The formal test *acceptance test cases* have run successfully.
    - All formal testing procedures are written, inspected, *debugged* to the degree possible, and ready to be formally executed.

If any of these process-related requirements are not satisfied, the product should not progress to the next phase of the product development cycle until the necessary recoveries are made. Otherwise, problems that were expected to be solved in earlier phases will be passed to succeeding phases to show up as an increase to the planned workload. This situation will invalidate the basic project planning of people, duration of activities, and so on, that went into laying out the project's schedules, resources, and costs. A project in which participants continuously waive the fundamental need for all process requirements to be met will result in a project's activities becoming uncontrolled and its schedules unpredictable.

The Notion of Defects

A defect is a *deviation from product requirements*. For example, consider a case in which the product is in a test phase of the product development cycle. When a problem is discovered, it can be associated with some deviation from a requirement. This deviation might be that the code did not operate as the product specifications defined, or perhaps the product did not perform according to the design that was documented. In either case, it can be said that the product did not perform as expected, or according to the requirements. The problem is therefore classified as a **defect**.

Two Goals

Two goals of all product development cycles are:

1. To remove as many defects as is *reasonably* possible before the product is delivered to a customer
2. To remove as many of these defects as early in the product development cycle as possible

As a product is being defined, designed, and coded, the developers inadvertently introduce errors, called defects. Defects discovered and corrected during the product development cycle will obviously not be later found by a customer. Therefore, the more defects that can be found during the product development cycle, the fewer defects that will remain in the product when it is delivered to the customer.

Accelerating Costs

The cost of correcting a defect early in the product development cycle is less than the cost of correcting that same problem later in the cycle. In fact, the cost increases with each subsequent development phase or activity that is entered. As an example, visualize that you are involved in the development of an application that performs a very large number of file reads and writes. At an inspection of your low-level design, a defect is discovered in the algorithm that manages both the file reads and writes as well as in the allocation of memory required to hold the file records. After the inspection, you:

- Rework the algorithm to correct the defect.
- Verify the solution with several peers.

Say that this took you two full days. Had this defect gone undetected until the code inspection, the rework might have affected several hundred lines of code. The cost could then be a week, required to:

- Rework the algorithm to correct the defect.
- Verify the solution with several peers.
- Recode the affected portion of the program.
- Reinspect the code to ensure the proper coding implementation of the design.

Now suppose this defect had been found during the component test. The cost to the project is now much greater. In addition to the week of rework that was required when the defect was discovered in a code inspection, there are now these additional costs:

- The assistance of the tester to recreate the alleged defect
- The isolation of the exact cause of the defect within the application, possibly requiring several developers to locate the problem
- The machine time dedicated to support the debugging
- The blocking of additional test cases from being run
- Retest the fix to verify the defect has been corrected

These activities could easily represent the equivalent of yet another person-week or more of costs to the product. The message?

Find and remove defects *early*.

This is accomplished by defining the process to be followed for each phase of the product development cycle and by getting all participants to agree to follow that process. If these *process requirements* are met, it can be said that the development of the product followed a *quality process*.

The Quality Plan

It is much less expensive to prevent errors than to rework, scrap, or service them.

Philip B. Crosby
(American author, lecturer on quality)

A **quality plan** is a document that can be used to define, track, and measure product quality goals throughout the product development cycle. It requires the project leadership to consciously think about quality goals early in the product development cycle. The quality plan is *the* roadmap for an organization to follow in an attempt to *do it right the first time.*

The quality plan should be written and approved before the product specifications and the high-level design are completed. Figure 5.1 illus-

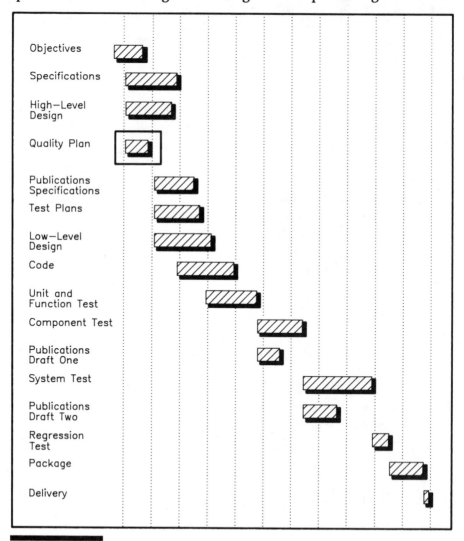

Figure 5.1. The quality plan within the product development cycle

trates the optimal point in the product development cycle for the creation and approval of the quality plan.

Can any organization write the quality plan? Yes, but: The strongly preferred group to write the plan is the one that has the most "skin" in the implementation of the plan. This is the development group (as opposed to the planners, testers, writers, and so on). If the development group does not write the plan, then they should at least take a lead role in drafting it. This participation is essential for a deeply rooted sense of commitment and ownership to be felt by the development group. Of course, once the plan has been written, it must be approved by *all* areas that are in any way impacted by the plan.

A quality plan contains the following information:

- **Defect removal activities.** This information identifies the phases and activities of the product development cycle that will be primary focus areas for finding and removing defects.
- **Requirements for each activity.** For each activity, the specific process-oriented requirements (i.e., entry, implementation, exit) used to support the discovery and removal of defects are identified.
- **Defect removal goals.** These goals identify the number of defects to be removed by each activity and by the project as a whole.

These items are discussed in the next several sections.

Defect Removal Activities

Figure 5.2 illustrates how the product phases, along with their more significant activities, can be defined. The activities have been selected based on their ability to yield major gains in removing defects. Note that other activities could be examined for the removal of defects (such as writing and reviewing publications, inspecting test procedures, or inspecting the module/link build process). However, the list of activities in Figure 5.2 includes many of the "heavy hitters," and therefore is sufficient for illustrative purposes. Most of these activities are introduced in Chapter 1. However, three activities need to be further clarified here:

- High-level design inspections
- Low-level design inspections
- Code inspections

These activities share an important element—inspection. An inspection typically consists of the following:

> A group of peers meets to inspect the design or code of a fellow peer. The data (e.g., document, design, code) to be inspected is distributed to the inspection participants a few days before the inspection meeting. This allows the inspection participants time to study the data and attend the inspection prepared to ask questions and identify suspected defects. A moderator controls the meeting and logs all the defects that are identified, as well as any questions that cannot be immediately answered. At the end of the meeting, the moderator declares that the inspection has either passed or failed. After the inspection meeting, a report summarizing the defects and questions is prepared and distributed. All unresolved defects and unanswered questions are tracked to ensure that they are satisfactorily resolved. If the inspection failed, a reinspection must occur.

At this point you probably have a general understanding of each of the activities shown in Figure 5.2. If not, you might want to review Chapter 1.

Requirements for Each Activity

Before specific requirements for each activity are identified, the first order of business is to understand the *need* to define the process require-

PRODUCT PHASE	ACTIVITY (SOURCE OF DEFECTS)
Product definition	Product objectives document Product specifications document
Product design	High-level design inspection Low-level design inspection
Code	Code inspection
Informal test	Unit test plan Unit test Function test plan Function test
Formal test	Component test plan Component test System test plan System test Regression test plan Regression test

Figure 5.2. Activities to be measured

ments for each activity. Again, an example of activities to focus upon is illustrated in Figure 5.2.

The model in figure 5.3 depicts a way to view an activity. In order to perform an activity, there must be input upon which the activity is dependent. For example, the "function test" activity requires the function test plan to be completed and approved before function testing can begin. Those elements that must be in place before an activity can be implemented are called **entry requirements**.

Each activity has **implementation requirements**. These are process requirements that help define how the activity will be implemented. For example, implementation requirements for the "function test plan" activity include a test plan that must have both a review and an approval phase. Another example: A meeting with all the approvers must be scheduled at the end of the review phase and at the end of the approval phase. Since there are many ways to implement an activity, these implementation requirements serve to bring order and efficiency in completing the activity.

Before an activity can be considered complete, certain things must occur. These are called **exit requirements**. For example the "function test" activity requires that all function test cases must have run successfully.

Benefits

After all the entry, implementation and exit requirements of each activity are defined, it is then a matter of tracking and adhering to these

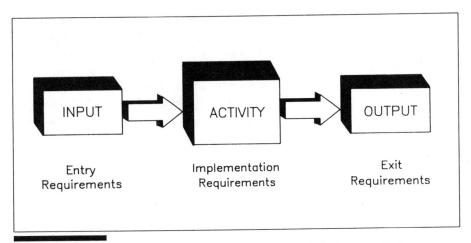

Figure 5.3. Process requirements model of an activity

process requirements. These requirements serve several useful purposes in a product development shop. In particular, they:

- Provide measurement criteria
- Force communications between groups
- Raise the quality consciousness level of the project

Process measurement criteria are often viewed as being subjective and, therefore, difficult to define and follow. Consequently, some projects may tend to staff too inadequately to address this area of a project. Such projects are more inclined to focus on the traditional, tangible areas of coding (measuring progress by counting the lines of code written) and testing (measuring progress by counting the number of test cases that have successfully run). However, the larger the project, the greater the need is to focus on the process aspects of *each* activity, not just the traditional ones. The saying, "If you don't know where you are going, then how will you know when you arrive?" applies nicely here. By having and applying measurement criteria at the entry and exit points of each activity, a heretofore subjective concept becomes an objective reality that can be readily measured.

To some, the term "force communications" might sound rather aggressive and unfriendly. However, the truly unfriendly act is not communicating. For example, if you are responsible for the implementation of an activity, then you must first make certain that all the entry criteria for your activity have been completed before you can start. If an entry requirement is an activity that is owned by another person (or group), then you must communicate that dependency to that person. Then, both parties must mutually agree on what, exactly, is being delivered and on what schedule. This situation conveniently forces groups to communicate early in the product development cycle and avoids uncomfortable and costly problems later. Now everyone knows precisely what is expected of them, and by whom and when.

Quality is something that everyone wants but many do not know how to achieve. With a clear definition of the activities and their entry and exit criteria, the employees in the trenches get a strong signal from the project leadership that quality is more than a word. It is defined and it is practiced. When quality is understood, it becomes contagious and similar measurements are developed for other aspects of a project.

Once the concept of entry, implementation, and exit requirements is accepted, the next step is to apply this concept to each of the project's activities that have been identified for measurement. This preplanning will later facilitate the discovery and removal of defects from each activity. This really is not as difficult as it might appear. It is just a matter of planning ahead what you want to do. Then, do it.

The following examples are provided only to illustrate the type of entry, implementation, and exit requirements that can be defined for a given activity. The requirements illustrated are not an exhaustive list. You might want to choose different requirements for the activities in your project.

Example 1: The Product Objectives Document

Process requirements for the product objectives document could be:

- Entry requirements:
  - The project must be funded or management approved.
- Implementation requirements:
  - There will be a review draft.
  - The contents of the review draft will be 90 percent complete before it is distributed for general review.
  - The contents of the approval draft will be 100 percent complete and will address all problems logged against the review draft.
  - There will be a meeting of the document owner and all approvers at the end of both the review and the approval phases. (The purpose is to reduce miscommunications of problems and to help the owner to better understand the problems reported. Also, these meetings allow many problems to be resolved on the spot.)
  - All problems discovered from the review draft and the approval draft must be recorded and tracked to closure. The answers must also be recorded. All approvers should receive the total problem/answer list.
- Exit requirements:
  - The approval draft must be approved by the people or organizations that are the recognized approvers.

If these requirements are met, a minimum number of defects will be passed along to the next activity: the product specifications. Notice that no mention has been made of the contents of the product objectives document. It is assumed that the contents already are defined in some *standards-related document* within the project. If this is not the case, the items that the product objectives document should address could be identified in the quality plan. (Chapter 8 identifies information that should be addressed in the product objectives document.)

Example 2: The Product Specifications Document

The second example is the product specifications document. Process requirements for this document are almost identical to those for the objectives document. Exceptions might include these implementation requirements:

- The review draft cannot be distributed before the product objectives document is approved.
- The product specifications cannot be approved until 100 percent of the high-level design has been completed.

The percentages used for some of these requirements can be arbitrary, based on variables such as the type and complexity of the product being built. But you will find it constructive and productive to strive for specific percentages as a way to both drive and measure progress.

Example 3: Low-Level Design Inspections

The third example is for low-level design inspections. Process requirements might be:

- Entry requirements:
  - The low-level design for any portion of the product cannot begin unless the corresponding high-level design has successfully completed an inspection.
  - An inspection must have a trained moderator.
  - The documents to be inspected must be in the following format and must address the following items: performance, memory/DASD storage requirements, messages and return codes, and so on.
  - The *design package* to be inspected must be distributed for review at least five working days before the inspection.
  - If any of the required participants fails to attend the inspection, the inspection is cancelled and rescheduled.

- Implementation requirements:
  - During an inspection meeting, the moderator is responsible for:
    - Recording all major problems (defects) found
    - Recording all minor problems (defects) found
    - Declaring that the inspection passed or failed (If an inspection fails, a reinspection is required and must be scheduled.)
- Exit requirements:
  - All major defects discovered must be resolved and the design documentation appropriately updated.

Other activities that would follow similar requirements are high-level design inspections and code inspections. When all the inspections of an activity—in this example, low-level design—have been completed, it is recommended that a composite inspection report summarizing all the data from the individual inspection reports be issued. This overall picture gives a clear view of the progress made and problems encountered.

If all guidelines for conducting an inspection are not already documented somewhere in the project, they could be listed here in the quality plan.

Example 4: Component Test

Consider one more example: the component test. The process requirements for component testing might be:

- Entry requirements:
  - The function test has been successfully completed.
  - The component test's acceptance test cases have successfully run.
  - All major defects found during the function test have been corrected in the code.
  - A committed plan must be in place to resolve all minor defects discovered in the function test.
  - A review draft of each product publication is available.
  - The component test plan has been approved.

- Implementation requirements:
  - Weekly test reports must be issued to selected groups. These reports must focus on:
    - *Planned* and *actual* progress for test cases attempted, test cases run successfully, and number of problems reported
    - Type of problems discovered
    - Severity of problems discovered
    - Response-time to fix different severities of problems discovered
- Exit requirements:
  - All test cases have been successfully run.
  - All major defects discovered have been corrected in the code.
  - A committed plan to resolve all minor defects discovered in the component test is in place.

The process requirements given in these four example, might not be strict enough for some projects or might be too strict for others. Whatever process requirements you choose for the activities of your project, it is important that they be enforced. If the project leadership is not serious about their enforcement, then do not bother to define them. But a note of caution: If a quality process is not defined for the project, the cost of producing a quality product will most assuredly increase. This increased cost will result from rework due to vague or nonexistent entry, implementation, and exit requirements for project activities. Also, with no defined quality process, it will be more difficult to know when you have *arrived* with a quality product.

Defect Removal Goals

It is better to aim at perfection and miss than it is to aim at imperfection and hit it.

Thomas J. Watson Jr.
(American past President and Chairman of
IBM Corporation)

Including a section on *defect removal goals* in the quality plan is optional. That is, although it is an exercise that offers some benefit, it is not required to ensure the development of a quality product. If all the recommendations discussed up to this point in this chapter are addressed in a quality plan and implemented within the project, a strong foundation will exist for an acceptable quality process. A section on defect removal goals offers a bonus to the already defined quality process. This section offers a methodology for anticipating the number of defects that must be removed from each designated activity in order to deliver a product with a predetermined, preapproved number of undiscovered defects. In other words, to ensure that a product will be judged acceptable by customers, the product owner can estimate how many undiscovered defects can acceptably be delivered with the product. From this number, the maintenance and support costs can also be projected.

A popular method used to describe defects in a product is to reference the number of defects against the lines of code for the product. The notation for this is *Defects per thousand lines of code*, abbreviated as *Defects/KLOC*.

Lines of code sometimes is defined to include comments and prologues. However, in this book, any discussion of lines of code does *not* include comments and prologues. The definition for lines of code includes only the instructions and data declarations that require some logic to create. When the code is tested, it is from the lines of code that problems, also called defects, will be discovered. Defects found in comments and prologues, by definition, will not prevent code from running successfully since compiled code does not generate executable instructions from comments and prologues.

There are many papers and books written that discuss how to predict the total number of defects/KLOC (pronounced *KAY-LOCK*) that a product can be expected to have from "cradle to grave." Then it can be shown how many of the total defects can be expected to be found and corrected in each phase of the product development cycle. From this algorithm, a prediction can be made for the number of defects that remain in the final product delivered to the customer. The product owner must decide if this number of defects will be acceptable to users. The product owner must also decide if this estimated number of defects will yield an acceptable cost to maintain and support the product after it has been delivered. Once the product owner decides on the number of undiscovered defects that are acceptable to ship with the product, the total-defect algorithm is then adjusted to reflect the number of defects that must be removed at each phase of the product development cycle.

Although some subjectivity is involved in defining any defect algorithm, the algorithm should be based on past project experiences. The methodology should have the confidence of project leaders before it is used as a planning tool.

The product owner must identify three variables before a defect removal plan can be completed. These are:

1. Number of undiscovered defects that will be delivered with the product
2. Total number of defects throughout the life of the product
3. Number of defects that will be removed for each designated activity

Delivered Defects

As discussed earlier, the product owner must determine the number of undiscovered defects that he or she views will yield an acceptable *level* of quality for delivery to customers. The number of defects remaining in the product can have a direct impact on the market success of the product. It will also have a direct impact on the costs required to maintain and support the product. Therefore, the product manager is motivated to remove defects throughout the development of the product.

But there is another side to this issue. Each defect removed from the product carries with it a cost. Time, and, therefore, real dollars are involved in discovering defects. Examples are preparing a design or code inspection package, reviewing the package, conducting the inspection, following up with an inspection report, and so on. Each discovered problem carries considerable overhead not only in the actual discovery of the problem, but in the rework and retest activities that must follow. If the requirement is to deliver a product with 100 percent of the defects removed, then the product might not sell. The selling price would have to be prohibitively high to recover the steep development costs. On the other hand, if a product is riddled with defects, customers will soon abandon the product—and even if customers continue to use the product, the maintenance and support costs will eventually sink it.

The product owner must find a balance between product costs and customer satisfaction. One such balance is revealed in the defect quality goal defined. For purposes of illustration, assume this goal is set at .5 defects/KLOC. This means a product that contains 100,000 lines of code is to be delivered with no more than 50 defects. Stated another way, no more than 50 unique defects will ever be reported during the field life of this product. These 50 defects are unknown at the time the product is delivered (with perhaps a few "last minute" exceptions). Identifying the estimated number of defects to be delivered with the product is the first of three variables that the product owner must declare before a defect removal plan can be completed.

Total Product Defects

The second variable to identify is the total number of defects that are in the product throughout its life cycle. The life cycle includes both the product development period and the period that the product is in use by customers. In defining this variable, some homework is required to determine the history of other, similar types of projects. Again, for purposes of illustration, assume the following number of defects: 20 defects/KLOC. This says a product that contains 100,000 lines of code has a total of 2000 defects that could be discovered.

Defects to be Removed

The third, and last, variable to identify, the number of defects to remove from each designated activity, is really several values—one for each activity. Figure 5.4 provides an example of the number of defects that must be removed from each activity if a product is to be delivered at the quality goal of .5 defects/KLOC. The "N/A" (not applicable) entries for the regression test plan mean that the number of defects expected to be removed is less than .1/KLOC and is therefore insignificant. Figure 5.5 shows more graphically the percentage of defects to be removed from across the product phases. This is only an example and might not be realistic for your project. The number of defects to be removed from each activity would be derived from experience—gained from counting the defects found during similar projects.

If the defect estimates are believed to be reasonable, yet significantly less defects were found in a certain activity, then a careful analysis must be made. Perhaps the defect removal process was not very efficient. Or maybe there was incomplete recording of defects. Or maybe the previous activity removed more defects than expected, thus leaving less for discovery later. Even the skill level of the programmers can have an effect on both the number of defects that were introduced into the product as well as the number of defects discovered.

PRODUCT PHASE	ACTIVITY (SOURCE OF DEFECTS)	DEFECTS /KLOC	% OF TOTAL
Product definition	Product objectives document Product specifications document	.2 1.8	1.0 9.0
Product design	High-level design inspection Low-level design inspection	1.2 3.8	6.0 19.0
Code	Code inspection	5.5	27.5
Informal test	Unit test plan Unit test Function test plan Function test	.2 1.9 .3 1.6	1.0 9.5 1.5 8.0
Formal test	Component test plan Component test System test plan System test Regression test plan Regression test	.3 1.5 .1 1.0 N/A .1	1.5 7.5 .5 5.0 N/A .5
After delivery	Customer-reported problems	.5	2.5
	Totals	20.0	100.0

Figure 5.4. Defects/KLOC to be removed per activity

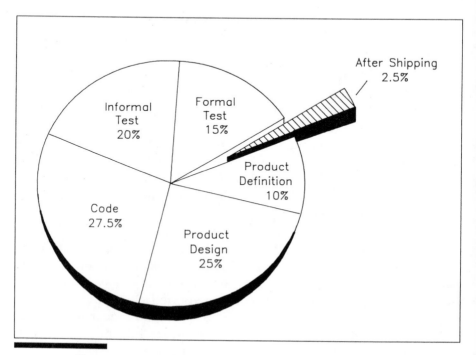

Figure 5.5. Defects removed from each product phase

Numerous measurement techniques are available for counting defects. For example, defects discovered in a document (e.g., the product specifications document) might be derived from the following algorithm:

$$\text{Defects/KLOC} = \frac{(\text{major defects} + (\text{medium defects}/3))}{\text{total KLOC for product}}$$

In this formula, major defects are considered to be severe errors or omissions that require entire sections to be written or rewritten. Medium defects are considered to be misleading statements that would cause the reader to draw the wrong conclusion. These statements must be rewritten. If desirable, recommendations and spelling/grammar items can also be weighted in an algorithm.

Defects counted from design and code inspections might only be those defects considered to be major. Major here means that the design or code implementation is definitely incorrect and would only result in a defect being propagated through the product development cycle.

Any problem found during a test of running code that results in a code change would be counted as a defect. These defects, as well as those found at inspections, would be tracked as:

$$\text{Defects/KLOC} = \frac{\text{problems}}{\text{total KLOC for product}}$$

Again, please note that the values and algorithms used in this section are strictly for illustrative purposes. They might not reflect what is right for your project. A considerable amount of homework must be done to develop a reasonable defect removal model for a product. Once again, it is my view that predicting and then tracking against defect goals is not a requirement for a good quality process. However, the added focus and care involved in removing and counting defects can have a positive influence both on the product and the people developing the product. By defining a defect measurement process, the project leadership can better track where the project has been, where it currently is, and where it is heading.

Quality Improvement Teams

The keynote of progress, we should remember, is not merely doing away with what is bad; it is replacing the best with something better.

Edward A. Filene
(American retail merchandising pioneer)

Among the people that make up a project, there is a tremendous creative energy that has only to be tapped. It is a frequently accepted assertion that people want to do what is right. All they ask is an environment that gives them the opportunity to participate and an environment that will listen to what they have to offer. Here enters the **quality improvement team**.

Quality improvement teams are called by many different names. Some of the more common labels are *quality circles, quality teams, improvement circles, quality control circles,* and *excellence teams.* The actual name used is not as important as the purpose for the quality improvement team. Simply put, a quality improvement team is *a group of people who meet to solve one or more problems.*

The group usually consists of a small number of participants, say, three to eight, but can also include a larger number of people. In addition to solving one or more problems, the group may also meet to identify a list of problems. This list would then be ordered so that the more important problems can be addressed first. The group might meet only once to solve a particular problem, or on a regular basis to take on any problems that come their way. The group might consist of people from the same department or from several departments representing various groups from across a project.

The ground rules for running a team can vary. But one very important ground rule of any quality improvement team is for every team member to be involved. Everyone, without exception, has something to offer. The team leader must allow everyone a chance to be heard and limit criticism to that which is constructive and properly used to support the goals of the team.

Every organization has its share of problems. How well an organization handles its problems has a direct relationship to its success. For example, when an organization encounters a problem it should do two things:

1. Fix the problem.
2. Fix the process or thing that caused the problem.

Take a look at two examples:

The communications are considered very poor in this project. Both the test and the product publications people are continuously learning too late about changes that the developers have made to the product specifications. Sometimes the test and publications people are not informed at all. There is a serious concern that the code and product publications will not accurately support one another and that the test cases will not test all the product functions. As testers and writers discover a new change in product function, they visit the developers to collect the new information. But it is recognized that some process needs to be established to better communicate, and perhaps even control, the changes being made in the product specifications. A quality improvement team is asked to evaluate the problem and recommend a process that will satisfy the project's needs. The final recommendation may be anything from "merge the testers and writers into the development departments that they are supporting" to "define and implement a product specifications change control board."

* * *

The product is in its formal test phase. During an analysis of the problems that have been discovered thus far, it was observed that three of the 100 modules that comprise the product have a significantly higher percentage of the errors. A quality improvement team is convened to recommend the course of action to be taken. The team identifies several options and then recommends its favorite to the project leadership. The list of options might include:

- Reinspect the error-prone modules and then redesign, recode, and retest them.
- Leave the modules as they are and predict and anticipate the defects that have yet to be discovered.
- Inspect the test cases to ensure 100 percent test coverage for the function of these three modules and find the remaining problems that way.
- Pursue some other action.

It is almost always the processes within a project that will make the difference between:

- Making or missing schedules
- A productive or a nonproductive project team

- A high or low employee morale
- Maintaining or exceeding product costs

The subject of quality improvement teams has been included in this chapter because it has a positive impact on maintaining a quality focus throughout the product development cycle. Quality improvement teams are great tools for focusing on improving processes within the organization. An added benefit is that people feel more ownership and pride in *change* when they have participated in making it come about.

One last note—this one to the project leadership. Quality improvements result from project leadership action and support. The easiest way to destroy the desire for quality improvement teams is to ignore the recommendations that you have asked the teams to make. It is not enough to put a recommendation in place. Many acts of change within an organization require ongoing support, tracking, and nurturing to help ensure their success.

Quality Recognition

If you want to be a winner you must think like a winner. If you want to produce quality then you must think quality. The visibility and support that project leaders expend on quality-related activities have a direct relationship to the employee commitment to quality. *Subtlety is not a virtue in the world of quality.* Because quality is viewed by most as being largely intangible and subjective, an assertive presence must be given to quality—a presence that begins at the highest levels of management. It usually takes a higher-management commitment before any true, sustained progress can be achieved at lower levels.

However, focus for a moment on what project-level leaders can accomplish. The project leadership must show its commitment and support for quality. Some tried and true approaches are:

- Public recognition
- Quality awards
- Performance evaluations
- Quality day
- Quality plan

Public Recognition

Providing public recognition to a person or a group of people for a noted quality achievement has several benefits. The person(s) receiving the recognition will likely feel a sense of pride for the accomplishment and for the praise from project leaders. This may inspire others to modify their work habits and place a greater emphasis on quality improvement. An added benefit is that the project leadership demonstrates its commitment to quality.

Quality Awards

Quality awards can be nonmonetary certificates of achievement that a recipient can display on his or her office desk or wall, or there can be a monetary amount given, or both. If nonmonetary certificates are the typical tangible form of recognition given, then it is suggested that the best of the best be awarded some cash as well. A company can save money and probably even make money when this higher level of attention is paid to quality on the job. Cash awards are not only appreciated but also demonstrate that the project leadership is willing to share some of the savings with the major contributors. This can be a great incentive. However, when possible, also include the certificate. After the money has been spent, the certificate offers an ongoing reminder of the achievement and, for some, an incentive for the future.

Performance Evaluations

Those who contribute the most should gain the most. Another way to do this is for an employee's performance evaluation to overtly give note to their attention to quality in their everyday duties.

Quality Day

A *quality day*, week, or month is another way to express both project leadership support and commitment. One or more seminars could be scheduled to explain what quality is and how real savings can be accrued from just being persistent and methodical in identifying and removing defects in a project. The more people learn about quality the more they can plan for achieving progress in their own activities. As Phil Crosby, author of *Quality Without Tears*, has often expressed, "Quality is free." It is usually less costly to prevent defects or identify and remove them earlier in a product development cycle than it is to scrap or rework them later.

Quality Plan

I have intentionally ended this section and this chapter with a few more words about the quality plan. There is so much to gain when a project defines its quality goals early and has defined the steps that will be taken to prevent and remove defects. The primary objective is product success, for only then can everyone win. The quality plan is a blueprint for ensuring that the product will be all that it was intended to be. Considering the keen competitiveness that exists in the software arena, can you really afford not to have a quality plan?

6

Project Tracking Made Easy

A software development project is like a living organism. To survive, all of its vital parts must function in harmony. If one of the parts fails to perform its mission, dependent parts will also soon begin to fail. Like a row of dominoes, the problem, if left unchecked, can topple the whole organism. Survival is not enough, however. The objective is to strive for a *healthy* survival. Getting a product "out the door" late, with poor quality, or with a higher cost is far from a healthy survival.

To an objective bystander, it would make no sense to plan your work, and then *not* work your plan. You might hear the same words from the leadership on a project. Unfortunately, you do not always see the necessary action required to enforce the words. To be able to say that a project has a successful tracking process, two elements are needed. The tracking process must be able to:

1. Identify potential problems before they happen.
2. Put recovery plans in place before unrecoverable harm occurs.

Many factors come into play in creating a tracking process that can satisfy these two criteria. This chapter discusses those factors.

Just Like Dominoes

The following scenario provides an example of how an otherwise well-planned project gets into trouble one day at a time.

The project appears to be off to a good start. The product objectives are written and approved. The product specifications are in the process of being written. The high-level design has started. Special attention was paid to developing the project schedule plan. All the project's work activities are defined, their dependencies identified, and their durations accepted. Now that an approved project schedule plan is in place it is just a matter of managing according to the plan.

The "top dog" on the project, Ralph Macho, is a project head who believes in taking charge. His motto is, "Let's not talk about it, let's do it!" It is the general belief that this assertive style probably gave this project its birth. Not many people on the project really know what to expect from Macho. He is a relative newcomer to the organization. The general view, however, is positive.

The word is out that this project is very important and *must* be a success. Macho declares that the project must be tracked closely. The first status meeting is called. All the project leaders are instructed to attend. They each portray the status of their activities on transparencies so others can follow the presentations from a projector screen. The meeting was scheduled to be three hours long. Four hours have passed and less than half the project leaders have made their presentations. During the first four hours, several problems are discovered that span across departments. The owners of those problems are told, "Go fix them." After eight tedious hours, the meeting ends. Several project leaders have still not reported their status, but Macho needs to end the meeting due to a prior commitment. He states that he wants to see the status reports that have not been presented. He will arrange a time tomorrow.

The project leaders attending the "three hour" day-long meeting have mixed feelings about the event. They feel they learned a lot about what the other departments are doing. In some cases problems were revealed in their own area. But the general feeling is that the benefits gained do not compensate for being tied up a full eight hours. Many project leaders had to miss meetings they had scheduled for later in the day.

The next morning, meeting notices are sent to the project leaders that have yet to present their status reports to Macho. The new meeting is scheduled for two hours that afternoon. A few minutes before the meeting is to start, Macho's secretary says he is "running late" and the meeting may be delayed by 30 minutes. It actually begins 90 minutes later and ends, once again, before everyone can present their status. Macho is quick to say, "We will have to catch the remaining presentations at some other time." This doesn't "sit well" with those project leaders who have yet to present their status reports, but they understand these things happen.

The next project status meeting is scheduled for a duration of four hours for the following week. Minutes before the meeting is to start, it is reset for two days later. Macho's secretary announces that changes had to be made to his calendar. When the meeting finally starts, it is quickly apparent that the people attending are not all the same attendees as last time. About 60 percent of the project leaders are present, but 30 percent sent representatives and 10 percent are not represented at all. The representatives do not all know the problems presented in previous meetings, so are unable to discuss them. There is an attempt to resolve some problems in the meeting, but the representatives are mostly unwilling to make commitments without their project leader's consent. To make matters worse, the project leaders had different "memories" regarding the action that was to be taken on several of the problems raised from the previous meeting. There were no minutes recorded for that meeting. Each person had only their own notes. This time, a summary of the problems to be acted upon are surveyed at the end of the meeting. The four-hour meeting ends in six hours.

The next few project status meetings follow a similar pattern. The scheduled time on the calendar is changed at the last moment. One meeting did not even take place since Macho was called out of town. Over time, fewer and fewer project leaders attend, with more and more representatives assigned to attend. The meetings continue to run longer than scheduled. Differences in opinions about the problems that have been identified at prior meetings and about their assigned owners continue to increase. The meeting attendees are having less and less success at getting commitments on work items from others in the meetings. Many of the dependencies and work items are beginning to be implemented later than required and the project schedules are slowly eroding.

A few project leaders get together and decide there must be a better way to track project status and get problems logged and tracked to completion. They list a half-dozen primary problems that exist with the current project status meetings. They also list recommendations to address these problems. They are able to be scheduled on Macho's calendar for a one-hour discussion. After two days of getting "bumped" from the project head's calendar, they finally meet with him. He appreciates their input and recognizes that some of these problems probably should be addressed. However, he asks, "Why can't the project leaders solve these problems on their own initiative? To get anywhere in a business you have got to take it upon yourself to make things happen."

Reluctantly, he agrees to adopt several of the recommendations. He assigns a person to conduct meetings when he is not available. This person will also issue minutes of each meeting and will make sure that all problems are recorded. These few project leaders feel partially relieved that some improvements will be made, and partially distressed that they had to sell so hard to get these improvements.

The project status meetings are now held at the same time each week. Macho rarely finds the time to attend, although he promises to be there "next time." Communication across the organization is improving. The actual resolution of problems is not. Dependencies between organizations continue to be missed on a more frequent basis. Most project leaders are not attending meetings. Each department's activities, as well as their dependencies on other departments, are being driven almost exclusively by the skills and motivations of each project leader. Some project leaders are not leading to the extent necessary, but the lack of leadership is not entirely intentional. Some just don't know how. It was agreed from the beginning that quick closure on higher priority problems may require an *escalation* to get the needed focus. (An escalation occurs when a person cannot get another person or organization to satisfactorily address a problem. The problem remains open until a mutually agreed to solution is arrived at. This sometimes requires higher-level project leaders from different organizations to be forced to meet until the problem is addressed and closed.)

The big problem here is that many of the escalations find their way to the project head's office. They may sit there for a week or longer, waiting for the availability of Macho. Occasionally more homework must be done and a follow-up meeting needs to be scheduled. It takes too long to get some problems resolved. Everyone knows this. Consequently, there is a tendency to not start the escalation process as quickly as a problem may require. There is a general feeling that things are out of control, that the *system* necessary to monitor project progress efficiently and to enforce corrective action just does not exist.

The project is falling further behind schedule. Because project status is not always accurately and completely reported, some activities that were thought to be on schedule one week ago are being reported, just one week later, to be *more* than one week behind schedule. Some groups are working considerable overtime, while others seem to be taking it all in stride. No one seems to be leading the organization. The question, "Who's in charge?" is often asked. The usual answer is that it probably is the project head—when he's available. An underlying tone can be heard, "Oh well, if our project head is not more interested, then we will just have to do the best we each know how and hope that things will improve." (Anytime there is an "oh, well" atmosphere, you can bet that a lot of commitment will be missing, along with its sidekick, productivity.) The lack of serious commitment by Macho to enforce the tracking process and ensure that problems are being identified early and resolved early is obvious to everyone. Morale is slowly eroding across the organization. Finger-pointing for scapegoats is becoming all too frequent. Everyone is now in agreement that the project will miss its product delivery date. To make matters worse, no one can agree on how deeply the project is "in the ditch."

How will this scenario end? How much damage has been done to project schedules? The events in this scenario, if left unchecked, only get worse. A few project leaders do care enough to try and right the wrongs. However, even these determined project leaders can get frustrated and begin to perform under their potential, or eventually may even seek to work for other organizations or other companies. The sad part is that this negative situation is curable. Not just patchable, but really curable. The remaining sections of this chapter offer guidelines for avoiding the traps shown in this scenario, as well as for avoiding other related, but common, pitfalls.

What Should Be Tracked?

Obviously, a man's judgment cannot be better than the information on which he has based it.

> Arthur Hays Sulzberger
> (American newspaper publisher)

Before we list the items that should be tracked, let's take a look again at the primary objectives for tracking:

1. Identify potential problems before they happen.
2. Put recovery plans in place before unrecoverable harm occurs.

Notice that the focus is on identifying and resolving problems. So, what in particular should be tracked to identify and resolve problems? The answer:

- Plans for work activities
- Known problems

Work activity plans are tracked in order to identify potential problems as early as possible. Once problems are identified, they are individually tracked to ensure they are resolved. The sections that follow discuss these two areas.

Plans for Work Activities

The recommended approach for identifying potential problems is simply to track a work activity against its plan. Work activities, discussed in Chapter 4, include such items as:

- Project documents (product specifications, test plans, project schedule plan, and so on)
- High-level design
- Low-level design
- Design inspections
- Coding
- Each test (unit, function, component, performance, and so on)

A project is laid out by work activities. Each work activity should have some defined method for allowing it to be tracked. In most cases, the method is defined in a corresponding plan. For example, the component test activity is defined in the component test plan. Before the component testing begins, the component test plan is written and approved. Included in the component test plan should be a list of all dependencies and charts depicting the duration of component testing, the number of test procedures to be run, a projection of how many test procedures should be attempted per week, how many tests should have run successfully each week, and so on. With this plan in place, it is a fairly trivial matter to gather the corresponding data each week and then to compare the actual progress against the planned progress.

Consider another example: coding. Long before coding begins, there should be a plan in place that defines the expected progress through the design and coding phases. Some projects call this a *development build plan*. It lists the modules to be created for the product; identifies the owner of each module; states when (with specific dates) the high-level design, low-level design and coding portions of each module will begin and end; identifies dependencies for each module; and so on. Now a plan exists against which programmers and their project leaders can track progress.

One more example: the product specifications. At the start of the preparation phase for the product specifications, a plan should be produced that identifies the chapters and sections to be written, who has the responsibility to write each piece, and the dates when each section will be started and completed. If internal reviews of the sections are to occur before the document is distributed for formal review, then the dates for these internal reviews, including updating the document with the corresponding feedback, must also be planned. Again, once this plan is completed, it will be used to track progress.

Known Problems

It was stated earlier that the recommended approach for identifying potential problems is simply to track a work activity against its plan. But what if there are already known problems? These problems must be individually tracked until they are resolved. These problems come in many forms. Some examples are:

- Issues holding up approval of the product specifications
- Problems blocking a design inspection from successfully completing
- Dependencies being late
- Defects prohibiting test cases from being completed
- Overlooked functions that must now be integrated into the product plan

Where Should Tracking Occur?

All projects have a hierarchy of organizational responsibilities. It is within this hierarchy that necessary tracking must occur.

Figure 6.1 represents a typical *project hierarchy*. The term *group level* can be exchanged for a term more typical in your organization. For example, each *group level 1* box might be a team (two to ten persons) and each *group level 2* box might be a department made up of two or more teams. Each *group level N-1* box might represent a uniquely defined organization made up of two or more departments of, say, developers, testers, writers, or support personnel. All the organizations of a project come together at the *group level N box*. In this example, a project leader is associated with each box—that is, *group levels 1* through *N*. The top project leader, called the **project head**, is associated with the *group level N* box. For purposes of discussion, the generic terms *teams, departments, organizations, and project*, as shown in Figure 6.1, will be used instead of *group levels 1* through *N*.

Work activities are usually performed at the team level. However, the first formal point of tracking typically occurs at the department level.

Departments are the first hierarchy point at which managers—those project leaders typically assigned the responsibility of evaluating the performance of personnel—are assigned. It is at the department level that the following should be tracked:

- All work activities within the scope of the department
- All problems that have an impact on the department's mission

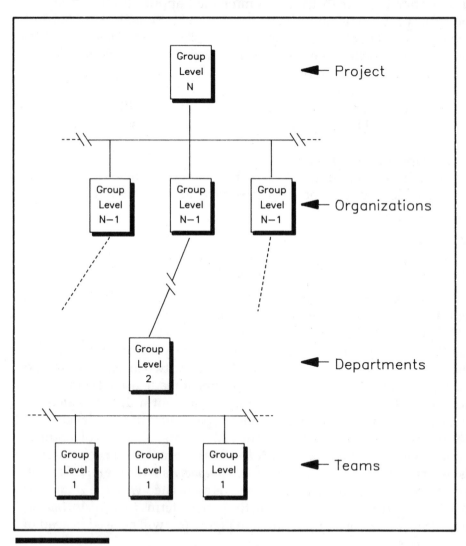

Figure 6.1. Project tracking hierarchy

The first item simply says that a department should track those work activities for which it is directly responsible. The second item, however, says that the department is also responsible for tracking any problems that could impact the department from successfully completing its commitments. If one department (shop A) depends on another department (shop B) for something, and shop B is going to be late on its commitment, then shop A should take the initiative to record and track the problem until the problem is resolved. Actually, shop B has the true responsibility to flag the problem. However, in reality, if the shop As of the world rely on the shop Bs to be self-policing, then the entire system would soon grind to a halt. If you are dependent on an item outside your direct span of control, *then track it*.

The second point of tracking in Figure 6.1 is the organization level. The areas tracked at this level are:

- All work activities within the scope of the organization
- All problems that have an impact on the organization's mission

Sound familiar? These are the same areas as for a department, only with a wider scope. Work activities should be tracked in less detail than at the department level. The problems tracked at an organization level need only be those that span across departments within the organization as well as any dependencies on outside organizations. Most problems isolated to within a single department in which the cause, cure and impact all reside, usually only need to be tracked within that department.

The last point of tracking in Figure 6.1 is the project level. The areas tracked at this highest level are:

- All work activities within the scope of the project
- All problems that have an impact on the project's mission

This is getting easy. And it should. There is nothing mysterious about tracking projects once you know the primary points to be sensitive to. Some tradeoffs can begin to be made when tracking at the project level. The tracking of work activities that was defined at the organizational level can optionally be deferred to this level. Problems that span across both departments and organizations are best tracked from a single database. This database is best managed at the project level.

Frequency of Tracking

There are many opinions on how often to track elements of a project. My experiences with projects and human nature make the answer to this question easy: Tracking should occur once per week. This rule of thumb applies to team tracking, department tracking, organization tracking, and project tracking. Tracking at a level higher than the project level should be less frequent than weekly. Beyond the project level, the higher the management involved in the tracking, the less frequently the tracking meetings should occur.

In tracking, up through the project level, meetings should be held at the same time each week. Participants who are required at tracking meetings are usually very busy. They need to be able to plan their time and manage their calendars. Regularly scheduled tracking meetings allow participants to plan their other activities and to prepare for the tracking meetings. Part of the preparation involves gathering the necessary status information for their own area's work activities, and might also involve negotiating problem resolutions with other groups.

Another important reason for regularly scheduled tracking meetings is the human need to pace oneself for effective productivity. Most people work more intelligently and with more conviction when they are being measured against schedules for which they feel a personal sense of ownership. Infrequent or irregular tracking typically results in occasional spurts of improved productivity. When the progress of people is tracked at frequent and predictable intervals, those being tracked are conditioned to maintain a fairly constant and predictably high level of productivity.

Tracking Charts

The appropriate level of detail that should appear in tracking charts varies, depending on the size of the project and the level at which the tracking occurs (department, organization, or project, for instance).

Consider a case in which a department is interested in tracking the progress of the coding. The department project leader will want to understand how many modules are being coded, the planned start and finish dates of each module, and the status of actual progress compared with planned progress. Additionally, the project leader will want to know the programmers, by name, that are ahead of and behind schedule. For those behind schedule, the project leader will want to know why the work is overdue and what plan is in place to pull the activity back on schedule. Those ahead of schedule might be able to assist those behind schedule. The status information the project leader must work with is considerably detailed, but is necessary to manage department commitments effectively.

Now consider the detail to be tracked at a project level for the same activity: coding. At this level the forest is more important than the individual trees. The project leadership is more interested in the total number of lines of code to be coded within the project, when that coding must begin and finish, and the actual progress of coding compared with the plan. Little detail about coding activities is required if the coding is on schedule. However, if coding is behind schedule, the functional areas that are late must be identified, the reason(s) for being late must be presented, and the recovery plan must be understood. More information might be necessary, depending on the severity of the schedule slip and the ability to recover.

The remainder of this section will focus on project level status. Department level status must be at a more detailed level and is considered to be less difficult to identify and manage than at a project level. At a project level more skill is required in presenting status that is informative, accurate, not-too-detailed, and in an acceptable summarized format.

The level of detail and format of tracking charts should be as consistent as possible in tracking at the project level. The charts should present a picture, whenever possible, to aid the project leadership in quickly understanding the overall health of the project. The higher the level of project leadership involved in comprehending the project's status, the shorter the time that is available for discussion.

It is recommended that one or more charts be developed for each major activity area of the project. Examples of major activity areas are:

- Project schedule milestones
- Writing the product specifications
- Design
- Coding
- Unit test
- Function test
- Component test
- Writing the first draft of the publications

The fewer the charts necessary to convey the status, the better. Of course, in some cases, this might require that status information on a particular chart must represent multiple departments. Therefore, a means of coordinating the data across departments is necessary.

Several examples of charts are included in this section. The first example, Figure 6.2, shows a bar chart that tracks actual and planned coding progress. The time, in this case shown as relative weeks, is represented along the horizontal scale of the graph chart, while the number of modules to be coded is shown along the vertical scale. If there are not many modules to code, or you are looking for a different way to measure progress, then the vertical scale could show the number of lines of code to be written rather than the number of modules to be coded. The decision should be based upon a method of measurement that you feel can best track your progress. Planned progress is shown in this bar chart as a straight, linear progression. Actual progress has been added to demonstrate the level of accomplishment that would be seen by the

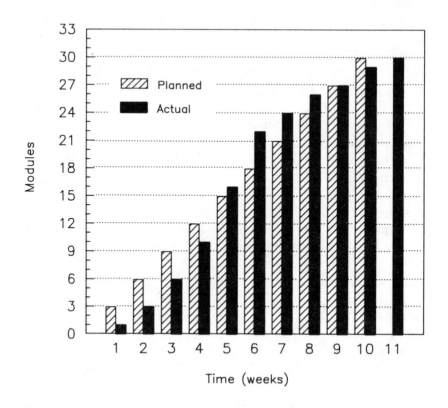

Figure 6.2. Coding progress

project leadership at each status meeting (one-week intervals are used here). Notice that coding was expected to be completed in ten weeks, but actually finished in eleven weeks.

Figure 6.3 is a line chart that shows the actual and expected progress within a test phase—in this example, component testing. The number of test cases to be successfully run are shown along the vertical scale. Notice that the planned curve looks like a flattened "S." This is more typical of the progress made for most items to be tracked. The start of the activity usually begins somewhat slowly, picks up speed as it proceeds, and then noticeably slows as the activity nears completion. Also notice that the plan expects 70 percent of the test cases to be successfully run when 50 percent of the time has elapsed. This allows proportionally more time to be planned into the end of the schedule to complete the remaining and frequently most difficult test cases. Again, actual progress is shown for illustrative purposes.

The next example, Figure 6.4, illustrates another useful type of chart that, in this case, is used with Figure 6.3. This chart shows the number

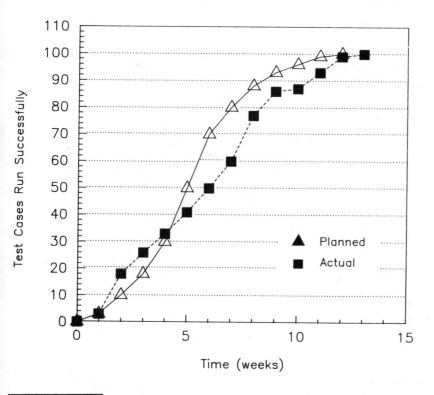

Figure 6.3. Component test cases

of problems reported, answered, and verified as closed as the component test cases are being run. Notice that the reported line, the answered
line, and the closed line occasionally diverge (not good) and converge
(good). This data is useful to the project leadership in helping them
determine where best to deploy the project's people/machine resources. For example, notice that in the fifth week of testing, almost
twice as many problems are reported than are answered (fixed). If this
trend continues then the testing personnel will soon have little to test
while they wait on the developers to answer the problems. Realizing
this, the project leaders might assign some of the test personnel to help
with answering the problems. Looking at the results in the sixth week of
testing, it is clear that more problems are now being answered than
reported. As the test phase draws to a close, the resources might be
further balanced in favor of verifying that the answered problems did
indeed fix the reported problems.

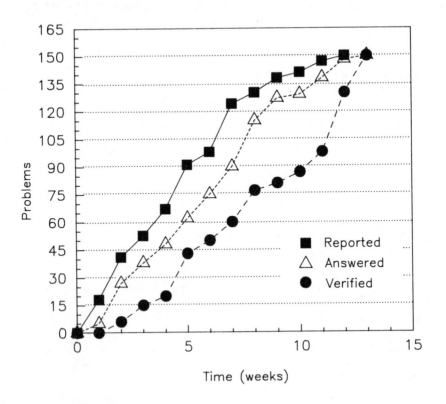

Figure 6.4. Problem status

Figure 6.4 shows only the *actual* status. For workload planning purposes it may be useful to create a *plan* chart of the same three variables: reported, answered, and verified. This plan chart, when used alongside Figure 6.4, can help to identify deviations from the expected.

You may find that picture charts are not always informative enough. The chart shown in Figure 6.5 is representative of a type of chart that is often required. This chart provides some data on specific activities that might not be easily or effectively represented in some other fashion. It provides a look at the activities that are currently in progress. It also enables you to look ahead in order to anticipate readiness for future activities, thus anticipating potential problems before they become real

NUM	ACTIVITY	DUR	FLT	PLANNED		ACTUAL		OWNER
				START	END	START	END	
200	Pubs plan preparation	15	0	01/30	02/17	01/30	02/20	Williams
201	Pubs plan review	10	0	02/20	03/03	02/21	03/06	Williams
202	Pubs plan update	5	0	03/06	03/10	03/07	03/10	Williams
203	Pubs plan approval	5	0	03/13	03/17	03/13	03/17	Williams
204	Pubs plan information	5	0	03/20	03/24	03/20	03/24	Williams
210	Pubs content plan prep.	20	0	03/20	04/14	03/20	04/19	Williams
211	Pubs content plan review	10	0	04/17	04/28	04/20		Williams
212	Pubs content plan update	5	0	05/01	05/05			Williams
213	Pubs content plan approval	5	0	05/08	05/12			Williams
220	Pubs test plan preparation	20	20	04/17	05/12			Williams
214	Pubs content plan info.	5	0	05/15	05/19			Williams
221	Pubs test plan review	10	20	05/15	05/26			Williams
222	Pubs test plan update	5	20	05/29	06/02			Williams
223	Pubs test plan approval	5	20	06/05	06/09			Williams
224	Pubs test plan information	5	20	06/12	06/16			Williams
230	Pubs initial draft prep.	40	0	05/15	07/07			Williams
231	Pubs initial draft review	10	0	07/10	07/21			Williams
232	Pubs update	20	0	07/24	08/18			Williams
233	Pubs final draft review	10	0	08/21	09/01			Williams
225	Pubs test	50	10	07/10	09/15			Williams
234	Pubs final update	10	10	09/04	09/15			Williams
240	Pubs to production	30	0	10/02	11/10			Williams

Figure 6.5. Scheduled activities by owner

problems. Each project leader or the representative for an organization would present a chart like Figure 6.5, if needed. The chart would list the activities, the duration (in work days) of the activity, the planned start and finish dates, the actual dates as they occur, and the project leader responsible. The FLOAT column, abbreviated FLT, shows any slack that can safely exist between the time an activity is scheduled to be completed and when the next activity depends on the first activity to be completed. A float of 10 (work days) means that this activity could slip up to 10 work days without seriously impacting any dependent activities. (It is possible that people resources will be impacted if an activity finishes later than expected, even though the activity technically does not impact another activity.) A float of zero means that this activity must be completed by the planned end date to avoid impacting one or more succeeding activities.

The activities in Figure 6.5 are owned by the project leader named Williams. These activities have been sorted according to planned end dates. The NUM column is the number that is associated with an activity. This chart shows that the publications-related activities have been assigned the numbers 200 through 240. The actual status through April 20 has been filled in to illustrate how the ACTUAL columns can be used. Notice, for example, that the activity numbered 202 actually started one day later than planned. Since this activity has a float of 0, some corrective action must occur to recover the schedule so that the impact does not continue to the following activities. In this case, the activity was able to be completed with a duration one day less than planned. This corrected a potential schedule slippage problem.

(Note: Figures 4.3 and 4.4 of Chapter 4 also use these publications-related activities and their assigned numbers (200 through 240) and durations. However, the floats that can be derived from Figure 4.4 do not identically match those in Figure 6.5. Although these figures represent potentially realistic data, all figures are for illustrative purposes only.)

Tracking charts do not have to be fancy, colorful, or published masterpieces in order to be useful. Keep in mind that the project leadership needs the "big picture" to help anticipate where an activity, or for that matter, the project, is heading. It is not important to spend great amounts of time updating charts. What is important, however, is to know what you want tracked, how you want the data presented, and, of course, where you need to be against your plan. You might find that what you are interested in presenting might not be what your audience is interested in seeing. In most cases the charts will evolve over weeks or months.

The Project Tracking Meeting

Earlier in the product development cycle you planned your upcoming work. Now you are working your plan. The project tracking meeting is the best tool for tracking yourself against your plan. As stated earlier, project tracking meetings should be conducted at the same time, and on a regular basis. Once per week is recommended.

If the project is small in terms of the number of participants, then tracking meetings might be run by the project head. If the project is medium to large, it is recommended that one or more persons are assigned full time to administer these meetings. A project tracking meeting can be a very large task to prepare for, conduct, and follow up. The investment in this meeting is very important. This meeting is the *communications backbone* that holds the project together and keeps it on a productive course. It is the primary communications medium for conveying status information and problems. Many people will depend on this meeting to acquire necessary information for performing their job.

To be effective, the project tracking meeting must:

- Be attended by participants who can make commitments
- Be fully supported by the project leadership

It is unacceptable to have participants at tracking meetings who cannot represent their area by fielding expected questions. This weak representation will have a serious, negative impact on the meeting. A project leader is usually the best person to attend tracking meetings. However, there are times when some things must be delegated. In these cases, project leaders should work with their representatives to give them the authority and support they need. Project leaders who genuinely work closely with their people to help them grow are usually the project leaders who are also recognized as more willing to take on risk and who are the greater contributors on a project.

There is no point in tracking a project if the project leadership will not enforce *the system*. Some examples of situations that must be swiftly addressed:

- Representatives continually show up for a tracking meeting late or infrequently.
- The participants are frequently not prepared to give status reports.

• The participants are frequently late in resolving problems assigned to them.

The entire organization wants to be successful. Everyone looks to the project leadership to provide the environment necessary to attain this success. The disciplined tracking of a project helps to create an environment for success.

Ground Rules

The meeting should have a simple set of "ground rules" for all to follow. These rules should include:

- Come to the meeting on time.
- Come to the meeting prepared to present your status.
- If you are behind on an activity, then address the following:
  - Why the activity is late
  - What other areas are/might become impacted
  - What recovery plan will be/is in place
  - Whether you need help
- Time-consuming problems are to be solved outside of the meeting.
- Encourage open and candid status reports and discussion.

The first two ground rules, attendance and preparation, may seem too trivial to record. However, lack of discipline in these areas will quickly spread to other aspects of the project. Violators must not be tolerated.

If an activity is reported behind schedule or potentially falling behind schedule, then certain information about that activity must be understood. First, the problem must be understood, not assumed. Any areas that are or could be impacted must also be understood. The recovery plan must not only address ways to get the activity back on schedule (if possible), but must address ways to satisfy the areas that are impacted.

The question, "Do you need help?" often reveals cases in which the owner of a problem does not have the resources or authority to correct the problem and requests help. This should be viewed as positive. Too often, project leaders will show a reluctance to get help. As a result, the problem will linger longer than the project can afford. There is a saying that is old but so, so true:

How does a project get to be a year late? ... One day at a time.
Frederick P. Brooks Jr.
(American author of The Mythical Man-Month*)*

Problems should not be dealt with in depth during the meeting. If they are, the result will be constant tangential discussions. Also, the meeting's end-time will become a random variable, and therefore will make it impossible for people to predict when the meeting will end. In response, people will leave at different times throughout the meeting. Tangents are the single biggest cause of unnecessarily long meetings. A technique that can help is for the meeting moderator to request that anyone, at any time, who believes that the meeting is on a tangent should raise his or her hand, without speaking. This will help the moderator to better gauge when the meeting is perceived to be off track. It is then up to the moderator to end the discussion quickly or to allow the discussion to continue a short time longer. It can be useful to solve problems in a project tracking meeting if no more than one or two minutes are required. Because of the select type of people gathered in one place— that is, people who have the authority to commit actions—this situation can be exploited in a positive fashion.

All participants should be encouraged to respect one another. A tracking meeting should not become a "lion's den," where people are verbally attacked and put on the defensive, nor should participants become intimidated when speaking out. Participants should be made to feel at ease. The respect enforced during these meetings will have an impact on the working environment for the entire project.

These ground rules can be expanded to suit the particular project at hand. But keep ground rules to one page. Having too many rules distracts attention from the truly key ones. And enforce the ones you have.

Length of Meeting

A project tracking meeting may last anywhere from 30 minutes to all day, depending on two factors:

- Size of the project
- How efficiently the meeting is run

The relative size of a project will not change during the course of the project. However, for very large projects it might be desirable to divide a project tracking meeting into multiple smaller meetings with unique attendance for each meeting.

The efficiency of meetings is a variable and must be addressed. Otherwise, not only are a lot of people wasting their valuable time, but impatience and hostility toward the meetings will grow. The result can be a self-fulfilling prophecy of "this meeting is a waste of time and should be disbanded," which can lead to actions that will later be regretted. Tracking meetings are critical to the project. Don't "throw the baby out with the bath water." Take corrective action if meetings are being run inefficiently.

It may be useful to set a time limit for each organization or each project leader making a presentation. This will give presenters something to strive for and, over time, will probably be followed more closely than might be expected.

Publish an agenda each week. The order of presenters should follow some logical pattern and should not vary from week to week. Those who are presenting major status reports should present first. For example, if a project is in the midst of the coding phase, the status of the coding progress should be one of the first presentations. The sequence of presenters can be adjusted for logical reasons, but it should be predictable and planned. For a case in which a person from outside the project has something to report each week, but has no need to sit through the entire meeting, this person could present at the beginning of the meeting and then leave.

Although people tend to be sharper and more alert during morning meetings, afternoon meetings are recommended for large project tracking meetings. Because many people will want to leave the office at a respectable time or some may have prior evening commitments, this can result in a self-policing action by the participants. Perhaps you have heard this more than once: "Hey, I'm on my own time. Let's get this done!"

Identifying and Tracking Problems

Project tracking meetings should focus on:

- Tracking of actual status against the plan
- Status of known problems being tracked
- New problems

The tracking of actual progress compared with plans is rather straightforward. The tracking charts introduced earlier in this chapter are great tools to use for this. Periodically, whether each week or each month, a conscious effort should be made to look ahead by at least one month. This exercise can provide an early warning to potential problems.

As problems are uncovered, they should be logged and tracked. Whenever an activity is recognized as being behind schedule, this should result in the logging of a new problem. A project tracking process begins to take shape when a recognized forum or medium is in place to log and track problems to closure. This widespread visibility of problems helps to get an organization thinking *as an organization* rather than as disparate groups. Everybody should feel they can bring up a new problem. Only when a problem is known and understood can it begin to be resolved.

Figure 6.6 is a sample problem reporting form. It requests the basic information that must be known about a new problem so that the

```
            ***   PROBLEM REPORTING FORM   ***


OPENED BY ----------------->        _____

DATE OPENED --------------->        _____

PROBLEM TITLE ------------->        _____

REQUIRED CLOSE DATE ------->        _____

SUGGESTED ASSIGNED PERSON --->      _____

SCHEDULED ACTIVITY IMPACTED ->      _____

DESCRIPTION OF PROBLEM ------>      _____

   _____

   _____

   _____

   _____

   _____
```

Figure 6.6. Problem reporting form

problem can be properly logged and tracked. You can add additional fields that may fit your tracking needs (such as severity of the problem). Once the problem has been logged, it can be tracked to ensure it receives the proper visibility and priority. Figure 6.7 shows the basic information to be tracked. This figure presents a problem that has been tracked for five consecutive weeks. Notice that fields have been added to facilitate status tracking. For example, a target closure date is provided by the person assigned to resolve the problem. If this date is past the required date, a special meeting may be called to resolve the conflict. A status field

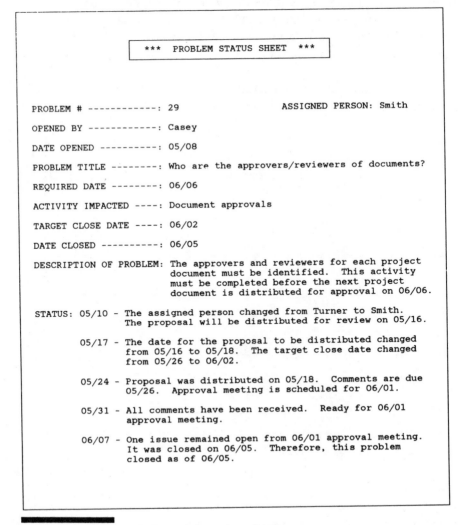

Figure 6.7. Problem status sheet

is also used so that the history resolution of the problem can be easily followed.

Recording the Meeting

Minutes from the project tracking meeting must be written and distributed as soon after the meeting as possible, preferably by the end of the next work day. This ensures that everyone operates from the same information. The minutes should record all new status, all new problems, and all new commitments. These minutes will also provide the baseline information against which the next week's meeting will be reported.

Recovery Plans

Recovery plans define the journey to be followed to recover from a problem. They outline how a problem situation will be corrected. Some activities in a project of multiple activities and multiple people can be expected to fall behind schedule. Often, even with a recovery plan, an activity's schedule will still fall behind, although not as far behind as it otherwise might. Many recovery plans are not complete unless they also address those activities that are dependent on the partial or total completion of the activity in trouble. The objective of a recovery plan is to fix a problem in the most efficient manner deemed reasonable and to limit the damage to the smallest area. Of course, the first rule of thumb is to protect the overall integrity of the project plan. This also protects the committed project end-date from slipping. The end-date is the day on which the product is committed to be available for delivery to the first customer.

After a problem has been identified, the next goal is to understand the cause. Except for the most simple of problems (are there any?), do not assume you know the answer. Trust the people assigned to address the problem to recommend the right solution — and also trust your instincts. Instincts are rarely wrong for most people. There is a counter problem that can occur here: indecision. Indecision is, overall, far more damaging to a project than the occasional wrong decision. As Thomas J. Watson Jr. had been known to say: "Better to do something—even the wrong thing—than to do nothing at all."

Once a problem is fully understood, the recovery plan can be completed. The plan must address the following areas:

- Identify the owner of both the problem and its resolution.
- Identify the sequence of activities that must occur in order to complete the resolution.
- Determine the dates when each element of the plan will be completed.
- Ensure that the appropriate people or groups approve the plan.

One person must own the problem. The same person must own the solution. Accountability and authority are key here. Don't allow the problem to have joint owners with equal responsibility. You can expect the best performance in closing the problem when the accountability and authority have a single focus. It is okay and even necessary, at times, for several people to solve a problem, but maintain one chief.

Lay out the activities that must occur to reach a final solution. Which of these activities must finish first? Which can be worked in parallel? Which must be done by the same person or persons? Where is the critical path? How can it be shortened?

Now declare dates to start and finish each activity. Be aggressive with these dates—but make them achievable. Remember, these dates will become commitments; others will depend on them.

The plan should be approved by the owning project leader and should have the commitment of the performers of the plan. The plan must also be agreed upon by those people or organizations that depend on the date of the recovery of the activity. Optionally, the quality assurance group, or some other person or group that can provide a check-and-balance role, could be requested to review the plan.

Next, the recovery plan must be implemented and tracked with a committed regularity. Tracking the recovery plan should not be overlooked; otherwise, you could be faced with a failing plan that only "might have" succeeded. If the recovery plan begins to fail, then you might need to redo a part or all of the plan. To maintain the necessary attention on those recovery plans that are particularly critical, or to deal with owners who have demonstrated a pattern of missing commitments, the following approach should prove helpful: When an element of the recovery plan in question is nearing its due date, schedule a meeting on that day for the owner to present status information to his or her project leader or even to the project head. The meeting might only require fifteen minutes, but this short investment in time can result in large payoffs.

Escalate to Consensus

What does it mean to escalate? Briefly:

> When two parties cannot agree on an item that must be resolved, and an earnest attempt to negotiate a resolution has occurred, then higher levels of the project leadership must be called upon to help resolve the issue.

Typically the next higher level of project leadership, from both sides of the issue, are called together to understand the issue. Then, through consensus, it is hoped that the problem will be finally and mutually resolved.

If the problem is still not resolved, the next levels of the project leadership are called upon. Eventually the two organizational chains will come together at the same boss. Then, the buck finally stops and the decision is made. Most escalations do not go this high. Moreover, experience has shown that the most agreeable solutions are those reached at the lower levels.

To some, "escalate" is a dirty word because they either don't understand its purpose or the project leadership has a reputation of punishing one or both of the parties involved.

Escalating an issue must be viewed as a healthy form of doing business. Emotions must be removed from the escalation process. The solution must be the right one for the business, not for a given person. Project leaders who might punish one or both parties for allowing an escalation to reach them should reconsider. There are many times when both parties might be making the *right* business decision from their respective viewpoints. Someone higher in the chain must make a decision from a different perspective or from a position of additional information. Project members and lower level project leaders must be encouraged to work things out at their levels. However, escalating, at times, is the proper and healthy course of action to follow.

The following scenario illustrates how some project members might view escalations:

> Dorothy Casey, a project leader of a development organization, called a meeting of about 10 persons who were all outside of her direct authority. These people represented several different organizations, all of which provide some form of service to her organization. Casey viewed the meeting as a way to understand the status of several work activities in progress. In one case, a group had missed its commitments three times in as many

weeks. Casey was growing uneasy because her shop needed support that it was not getting.

She looked at Barney Sullivan, who represented the group that was consistently making and then missing the commitments, and asked what he had planned as his next action. Sullivan said he was dependent on a person in another department and that person kept missing the commitment. Sullivan also said that "the person is very busy and was doing the best that he can." Casey asked Sullivan if he had escalated (as he had said he would). He had not. When Casey asked why not, Sullivan said, "I need to work with this person and we have a good working relationship now. I don't want to upset that."

Casey replied, "Have I ever escalated you over an issue?" The replying nod was a yes, followed by, "Two or three times." Casey continued, "Are we still working together and managing to negotiate and do what's right for the business?"

Sullivan said, "Yes, but that's different—" then stopped, realizing that it wasn't any different. Sullivan got the point. The project leader got the commitment for the final time.

Frequently, you can actually help people by escalating an issue *over their heads* and, assuming you win, have their priorities officially redirected. The issue may have been something that they wanted to do all along, but they did not feel they had the authority to alter their current priorities.

When two parties cannot agree on an important issue, escalations should be set up quickly. If the issue is truly important, a decision must be reached so that everyone can get on with their business. As a guideline, escalations should occur within two working days of being identified. Immediately, the next levels of project leadership (or whoever gets involved in your organization) must reserve time on their calendars for the escalation meeting. Although an advance notice of two work days might not always be enough time to get an appointment on some calendars, management must support the expedient resolution of escalated issues.

The Risk Management Plan

Risk management fits into the project picture when the schedules are in place and committed, and the project personnel are working according to the new plan. At this point, it is expected that the project leadership has a good understanding of the high, medium, and low risk areas of the new plan. Two options are now at hand:

1. A conscious mental note can be made by the project leadership to watch for the higher risk areas at the weekly project tracking meetings.
2. A risk management plan can be developed.

The first approach is business as usual for most project shops. The thinking goes like this: "If a problem is discovered, then it will be addressed at that point. Why work on something that just isn't recognized as a real problem today?"

The second approach requires some planning today for what may become tomorrow's problem. A risk management plan:

• Identifies the higher risk areas in the project
• Identifies the owner of each risk area
• Documents a plan for reducing the risk for each area

To identify the higher risk areas of a project, it is first useful to list all perceived risks. A brainstorming meeting among several of the project leaders can be an effective way to develop a *risk list*. (Brainstorming is a problem-solving technique whereby a group of people collectively pool their knowledge and experiences to solve a problem.) Once this list is compiled, the highest risks must be singled out. Assigning a high, medium, or low risk value to each identified risk helps to put it in a perspective that allows it to be more easily judged. It is then up to the project leadership to agree on identified risks and to decide which risks should require a plan. If this is the first time a project employs the risk management plan technique, it is suggested to focus only on the high risk areas. The list of risks to track should not exceed ten, while three to five is preferred. If there are too many risks, not only is it tedious and painful to plan and track them, it is also indicative that the project schedules were planned too aggressively and might not be achievable. Examples of some items that could make the risk list are:

• Completing the product objectives
• Completing the product specifications
• Completing the product design in a particular component
• Acquiring special test hardware or software by the time the testing begins
• Achieving full compatibility with the output files of another product

- Staffing with skilled personnel at the rate the project plan requires
- Completing the project on time
- Completing the project within budget

Note that the last two risk areas might be too broad to tackle. In these cases the project could be divided into phases or major activities (see Chapter 1) and a plan developed to address the riskier activities.

The next step is to assign an owner for each risk area. The owner will be responsible for putting a plan together for that risk and for executing that plan. It is recommended that a risk have only one owner. As discussed earlier, shared ownership of a responsibility often prevents the responsibility from receiving the attention it requires.

The assigned owner must develop a plan to contain the risk to a point where it is no longer viewed as a threat to the overall health of the project. The plan should be reviewed by others to help ensure that it is achievable and trackable. The plan then should be tracked at the project tracking meetings, along with the plans for the other risk areas. The risk management plan contains the collection of these plans—one plan for each risk area.

A risk management plan can be a useful tool. If the probability is high that certain risk areas will cause problems somewhere in the project, then it simply makes good business sense to confront these potential problem areas as soon as possible. This early investment could make the difference between the overall success or failure of the project.

7

Managing Priorities Effectively

In every project, there are problems and there are PROBLEMS. Whenever a project's known problems are listed, there are always some that stand out as being urgent. These high-priority problems might change many times throughout the life of the project, but the level of attention they receive will have a major impact on the health of the project. Neglecting these problems for lower-priority problems is like buckling your seat belt at the end of a trip. Some items demand attention first—to ensure a successful journey.

If a project's leadership is unable or unwilling to focus the project's resources on solving the most important problems first, then the project and its participants will *drift*. Drifting has a serious, negative effect on many areas of the project. These effects include lower productivity, longer schedules, lower morale, lower quality, increased rework, and maybe even the eventual death of the project. The death knell might arrive before the first line of code is written or soon after the final product is delivered to the first customer.

Project success doesn't just happen. For the most part, it is predictable, controllable, and implementable. This chapter explains why working intelligently has a lot more going for it than just working hard.

Priorities Adrift

The following scenario describes an example of a project that gets caught up in drift. This drift can cause or accelerate the erosion of a project, an erosion that can eventually undermine the health of the project.

The project is several months into an estimated two-year product development cycle. Many project activities have been started. Among these are the product objectives, the product specifications, the project schedule plan, the product design, and even some code. No activities have been completed.

Staffing of project personnel is judged to be 60 percent complete. The project members are uncertain about what, specifically, they are supposed to be accomplishing and when. But this does not stop them from working on tasks they believe must get done anyway. Enthusiasm abounds. Optimism can be seen and felt everywhere.

Two months pass. More activities are started. Sixty-five percent of staffing has now been completed. The project leadership is under increased pressure to complete some key activities. The first completed activity is the project schedule plan. Many people feel some relief now that an agreement has been reached on a defined set of schedules. Everyone now knows what activities must be completed and when.

Two more months pass. Almost every activity that has been started is shown to be behind schedule. The code that has been unit and function tested has some serious function and interface problems. The design was not properly inspected, under the excuse that no inspection process has yet been approved. Also, the programmers made assumptions about the contents of the product specifications, but the product specifications have not yet been approved. The approvers of the specifications cannot agree on the full set of product functions, in part because the product objectives have also not been approved. The objectives have been written but have not been approved because the various organizations with approval rights either cannot settle on the precise product to build or fear the current architecture and design assumptions that are being implemented cannot support the full set of product objectives.

The project head declares, "Enough is enough. I want to know the major obstacles to progress in this shop. I want these problems resolved immediately. This logjam must be broken, and broken now."

A list of the major project obstacles is compiled. These problems are then ordered according to priority. An owner is assigned to each of the top ten problems. The owners are directed to correct their assigned problems by specified dates. A mix of apprehension and relief is felt throughout the project. Apprehension is felt about the large number of problems that have been identified and the complexity of some of these problems. Relief is felt because the list appears to be comprehensive and for once the project leaders seem to be working together and gaining some semblance of control.

Another two months pass. The product objectives are finally approved. This approval took longer than expected. Because the development organization had already made considerable progress with the product specifications, design and coding, numerous compromises were made in approving the product objectives. The major challenge was to ensure conformity between the product objectives document and the product specifications document. Unfortunately, the product specifications are now locked in controversy. Agreement cannot be reached on how to resolve several product specifications issues. These issues include the ability to reach agreement on product performance characteristics, the degree of product usability, and some major functional definitions. Those approvers who had been reluctant to approve the product objectives were expecting to have more success in negotiating the content of product specifications. However, since a large portion of the product has already been coded and informally tested, it is argued that a functional change at this point would require major rework and further schedule slippages.

Another month passes. The product specifications are finally approved. Significant areas of the code are being reworked to match those changes that were negotiated in the final specifications. The schedules continue to slide. A brief analysis is made by the project leadership to determine the root causes behind the sliding schedules. The major problems are singled out to be:

- Failure of the project leadership to resolve major product issues
- Conflicting project priorities, which are further compounded by limited people and equipment resources
- Lack of discipline from the project leaders in meeting their schedule commitments

Some frustration is evident among the project leadership. One project leader is overheard saying to another, "There just doesn't seem to be enough hours in a day. If only the leadership across this project could reach a consensus on which problems are most important, and if the whole project would unite and support this list of priorities, then the needed project structure and progress would follow."

The decision is made to reset the project schedules and to get a commitment from the project leaders to make the new schedule plan happen. It is also acknowledged that staffing is significantly behind planned levels. Staffing was expected to be 98 percent complete, but is only at 75 percent of expectations. The delay is blamed on the multiple tasks that project leaders have had to focus on and, therefore, the limited time remaining for them to solve other problems. The project leaders are again told to fix this. One project leader confesses to his manager, "Along with all the other problems I am solving, I don't have sufficient time to work on staffing."

The reply is, "If you had made recruitment a priority among your work activities, then you would now have the people necessary to deal with many of the problems you are currently experiencing."

The new schedule plan is finalized and brings a long awaited sigh of relief from both the project leaders and the project members. Some of the project members voice their concern that the new plan, which is viewed as achievable, might not be attainable with the current project leadership style. Nevertheless, everyone accepts the new plan and is determined to make it work.

Two more months pass. Six weeks of progress have been made. This progress is viewed as being slow, yet better than before. The current issues of the day are:

- Staffing delays
- No well-defined usability requirements
- No approved control process for making changes to the product specifications
- Inconsistent and incomplete design and code inspections
- "Off-spec" product performance characteristics
- Major rework required against the first drafts of the product publications
- No firm commitment for needed hardware equipment
- No regularly scheduled project tracking meetings

As before, these work items, and others, are assigned to individual project leaders to fix. No formal plans for any items are requested and the items are not tracked over the course of the next month. The project head assumes that, as professionals, the project leaders will complete these work items on a timely basis.

One month later there is a request for status reports on the issues that were delegated a month earlier. Only one has been considered complete by its assigned owner: commitment for hardware equipment. Unfortunately, the commitment does not satisfy the schedule requirements. The owner of the work item had not pursued this item further because she believed this was the best the hardware people could do. It is discovered that the current issues of the day are almost identical to those of one month earlier and of the month before that.

The project head is furious and requests a personal accounting on each issue. These unresolved issues continue to cause the organization to drift away from its ability to function as an effective, working unit. They are also causing further schedule delays, and in some cases are resulting in significant rework time having to be added to the schedule plan. Confusion abounds over which problems to deal with first, second, and so on. The ongoing mismatch of priorities being handled across the project continues to erode overall project progress.

The project continues in much the same misguided way until the final product is delivered to customers. Yes, it *is* shipped, although nearly nine months later than the original two-year plan had specified. And it is shipped with some of the same problems that were known from the start, problems in product performance, usability, incomplete and inaccurate publications, and design. All of which has left the product on shaky ground for customer acceptance as well as for additional funding required to support the problems that will be found by the product's users.

What went wrong? Almost everyone on the project could see that the issues were not receiving the attention they required. Yet everyone had a "valid" excuse: They were too busy to take time to identify and then deal with the most important issues. The claims were that, if the main issues were focused on with the intensity required, then too many other areas of the project would suffer. As one of the newer project leaders put it, "If I had to do it all over on the next project, I would probably do it the same way. It was just an aggressive project."

Don't believe it!

Solve the Most Important Problems First

It is easy to get caught up in the day-to-day flurry of activities, allowing the onslaught of daily problems to consume every inch of each day's mile. When this happens, there is a strong tendency to delegate more and to become further removed from the endless, revolving list of problems. This situation can lead to a loss of control. If you are a project leader, you cannot afford to be too far removed from major problems and decisions. The further removed you are, the greater the chances for the project to enter the *drift zone*. The drift zone is recognizable when:

- No one appears to be in control of the project.
- Activities are not completed.
- Wheel spinning and rework become the norm.
- Schedules slide.

There is another, although opposite, reaction to the endless emergence of problem after problem. That reaction is to actually get closer to all the problems, to actively cultivate the view that "Unless I personally fix these problems, they won't be fixed correctly and a bad situation will get worse." Unfortunately, this approach is also disastrous. The project head or a project leader becomes a critical path to getting problems resolved. Progress will ultimately slow down, not speed up. Displays of ownership from those who should be solving these problems will wane, as will the morale, productivity, and schedules.

What option is left? Stay abreast of the most important problems and allow those around you to handle all other problems. Frequent and regular tracking meetings will keep you as informed about the problems of lesser importance as you need to be. It is the more important problems that can cause the most harm to the project. The project leadership must manage these problems directly or be confident that they are being properly managed by others.

How do you decide which problems to get directly involved with and to what extent you should be involved? The following list identifies the steps to follow. Adherence to these steps will allow you to maintain the control necessary to yield the successful closure of your most critical problems.

- Step 1. Pinpoint Priorities: Identify and prioritize the most important problems.
- Step 2. Assign One Owner: Assign an owner to each priority problem.
- Step 3. Commit to a Course: Develop a plan that will successfully resolve each priority problem
- Step 4. Review Daily Dumps: Review the priority problems daily.

These steps, summarized in Figure 7.1, are discussed in the sections that follow.

Step 1: Pinpoint Priorities

At any given point in a medium or large project, there can be literally hundreds of problems that are known and being solved. Most of these are typical, business-as-usual problems. Examples of business-as-usual problems are those found while:

- Reviewing or using the product specifications
- Inspecting the design
- Correcting defects in the code
- Writing and updating the product publications

There are also the major problems, those problems that inhibit others from doing their job, problems that have a major impact on the well-being of the project, the product, and the people involved. These problems are similar to those revealed in the opening chapter scenario. Examples of major-impact problems are:

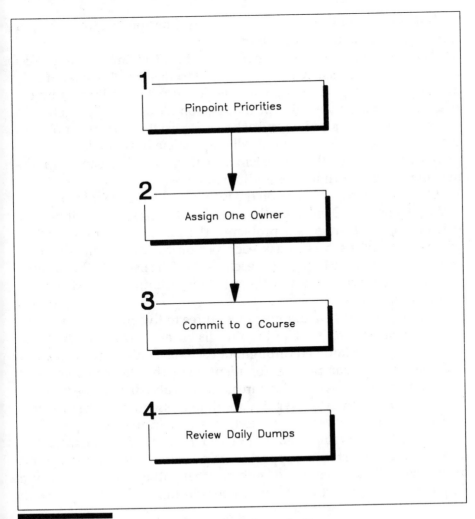

Figure 7.1. Steps for managing priorities

- Incomplete and unclear product objectives
- Incomplete and uncommitted project schedule plans
- Inability to meet product performance specifications
- Ineffective change-control process for making changes to the product objectives and product specifications
- Ineffective project-tracking process
- Late staffing of project personnel
- Inadequate hardware equipment delivery commitments
- Untimely closing of contracts with outside companies for deliverables required to complete the project successfully

This important-problems list may vary from project to project, or from one phase of the project to the next.

The first thing to do in managing the most important project problems is to list them. One person can start this list. However, if only one person is assigned to generate the list, it might be limited by the relatively narrow viewpoint of that person. A useful approach is to assemble the project leaders and ask them to list the top three problems that they recognize. Then compile all the problems on a single list. Using this list as a base, and the synergism from the assembled team, open the meeting to brainstorming for additional items.

Of course, every problem on the list will not have the same priority within the project. Once the list is considered complete, prioritize it by placing the most important problems, the priorities, at the top. One prioritizing approach is to ask each person to select their top three problems from the list. Then, for each item on the list, note the number of votes it received. The top three to five priorities should quickly become apparent.

The project head should post these three to five priorities on his or her office blackboard, wall, or in some visible area near or in the office so that they are reinforced throughout each day. Other project leaders can follow a similar process for identifying the three to five most important problems within their areas and can also display the list in an easily seen location. However, it is absolutely essential for the top three to five problems across the project area to which they apply to be publicized for every impacted project leader to see and understand. The project leaders must fully support these priorities when applying their resources. They must also ensure that other activities being implemented do not conflict with these priorities.

Step 2: Assign One Owner

This section and the next section follow the same basic guidelines that were presented in the "Recovery Plans" section of Chapter 6. Rather than repeat the full text here, only a few words will be added in support of the "Recovery Plans" section.

Assign lead people to own major problems. The same person must also own the proposed solution. The notion of *accountability* is key here. Also, only one owner should be assigned for each problem. Often, the effectiveness in resolving a problem quickly and efficiently is inhibited when two or more people jointly share responsibility for solving it.

Step 3: Commit to a Course

The following example illustrates an error that causes many projects to "miss the mark":

> Ron Clark is assigned to fix a problem. It is an urgent matter that must be corrected within two weeks. This is considered a very short time period, but with the proper attention, it should be able to be closed within the two weeks. It is obvious what the journey to reach a solution must be. Therefore, Clark is left to his own devices to close the problem.
>
> One week later, Clark presents the status of the problem resolution. It doesn't appear that the problem can be closed within the remaining week. Perhaps, if more time and a more intelligent effort had been spent on the problem during the first week, it could have been closed within the two-week goal. The project leadership reviewing the status information suggests that the approach be reset and asks for a status update at the end of the following week.
>
> At the end of the next week Clark declares he is still a few days away from closing the problem. Some refinements are suggested to his approach and no additional status meeting is scheduled. It is assumed that the problem will be closed during the following week. No further status meeting is scheduled. The problem *will not* be closed.

What is missing in the above scenario? No detailed plan or course of action was required. An issue that is recognized as one of the hottest in the project and, to boot, must be closed in just two weeks, should be a clear signal that each day counts. Therefore, a committed, detailed plan must be required from the person assigned to solve the issue. Do not accept the comeback, "With the time it will take me to build a detailed plan, I could have had most of the problem solved." This response only reinforces the need for a detailed plan—if not out of necessity, then for insurance. This plan should spell out not only the events to be completed each day, but also the dependent parties who are required to resolve the issue successfully. The plan should be approved by the project head as well as by those who are performers. All of this preparation helps to ensure that the problem is solved *the first time.*

Do not neglect to seek help from outside the project or even outside the company. These important project problems must not be allowed to linger. It may be that outside resources of equipment, consultants, or even uniquely skilled people may be needed. The cost to procure them can be more than offset by the importance of solving the problem on a timely basis.

Step 4: Review Daily Dumps

Time is scarce for a project head and project leaders. That is why it must be wisely invested. Project leaders should not spend 80 percent of their time on low-priority project problems and 20 percent on high-priority problems. Eighty percent of a leader's time should be spent on the most important problems. However, there is a strong attraction to work almost exclusively on the lesser problems. Minor problems tend to be easier to solve than major problems, and it is satisfying to see frequent accomplishments. But resist! Deal with important issues first.

Some form of status report, or dump, must be pursued each day on each of the "hot" problems. If your project has weekly project tracking meetings, the status of the hot issues should be shared with everyone. However, these problems and their progress toward resolution must be traced daily to help ensure success. The daily meetings can be formal or simply a five-minute briefing against the established plan.

Measure of Success

The top-priority problems in a project will likely change many times throughout the life of the project. This "hit" list must be reevaluated at regular intervals. Weekly evaluations are preferred, although twice-weekly evaluations can be best for projects that are starting a hit list for the first time. Evaluations can be as infrequent as once every two weeks for mature, structured projects that have been managed according to a hit list for some time. Of course, a meeting is not always required to determine whether a new addition should be made to the hit list. The project head must exercise authority in changing the problems on the hit list when the need to do so arises. However, any changes made must be clearly and timely communicated to the staff. This is essential in maintaining control and a respectable productivity within the project. After awhile, the use of the hit list will be an established activity and focusing on it will become automatic.

A good way to measure how effective an organization is at responding to its major problems is to compare the hit list from one month to the next. If the same items are present, something is wrong and the organization is still suffering from *drift*. That is, too much time is spent doing rework and too little in working effectively. The organization is drifting from one activity to the next without achieving a clear closure on earlier activities. Or it may be entering the next set of activities before those activities are fully ready.

Don't lose sight of the forest...

A side benefit in focusing so intensely on the hit list is that participants learn how to see the whole picture and, therefore, become less susceptible to spending too much attention on tangents of lesser value. This skill is one that project heads require in order to manage effectively. It is also a skill seen most often in the more productive and effective project leaders.

8

Product Objectives: Providing Direction

"If you don't know where you are going, then how will you know when you get there?" These familiar lines could have been written about software projects in general and product objectives in particular. Every project, when it is conceived, has a set of objectives. Making money is not the type of objective referred to here (although that is certainly one of the usual end goals and is not to be slighted). The focus here is on a set of objectives that provide *direction* in the creation of the new product. As a program product is developed it can take on a thousand different faces, all of which have a schedule cost, a complexity cost, and a dollar cost. Also, each face has an associated level of customer satisfaction. The goal, of course, is to choose the right set of faces, called *basic product functions and features*, at the *beginning* of the product development cycle. These faces should be sufficiently defined to ensure they are understood and followed, but not defined in such detail that the creative energy of the builders is inhibited.

If, at the beginning of a product development cycle, the product objectives are not complete and the participating organizations are not in agreement about what to build, then a lot can go wrong—and usually will. Several major restarts could be necessary, leaving an aftermath of throwaway work, frustrated participants, poor communications across the project, slipped schedules, and increased costs—or, worse, the cancellation of the project.

Not Doing It Right the First Time

The following scenario shows how inattention to product objectives can have an unwelcome toll on a software development project.

No one remembers there ever being a formal agreement about the basic requirements for this new product. But a lot of people had their own ideas on what the requirements should be. After all, many of the requirements were "common sense." Since software development cycles always seem to take too long, the project leadership had decided to take that "calculated" risk and dispense with formal product objectives. Instead of creating a document that addresses the major product considerations, it was decided that a small set of charts would do just as well, as long as certain project leaders in the direct chain of command could reach a consensus on the contents of these charts. Anyone outside of this direct chain of command could log an objection, or **issue**, and there would be plenty of time to work on these issues later.

Several product designers are quickly recruited to form a product development team to begin work on the product specifications and design. The team's size is intentionally small to limit the number of people interfaces among team members. The team is also told to work primarily in a "vacuum"—that is, as a self-contained team with little-to-no communications with any groups outside the team. This is viewed as a "productive" way to streamline the decision-making process for the new product. In lieu of having no completed product objectives to reference when confronted by potential product tradeoffs, the team attempts to reach a consensus for many decisions. Frequently, a consensus cannot be reached, due to conflicting perceptions of product objectives. When this happens, the team leader or his project leader makes the decision. It appears that something must be going right because the product specifications are on schedule for review. Several groups outside of the small product development team have waited anxiously to review the product specifications.

However, the product defined in the review draft of the product specifications would have been fine for a product of five years ago. But today's users are looking for increased ease of use. Information systems (IS) managers are looking for connectivity to computers already purchased and in use by their companies. Company managers are looking for compatibility with their existing hardware and software. Retailers are looking for something that sets a new product apart from competitors. The customer service department is looking for improved serviceability aids.

But the developers like this product. After all, they defined it. It was their creation. It can always be enhanced in the next release offering of the product. Isn't that what new releases are for?

Upon closer examination of the product specifications, there appears to be some inconsistencies in the product functions. Some parts are strong in function, while others are weak. All issues raised against the product specifications are logged. A third of the issues are accepted as work items to resolve. A third are negotiated to a future release of the product. And the remaining third are rejected.

Several weeks later, the product specifications are reworked and reissued. These revised specifications are definitely an improvement. But new issues surface, issues that should have been resolved with the product objectives. Marketing learns that it must sell "X" number of packages of this product in order to meet the forecast, a forecast that is based on a minimum return-on-investment figure. Several of the issues that had been negotiated to a future release now seem too important to be ignored until then. To make matters worse, the next release will follow this one by at least a year, and a lot can happen in the software industry in one year. After more compromises are made, mostly by the marketers, the specifications are deemed to be at an acceptable level of completeness. The detailed design of the product begins.

By now the project is fully staffed. The developers are halfway through the coding phase. The testers are defining, designing, and writing test cases from the product specifications. The product publications writers are working on the initial drafts. The marketing and support people are preparing their brochures, tutorials, and support plans. Then, reports are heard that the competitor, who currently dominates the industry among this product's target audience, has just announced the ability to connect its product to other programs in other machines.

The company's marketers had predicted this. Now major product changes must be made to add this enhancement into the first release of the product. This addition will impact product schedules and will increase the selling price of the product. Also work that had been completed now must be thrown away. This change in direction for the product has caused the project leadership to take a closer look at the plans for the next release. It is discovered that the enhancements in the next release will cause up to 25 percent of the code in the first release to be discarded. Unfortunately, most of this code has already been written.

Several months pass. The product is now in system testing. The original schedules have been extended by several months. Marketing has decided that the product is, once again, no longer desirable at the current level of function. Either the project must be scrapped or some of the enhancements that were to be provided in the next release must be moved into this first release. A scramble takes place to reissue an updated product specifications document and to turn around the momentum that has taken months to build.

How does this scenario end? The damage is high. Schedules, costs, and resources, have all been negatively impacted. Could this scenario have been avoided? Nobody can say for sure. But it could definitely have fared better had the product objectives homework been done up front, when mistakes and delays are much less costly.

The Good Sense ($ Dollars and Cents $) for Product Objectives

The beginning is the most important part of the work.

Plato

Take a look at Figure 8.1. Of all the major activities in the product development cycle, the creation and approval of the product objectives document is the first. This should suggest how to start out on the right foot. Depending on the size and complexity of the product being developed, there might be anywhere from one to a dozen people working on product objectives. But the product objectives might directly affect well over ten times this many people, most of whom will be assigned to build the product. Furthermore, these people might be working on the product more than ten times longer than the time it took to write and get agreement on the product objectives document. From these simple analogies, you probably can feel the sense of importance and influence that the product objectives document has over the entire product cycle. No other aspect of the product development cycle has such a magnified return on its investment (or lack of return).

Suppose, for a moment, that a product objectives document was not completely written and approved for a given project. Without approved product objectives, the project participants will continually wrestle among themselves to determine the proper tradeoffs to make between the functions and features of the product. This product content must be balanced against project schedules, project costs, and intended user needs. How valid are project schedules that are committed early in the product cycle if full product objectives are incomplete and lack agreement among the principal project groups? And the most important element in this equation should not be overlooked: the user. If the intended users of a product have not participated in some significant fashion in defining and approving the product's full set of objectives, how can there be any certainty that the product will meet user requirements? This reasoning applies to a product built for a single customer, a product intended for use only within the company that built the product, or a product targeted for multiple user groups and customers. No matter what type or volume of customer applies, some valid representative sample of the targeted *user set* must be included in the product objectives process. If this user involvement is weak or missing, you can expect rough going throughout the product development cycle—and beyond.

Waste is what typically results when product objectives are incomplete, waste in the form of the following items over the course of the project:

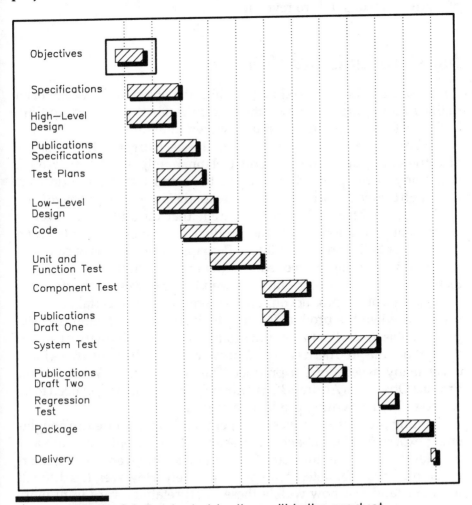

Figure 8.1. Product objectives within the product development cycle

- Extended schedules
- Continuous rework of design, code, and testing
- Increased person-months of overall work
- Decreased morale
- Increased product costs

These wastes are confined to the project. But consider the waste brought about by the resulting increased product costs to the user as well as the inevitable loss of revenue to the product's builder. Or consider the ultimate waste, the cancellation of the project brought about by poor product planning and by cost overruns. The cancellation of a project results in zero revenue.

Invest Today to Reap Tomorrow

It is wasteful to build a product for which the objectives have not been defined and approved. Know the objectives for the product you are building. Follow the simple process shown in Figure 8.2.

Interesting and often unexpected things happen when product objectives are put to paper. Product planners might suddenly realize that many of the product's basic functions and features are unclear. Although the overall scope of objectives for the product might have been known, it might now become apparent that an additional level of refinement is needed before the product objectives are ready to be turned over to the product builders. Perhaps more analysis of competitive product offerings is needed to better ensure that the functions and features chosen for this product will lead to the success of the product. If any aspect of the product objectives is omitted, this is certain to cause problems when the product is being built from interpretations of the product objectives. For maximum productivity and minimal disruption throughout the product development cycle, the product objectives must cover many aspects of the product. The next section, "What Should Product Objectives Address?" will identify specific areas that need to be addressed when writing product objectives.

Putting product objectives on paper for all to see is often an enlightening experience for yet another reason: When the objectives are at a high level, perhaps written simply as "bullets" on several charts, interpretations of each bulleted item can vary widely. However, it is difficult to understand just how widely these interpretations vary until more detail behind the bullets is documented and studied. With the documentation in hand, a sudden unexpected flurry of issues may appear. When everyone has had the chance to study the product objectives thoroughly and realize that they will share responsibility for the success of the product it defines, a very careful and interested group of participants emerges. The marketers suddenly recognize that the product is insufficiently function-rich to be competitive. The service group sees it deficient in serviceability aids and believes these deficiencies will restrict their profit margins. The human interface "gurus" believe the product

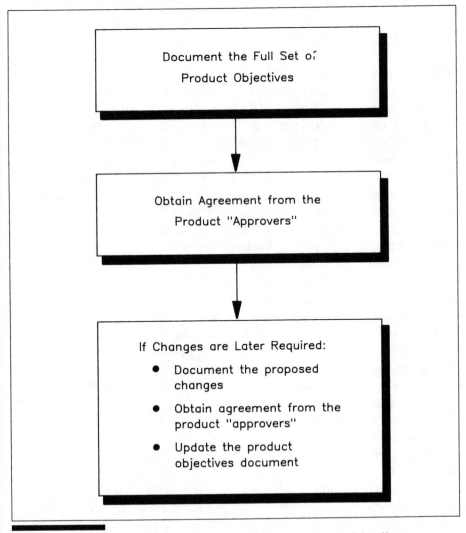

Figure 8.2. Know, and control, the product objectives

is not intuitive enough for the typical user. The financial and forecast departments say it won't generate enough revenue. Representative users feel the product won't satisfy their primary needs and priorities. And the development shop views the product as too much to deliver too soon.

So who's right? Not the point. The point is that, before this project gets on the road, a consensus of the right people or groups must be reached in order to avoid serious roadblocks later, or worse, the project being scrapped. A contentious environment is almost always healthy for the product. It can challenge a team to run lean and make decisions early—when they are the least expensive and the least emotional. Getting the *right people* to agree and feel ownership is like buying stocks low in an emerging bull market. It feels good and significantly increases the project's chance for success.

If "new" news appears later in the project and it is felt that a change must be made to the product objectives, then this alteration must go through a **change control process**. This is a defined process that can be followed when a change is proposed in a critical, and therefore *controlled*, document—in this case, the product objectives document. The change control process ensures that the proper documentation and approvals are obtained; otherwise, the proposed change is rejected.

Remember, the objectives literally define the basic direction of the entire project. They must be sufficiently complete and have the necessary agreement to risk betting the company's allocated financial investment against—because that is exactly what is being done. Every time a product takes a departure from the objectives, it costs. The further into the product cycle, the greater the cost. Therefore, any changes made to the product objectives should be carefully controlled once they have been approved. The recommended change control process is presented in Chapter 9, along with a discussion of product specifications. The change control process discussion is deferred to that chapter because it takes on a greater importance once the product specifications are approved, the project is nearly staffed to its maximum level, and the efficiency of communications among the project members requires greater attention.

Look again at Figure 8.1. Notice that the high-level design can begin shortly after the product objectives have been started. The earliest practical starting point for beginning high-level design is after the product objectives have been distributed for their initial review, called the document *review phase*. (See the "Review Cycle for Project Documents" section of Chapter 4 for more about the phases in developing a project document). However, high-level design should be reasonably understood *before* the product objectives are completed. This intentional overlap between the development of product objectives and early high-level design will help to prevent the product objectives from defining a product that could not technically be built in a satisfactory manner. There must be confidence that a high-level design supports the objectives before the product objectives document is completed. This approach is not meant to imply that high-level design must be completed, or be even near completion. In fact, the high-level design cannot be completed until the product's description, documented in the product specifications, has been all but finalized. The result of an early high-level design activity, called *preliminary high-level design*, is vital knowledge for the approving organizations, particularly those organizations that are responsible for developing the product specifications and the high-level design.

It literally pays to do the required homework up front, before the full deployment of dollars, people, material, and time has occurred. No activity in the product development cycle should be rushed, but of those activities *not* to rush, building complete product objectives leads the list.

What Should Product Objectives Address?

Product objectives should address several different aspects of the product it defines. These topics and the extent to which they are discussed can vary, depending on the type of product to be built. Compare the product objectives for a real-time, multitasking network program to handle the routing of telephone calls throughout the Southeastern United States with the product objectives for a standalone, sort utility program that runs on a personal computer. Obviously there are many more factors to consider in defining the product objectives for the network program than those for the standalone, sort utility program.

Also keep in mind that product objectives are just that—objectives. They do not describe the product in detail. Certain areas might be defined in detail, such as the intended audience for the product or the exact hardware it will support, but the way in which the product will be built and the syntax and semantics of the function it will provide should not be part of the product objectives. As you can see, this leaves wide room for the builders of the product to exercise their creative energy in developing the best possible product description and design.

The following categories, while not exhaustive, represent the more common elements to address in a product objectives document. Some of these categories are more important than others in that they are defined and agreed to very early in the product development cycle. Examples of these relatively important categories include definitions of the product audience, basic function, and ease-of-use considerations. These items need to be understood before the product design and detailed function can be described. Categories in which objectives can be delayed a bit might include product license agreements and packaging. If the objectives for these items will not be fully defined in the product objectives document, then a *place-holder* for these items should, at minimum, appear in the product objectives. This place-holder would then act to reference a forthcoming document of objectives for these items.

With each category listed below, a supportive example is used to further illustrate information that should be addressed in product objectives. A word processor program has been chosen as the product example.

Audience

Define both the customer and the customer's environment for the product.

> Is the word processor user expected to be computer literate? And if so, how much computer and word processing experience is assumed? For what reading grade level should the publications be targeted? Will the product user be expected to install the product or will a data processing staff or even the authorized product dealer perform the installation? What level of problem determination is the user expected to handle? The dealer? The manufacturer?

Function

Present the fundamental capabilities that the product should provide for its intended audience.

> For a word processor product, the basic required functions to be defined could include:
>
> * Delete character, word, line, block
> * Insert character, word, line, block

- Copy character, word, line, block
- Move character, word, line, block
- Set new page
- Set top/bottom margin
- Set page width/length
- Set left/right margin
- Define heading

Ease of Use

List all ease-of-use requirements. These requirements should be stated in terms of typical tasks that the user is expected to perform with the product. These tasks should be defined in terms of examples of typical customer hardware/software configurations and ease-of-use criteria that are measurable in a test environment. (See Chapter 10 for more on this topic.)

How much time, and with what assistance, if any, should it take for the customer to install the word processor? To begin to be productive? To recover from specific error situations? To learn how to use a specific function? To retrieve information from the product publications?

Hardware Supported

List all hardware devices to be supported, as well as the specific features of each device to be supported. Also, state the minimum machine configuration to be supported.

What printer models will the word processor support? What video display modes will be supported? What is the minimum memory size required?

Performance

Define the critical performance requirements that the product builders must satisfy. These requirements should be stated in specific, measurable terms. It is here that any memory or DASD storage size requirements or program execution path performance requirements are listed.

How much time, expressed in user terms, will it take the word processor product to perform such actions as initializing and becoming ready for use, switching from one screen to another, getting or saving a file, or searching and replacing character strings?

Publications

Define the number, size, and types of publications, define what each publication will address, and its specific audience. Also, list any special considerations, such as color or black-and-white publications and physical page size. This Publications section must also satisfy those requirements that apply from other sections defined in the product objectives. For example, the publications must be written to the proper reading grade level and experience level of the intended audience.

What consideration is being given to the layout of each publication in order to support ease of use for readers? What is the goal in providing examples? Will there be none, some, or many? For just some sections or all sections? What areas of the publications, if any, will be provided on-line? What special accommodations are provided for the new user? For the experienced user?

Standards

List the standards that must be followed. These standards may be the manufacturer's or specific industry standards, or both.

What data format types will the word processor product support? If documents will be distributed over a network, then what voice, graphics, imagery, and other data standards must be supported?

Reliability

Define the level of reliability of the final product.

What is the acceptable failure rate for the word processor in the user's establishment? How many problems are expected to be reported to the manufacturer for correction? What percentage and types of problems are expected to be corrected by the user? In the event of a failure, to what extent will the data files be preserved?

Serviceability

State how and where the product will be serviced and by whom.

Will the word processor customer and/or dealer have tools to aid in identifying problems? In resolving problems? Will failing modules be field replaceable? Will a HOTLINE number be available to handle problems by telephone? If so, for how many hours per day? Days per week?

Compatibility/Migration

State the level of compatibility that this product will have with other software and hardware products currently in use. If follow-on releases are planned, state the degree of upward compatibility expected.

Will the word processor user be able to use existing data and document files in their current format or will a migration path be defined? Will this migration path require new software or hardware tools? To what degree will the user's existing hardware investment be protected? Will any new hardware be required? Software? With what release levels of existing and new software, including operating systems, will the word processor product run?

Pricing/License Agreements

State the acceptable pricing range. Also, state the terms and conditions that apply to the purchaser, the seller, and the manufacturer.

How will a buyer of the word processor product be charged to allow one copy of the product to be used by multiple users within a network? Can the publications be purchased separately?

Competitiveness

State the degree of competitiveness this product has with similar products that are already available and with those that are anticipated to be available.

> Will the word processor be a competitive price/performance product? What is its anticipated lifespan? Is this a one-time product or will it be replaced by follow-up products?

Packaging

Define all the options to be made available in packaging the product. State all media on which it will be distributed.

> Will the word processor be made available on a personal computer with 3.5- inch diskette drives, 5.25- inch floppy drives, or both? Will the product be packaged as one unit or will it consist of multiple, individually packaged units? Will the product have the capability to be electronically distributed?

Security

Define security-related requirements.

> Will the word processor generate and use documents that have been encrypted? Will the user be required to enter a password before retrieving files?

Futures

List future enhancements expected.

> Will the word processor be enhanced to support the new generation of graphics displays anticipated to be available the following year?

The "Futures" category is useful in helping guide developers in selection of the design that will best support future enhancements. A list of future enhancements also provides a way to satisfy those approvers of the objectives who do not get everything they want in the first release, but at least feel that their desires are being planned for as the product evolves.

You might have noticed that several of these categories have no direct relevance to the programmers who design, code, and test the product, or to the writers who write the product's publications. Many different organizations and skills are required to successfully launch and support a new product. The product objectives must give direction to *all* participating organizations so that each organization is "singing from the same hymnal." This direction serves to ensure a unified, consistent, and complementary approach to building the product.

Invest the time very early in the product development cycle to create completed and approved product objectives. You will find the returns to be handsome indeed.

9

Product Specifications: Defining the Final Product

The continual addition of function enhancements to a product, throughout the product development cycle, is called **creeping function**. These enhancements creep into the product, line-of-code by line-of-code, until the weight of the code exceeds the committed schedule capacity of the project. It does not matter what the intentions are for accepting these changes into the product. The result is that these constant changes can literally destroy a project, a product, and the morale of the people building that product.

It is essential that the answer to the following question is understood early in the product development cycle:

"What is the product to be built?"

When the answer to this question is spread across the entire development cycle, it usually will come in the form of bad news. Why bad news? It is impossible to schedule a project's activities, to commit deliverables, to anticipate problems with the expectation of avoiding them, or just plain act responsibly when certain planning-related activities have been neglected. These important activities are:

- Describe the product, in detail, early in the product cycle.
- Get agreement from the right people or organizations on the functional detail of the product to be built.

- Define and implement an orderly process to follow when a functional change must be made to the product.

Out of Control

The following comprehensive scenario is an example of the ways in which creeping function can undermine a project. Does the detail revealed in this story sound familiar?

A new project has started. The product objectives have already been written. Furthermore, all the right people and organizations have agreed to the direction that the product objectives prescribe. The product definition is off to a good start.

The detailed description of the product must now be defined. (This is typically accomplished through a document called the **product specifications**.) A small group of programmers has been working off to the side, prototyping the basic design and function of the desired product. With the help of a generous amount of **scaffolding** (temporary code that will later be discarded), a portion of the group's model is running. As with most projects, a great need exists to develop this product as soon as possible. Not only is there an attractive market for the product today, but the competition is allegedly planning to unveil a similar product. The company management is supportive of the project and, at the request of the project leadership, has already approved the required staffing of people for the project.

The project leaders have had experience in developing several other products, so there is a high level of confidence in their wisdom to plan and direct this project. Because the project is on a "fast track," the leaders decide that time restrictions do not allow the "luxury" of writing full product specifications and getting the early agreement of participating organizations. Instead, an *overview document* will be produced. This document will record the portion of the product that has already received general agreement and is also supported by the prototype work. The person writing the document is one of the more knowledgeable project members and, unfortunately, is also needed to help lead in the remaining design activities. Since his time is critical, the project leadership decides that he must complete the overview as soon as possible. The document is "completed" within two weeks. The new people on the project find the document to be extremely valuable as an educational aid in getting them "on board." Schedules are now firmly in place and committed throughout the project as well as up through the project leadership chain.

The leadership has divided the development organization into groups that will each work on developing specific components of the product. At this early juncture in the project, communication across the different groups is relatively easy to manage. The groups' leaders meet regularly to resolve problems and present status information. The overview document that was intended as a substitute for the product specifications continues to evolve into more detail to accommodate each of the groups' components. The leadership has decided that these changing product specifications must be frozen in order to stabilize the design activities. Even though schedules indicate that all changes to the product specifications were to be completed by now, more work is required. However, the groups believe that the remaining work is relatively minor.

Time passes and this "minor" work seems never to end. Increasingly, more of the design assumptions are proving to be incorrect, and additional design changes are necessary. This is recognized as a result of neglecting to finalize the product specifications. Some frustration is beginning to surface due to the changing design coupled with the fixed, committed schedules.

Several groups are now falling behind their schedules. No serious concern is shown since it is still relatively early in the overall project schedules and "There is plenty of time to recover." The project continues to recruit new people to take on activities not yet in full gear. The test organizations are being assembled. So too are the writers for the product's publications. Excitement for the project continues to mount as people are assigned to the various areas of the project.

Until now, the problem of incomplete product specifications has primarily been confined to the programmers charged with designing the product. But as the project grows in size and momentum, other groups have an increasing need to understand the specifications. The test group must design and write test procedures that verify the product performs as required. Members of this group need to know precisely how the user will install and use the product. They need to know what each screen will look like and what the product's responses to the user will be. The writers of the product's publications need the same information. In fact, the testers will verify the accuracy of the publications against the specifications.

The need for completed product specifications is growing urgent. Even though testing is not to start for quite some time, this period of the development cycle is expected to be productively used in writing the first set of test cases and in preparing the initial drafts of publications. Several options are explored to address the serious problem of incomplete product specifications. These options range from one extreme—the writers will create the product specifications under close direction from the designers—to another extreme—a large weekly education meeting will be included to share the latest information on specifications. The alternative chosen is to isolate the designers for three weeks so they can concentrate on completion of the product specifications. It is understood that this will leave many of the project's people idle during this three-week period, but it is decided that, over the long haul, this is the least painful approach.

Three weeks pass. The designers emerge with a document that they say is "All but complete." It is their view that, although remaining design activities might continue to impact some areas of product specifications, the specifications are now current and are sufficiently complete for the dependent organizations to proceed with their activities. The designers return to designing. This three-week slip has also meant at least a three-week delay in starting the detail design and coding. Several groups request that the product specifications be reviewed by all the dependent groups and updated until all groups approve its completeness and level of detail. The project leaders decide against this. Their rationale is the following: There is no time remaining in the schedules to allow for an approval cycle for the specifications, and that at least 80 percent of the specifications are not debatable. Debating the remaining 20 percent will only tie up the key designers. And if the key designers are consumed in meetings and debates, many people and groups dependent on the completion of their design work will suffer.

As the testers and writers begin their activities from the new product specifications, they freely admit that additional productive work can now be done. However, the further they proceed into their activities, the more questions they have about the specifications. It appears that the product specifications have numerous weak areas when one peels back information to view a lower level of detail. (These weak areas would have been identified and corrected had the product specifications been through an approval cycle.) The testers and writers are told they can have only minimal access to the designers. Frustrations abound, but restraint is shown. The designers are also getting increasingly frustrated by their inability to satisfy all the demands made on them to provide additional information and clarification. Adding to this frustration is the increasing requests they receive to include additional functions in the product. It seems some people just don't seem to understand or appreciate the designers' predicament. The designers rationalize that these people probably never experienced a product development cycle. (Or could they, instead, be people who sense something very wrong and are hopeful the same mistakes made on past projects will not be repeated here?)

As the designers continue to make changes to their copies of the product specifications, bits and pieces of their changes find their way to the dependent groups. It is becoming more apparent across the project that these changes must be given to everyone at the same time. A procedure is established to document and distribute changes to the product specifications. Everyone (except the designers) is ecstatic. Now changes are flowing from the source to the people who need them. While the designers recognize the need to do this, it is costing them time for which they had not planned. For everyone else, things begin to look up.

It is time to reevaluate schedules. There is, of course, much need (and pressure) to prevent schedule slippage. After several days of negotiations across the project, new schedules are established. Some relief is felt. But not enough to feel "right." Everybody will have their own challenges to overcome. Spirits, however, are reasonably high.

The product is now in the unit and function test phase. The first formal test, called **component testing**, is right around the corner. The initial drafts of the publications are also just around the corner. Things should be looking up. Unfortunately, this is not the case for all. It seems that the product specifications are still changing. Although the changes are not all major in magnitude, the collection of numerous, small changes is making it almost impossible for the writers and testers to maintain their schedule commitments. Something needs to be done to shut down, or at least significantly reduce, the number of these changes. The designers say the changes are necessary because "the schedule" never allowed them the time to complete the product specifications during the early stages of the product development cycle. Also, the designers say that, as they proceeded into the design activities, corresponding changes were required in the specifications.

The project leadership decides that drastic steps must be taken to reduce, if not eliminate, the number of changes being made to the product specifications. These leaders decide that all new changes must be personally and individually approved by them. This bureaucratic step is not welcomed by all. However, it does cause fewer changes to be proposed and accepted. Apparently, two conditions are causing the product specifications to change. The first is that specifications were never completed and locked tight by a strict change control process. The second condition is the eternal desire of programmers to make things better, to add things that are "nice to have" but are not required. A consensus cannot be reached to determine which condition is more at fault. A consensus is reached, however, that both are factors in the creeping function equation. Regardless, things are looking better again, not in the sense that current schedules are being met, but in the sense that progress is proceeding at a more productive and predictable pace.

The project is now several weeks into component testing. The first drafts of the publications are now available for review. A new concern is surfacing. Areas of the product specifications were misinterpreted due to the sketchy information available for some of the sections of the document. Misinterpretations also resulted because writers had restricted access to designers, who could have made necessary clarifications to the specifications. Also, many of the commands, display screens, and product responses to the user are not consistent across the product. Since the product specifications were not cast in concrete early, the different design groups evolved their pieces independently. This incompleteness and inconsistency must be corrected, which means more design, specification, coding, test case and publications changes—and, ultimately, more schedule slippage.

All these changes are made, including the revision of schedules—again. (Unfortunately, it will later be shown, the original project schedules bear no resemblance to the final product schedules.) Due to the need to maintain schedules throughout the project, compromises have been made continually in the functions defined in the product specifications. Testing and publications trade-offs are also made. The resulting product not only looks different than originally anticipated, there is now some pressure for the quality to be less than originally expected. No one specifically states or votes for lower quality. It is not an overt desire. It is a result—a result of the chaos brought about by incomplete product specifications and by a weak or missing process to control changes to product specifications.

Does this example have a happy ending? It is too late for that. Much irreversible damage has been done. The best that can be hoped is for the product to survive the cost overruns and to still be deliverable. Could this mess have been avoided? A definite "Yes." In ways that you might already have seen.

Controlling Creep

Three steps must be followed if you are serious about controlling creeping function. These steps are stated at the beginning of this chapter and are shown in Figure 9.1.

You first need to describe the product to be built. This description must be in sufficient detail to allow the many diverse project groups to proceed with their missions. These missions include designing and writing the code, developing test cases, writing product publications, and preparing the market and support plans for selling, distributing, and maintaining the product. The product description must be available early in the product development cycle so that all groups can proceed in a parallel and productive manner.

Because each group within the project needs the product definition for different purposes, all groups need to review and approve the product description, also called the product specifications. Each group needs to ensure that the proper level of information is documented. Also, there is a need to ensure that product specifications adequately reflect and support the product objectives.

It should be expected that some changes will need to be made to the product specifications as the product proceeds through the development cycle. A process must be defined and followed to ensure that all changes that must be made to either the product objectives or the product specifications are made in a controlled and effective manner.

The discussions in the sections that follow expand these three steps.

Step 1: Starting in Control

A previous chapter presents the importance of driving to approved product objectives early in the product development cycle. (See Chapter 8.) Briefly stated, product objectives are a crisp statement of direction, or framework, for which the project's money, people, material, and time will be committed. It is this early declaration of direction that uniformly focuses a project's resources.

But you cannot build a product from product objectives alone. The objectives are at too high a level. Much more detail about the product is

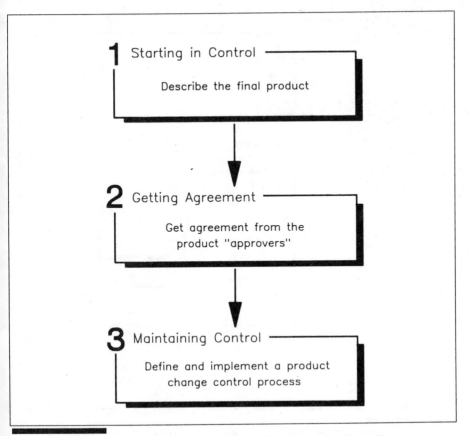

Figure 9.1. Steps in controlling the creeping function

required. This detail is provided in the product specifications document. Figure 9.2 illustrates the relative position of the product specifications in the product development cycle. The product detail found in the specifications is the same level of detail that the user of the product would require to understand and use the product. As previously mentioned, it is also the level of detail required by the many organizations within the project to proceed with their activities productively. With so many people and groups dependent on this detailed

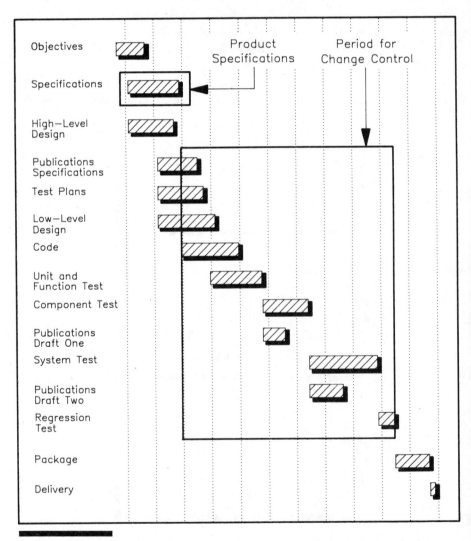

Figure 9.2. Product specifications and change control

description, it should be easy to understand why it is important to document product specifications for all to see.

Relationship: Product Specifications to Product Objectives

Looking again at Figure 9.2, notice that the product specifications can begin relatively soon after the product objectives have been started. The earliest practical point to begin product specifications is after product objectives have been distributed for initial review, called the document *review phase.* (See the "Review Cycle for Project Documents" section of Chapter 4 for more about the phases in developing a project document.) However, product objectives should be completed and approved before product specifications can be completed. The basic direction for the product must be decided before the detailed description of that product can be completed.

Relationship: High-Level Design to Product Specifications

Again, looking at Figure 9.2, also notice that high-level design can begin about the same time as the product specifications. To be practical, high-level design should also wait for the initial review draft of the product objectives document. There are two major reasons for starting high-level design at this point (rather than later) in the product development cycle. The first reason is to perform enough early high-level design (called preliminary high-level design) as is necessary to feel reasonably comfortable that the product defined in the product objectives document can, indeed, be technically built in a satisfactory manner. There must be confidence that a high-level design supports the objectives before the product objectives are completed and approved.

The second major reason for starting high-level design this soon is to complement the development of the product specifications. Notice from Figure 9.2 that high-level design is completed *before* the product specifications are completed and approved. This helps to ensure that any high-level design considerations that could impact the externals of the product are properly reflected in the product specifications. Figure 9.3 presents an example of how this overlap of high-level design and the development of product specifications might be scheduled. The goal is to create an approval draft of product specifications that essentially is supported by the high-level design. (Again, see the "Review Cycle for

Project Documents" section of Chapter 4 for a discussion of the phases in developing a project document.)

As you can see, the example provided in Figure 9.3 also shows how the product specifications and the high-level design overlap with the product objectives. For information on what is meant by **inspections** within the high-level design sequence of activities, see the "Defect Removal Activities" section of Chapter 5.

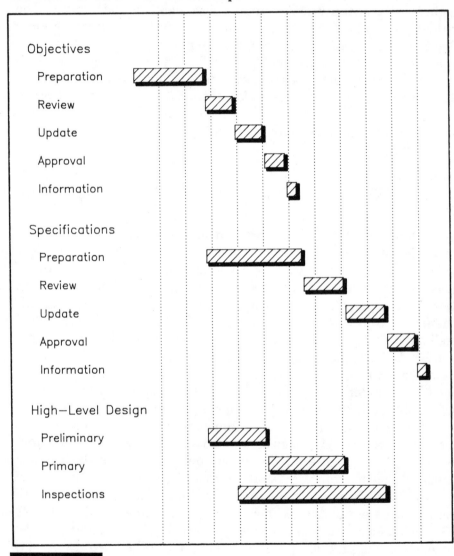

Figure 9.3. Overlap: Objectives, specifications, high-level design

Relationship: Prototype to Product Specifications

Now consider, for a moment, the role that a prototype can play in the development of product specifications. The concept of a prototype is introduced in Chapter 10. However, a brief discussion here is pertinent since a prototype can have significant value to the developers of product specifications. A prototype is defined as an early, running model of the product to be built. This model might represent only a small portion of the product or a substantial portion. The primary purpose for building a prototype is usually to demonstrate or prove the feasibility of a concept, such as:

- Applying new technology
- Obtaining an early start in developing a new product
- Optimizing a product's user interface
- Developing and fine-tuning design algorithms

Building a prototype is essential to the development of a product. Great benefits can be achieved by testing changes in a prototype before they are adopted into the product. The earlier in the product development cycle that you can study aspects of the product through a running model, make adjustments *"on the fly"* and examine their impact, and reflect those findings in the product specifications or soon thereafter, then the greater the likelihood that fewer product changes will have to be requested and made at the end. Figure 10.1 shows the relative position of the prototype activity in the product development cycle.

The Return on Investment

You should expect to spend a bit more schedule time (than is typical for some projects) while writing the product specifications to the level of detail recommended here. However, this investment should be more than recovered later in the development cycle. Why? Because the entire organization starts off on a more productive footing. Also, significantly less rework is expected since fewer functions should need to undergo change.

Once again, it is in the best interest of the product and the project to define *all* of the final product in the product specifications. People and organizations are dependent on complete and accurate information in order to do their work. The longer the development of *complete* product specifications is delayed, the longer it will take to complete the product. This translates to higher expenses and lower revenues. The investment in completing the product specifications as recommended here will likely draw interest for the remainder of the product development cycle, and beyond.

The recommended information to be included in the product specifications document is discussed in this chapter in a later section, "What Should Product Specifications Address?"

Step 2: Getting Agreement

The next step in controlling creeping function, as shown in Figure 9.1, is to get agreement from the product approvers. A defined review cycle for project documents is discussed in the "Review Cycle for Project Documents" section of Chapter 4. That discussion is relevant here because drafts of the product specifications are distributed for review.

Once the product specifications are written and distributed for review, you can expect some differences of opinion to emerge from various groups across the project. This should be viewed as healthy for the product and should be *welcomed input*. It is better to make changes now that are right for the product rather than to wait until the design, coding, and much of the testing has been completed. The cost of making product changes can increase dramatically the further along the product is in the product development cycle.

Literally every group in a project has some stake in the completeness and accuracy of the product specifications. Some groups will examine product specifications to ensure that the specifics and/or the spirit of the product objectives have been followed. Many other groups will have their productivity quickly go into a nose dive if the specifications do not have the data or detail that these groups require in order to fulfill their commitments. Therefore, it is especially vital that this important project document receive the approval of all groups participating in the product development cycle.

There is another value in getting agreement from the participating groups, though perhaps not as obvious: The more that people believe in the product, the more their ownership will be demonstrated. Ownership can be translated into commitment—and it is commitment that will greatly increase a product's chances for success. People are much more interested in working on a product that they feel a part of than on a product that they perceive was dictated to them.

Step 3: Maintaining Control

The final step in achieving victory over creeping function (see Figure 9.1) is to define and implement a process to follow for making changes to the product specifications.

The project that has, early in the product development cycle, documented product objectives and product specifications *and* has reached agreement on these documents is off to a strong start indeed. Starting a project with the product definition under control is an enviable (to projects that have failed to do this), but achievable, accomplishment. But what happens if some change in the approved functions is necessary? Even the sharpest minds cannot anticipate all future changes. Once the lowest level of design or the coding begins, deficiencies or oversights might be discovered. Also, product testing, particularly usability testing (see Chapter 10), might uncover undesirable user interfaces. Figure 9.2 shows the lengthy period of time that follows the approval of product specifications. Throughout this period, changes to the product specifications might be required.

When it is necessary to make a change to a product's description, it must be made with the following considerations in mind:

- Is the change necessary? In this release?
- What groups are impacted by the change? How will dependencies and schedules be impacted?
- Is there a more effective and preferred change than the one proposed?
- What documentation must be produced to document the change properly?
- How and when can the change best be made with the least negative impact?

A **change control process** should be followed to ensure that the following occur:

- Only necessary changes are made to the product.
- Changes are communicated to all.
- Changes are implemented in an orderly fashion.

There are many methods to choose from in implementing a change control process. An example of one method is shown in Figure 9.4. This example shows how a change to the product specifications might be made.

Representatives from across the project are chosen to form a group. This group is commonly called a committee or *board*. When a technical change is deemed necessary, the originator of the change brings the change proposal before the board and attempts to convince the board members of its need. If the board agrees to accept the change into the next step of the change control process, the programmer with the

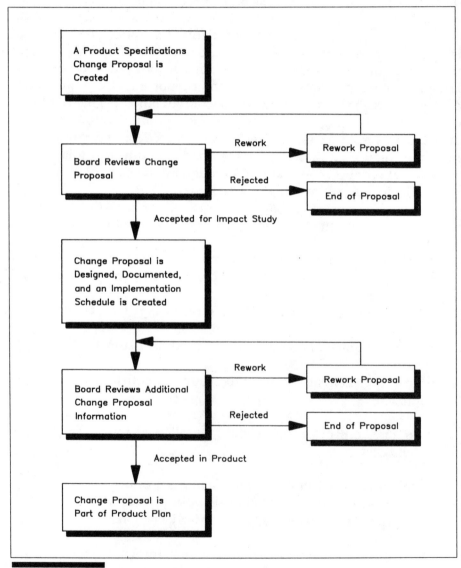

Figure 9.4. Change control process

responsibility to design and implement the change must then study the proposal. This study includes doing the following:

- Completing the high-level design
- Documenting the precise change that must be made to the product specifications
- Understanding the impact to all components of the product
- Developing an implementation schedule

This "homework" is done to ensure that the true impact of the change proposal is understood before a final vote is taken by the board. Now the board reviews this new information and can make a much more educated decision whether to accept or reject the change. If the change is accepted, the proposal becomes part of the product plan and is tracked along with other product work items.

If the change proposal is not accepted, then it is slated to be reworked and then resubmitted to the board, or it is rejected. If the change proposal is rejected at any time in the change control process, one of three actions can occur:

1. The originator can escalate the proposed change to higher management in an attempt to win support for the change proposal.
2. The change proposal can go into the *product outplan* and be considered for inclusion in a future release.
3. The change proposal is rejected, with no intention of future consideration.

If the change proposal is trivial, or the previously mentioned homework is completed before first taking the proposal to the board, then the board may act immediately on the fate of the proposal. This can save time in the change control process because the change proposal does not have to be brought before the board twice.

Figure 9.5 is a sample change control form. It requests the initial information that must be known about a change proposal being brought before the board. You can add additional fields that may fit your specific needs (such as severity of the problem and telephone number of the person opening the proposal). Notice that the justification for the change is required. This information is important to help ensure that only necessary changes are added to the product.

Figure 9.6 shows a completed form that has made it all the way through the change control process. The data filled in on the form originally submitted (Figure 9.5) can be input into a database. From this database, a form can be generated that includes several additional fields to be completed. When the board initially reviews the proposal, the following additional fields are filled in:

- Change control number
- Person assigned
- Target close date
- General comments (if any)

```
                    ┌─────────────────────────────────┐
                    │  ***   CHANGE CONTROL FORM   *** │
                    └─────────────────────────────────┘



    OPENED BY ----------------->    _____

    DATE OPENED --------------->    _____

    TITLE OF CHANGE ----------->    _____

    REQUIRED CLOSE DATE ------->    _____

    DESCRIPTION OF CHANGE ----->    _____

              _____

              _____

              _____

              _____

    JUSTIFICATION FOR CHANGE -->    _____

              _____

              _____

              _____

              _____

              _____
```

Figure 9.5. Change control form

For the simple example shown, assume that the board accepts the change proposal for an *impact study*. The date on which the board gives the go-ahead to proceed with the impact study is recorded on the form in the area designated by "accepted for impact study." The proposed

```
            ***  CHANGE CONTROL STATUS SHEET  ***

                                                     DATE
                                                     OCCURRED
                                                     ────────
CHANGE CONTROL # ----: 46        STATUS:
OPENED BY -----------: Rosenman  o ACCEPTED FOR IMPACT STUDY  01/17/90
DATE OPENED ---------: 01/17/90  o ACCEPTED IN PRODUCT        02/09/90
PERSON ASSIGNED -----: Forlenza  o REQUIRES REWORK            _/_/_
REQUIRED CLOSE DATE -: 02/14/90  o DEFERRED TO (DATE/RELEASE) _/_/_ (__/__)
TARGET CLOSE DATE ---: 02/07/90  o REJECTED                   _/_/_
DATE CLOSED ---------: 02/09/90  o CANCELLED                  _/_/_


TITLE OF CHANGE -----: Return Display Cursor to Former Position

DESCRIPTION OF CHANGE: Each time the user of the Word Processor returns to edit the
                       currently active file, the cursor should be placed at the same
                       character position that the user had left it.

JUSTIFICATION FOR CHANGE: Usability testing revealed that the Word Processor user prefers,
                       and often expects, the cursor to reappear at the same character
                       position on the display.  The usability task studied involved
                       the user temporarily exiting the "edit mode" to save or print
                       the currently active file, and then returning to the "edit mode"
                       to continue editing the file.  This change must be approved in
                       time to allow it to be implemented by the next usability test
                       that starts on 2/26.

IMPACT ASSESSMENT: CHANGED/NEW LOC    = 10                     COMPLETED BY
                   COMPONENTS/MODULES = 2 modules: "EDITOR" and "EDIT"
                   DESIGN             = 1/4 day                   02/19
                   CODE               = 1/4 day                   02/19
                   UNIT TEST          = 1/4 day                   02/19
                   FUNCTION TEST      = 1/4 day                   02/19
                   FORMAL TESTING     = 1 day  (Component Test)   02/22
                   DOCUMENTS          = 2 days (User's Guide)     02/23

UPDATED PRODUCT SPECIFICATIONS SECTION COMPLETED AND ATTACHED:  CHECK HERE  __

GENERAL COMMENTS: This change must be approved by 02/14 to be implemented by the next
                  usability test that starts on 2/26.
```

Figure 9.6. Change control status sheet

change is then designed and documented, and an implementation schedule is created. The following additional fields on the form are then filled in and the board reviews this new data:

- Impact assessment
- Check-mark to show that the product specifications section has been completed
- General comments (if any)

If the board accepts the change proposal, the date is recorded in the area on the form designated "accepted in product" and "date closed." In this simple example, the board might have approved the change proposal the first time it was reviewed. Why? Because the board may be able to recognize that the design, code, test and documentation impacted was minimal and needed no more study. (The 10 LOC depicted in Figure 9.6 means 10 lines of code.) However, some projects might insist that all changes undergo a thorough evaluation to prevent unexpected problems later.

The example just discussed is included to give you some insight into how the "board" operates. For some projects, the data gathered here might be too much; for others, too little. For instance, there are other factors you might want to consider before a change proposal is accepted in your product. These factors may include:

- What alternative solutions were investigated?
- What is the impact to the product's performance?
- What is the impact to the product's compatibility needs?
- How will the implementation be tracked to its completion?

A similar change control process should be followed in making changes to the product objectives. Whatever change control process is chosen, and whether it is for the product objectives, product specifications, or both, it is important that all changes to the product offering be made in a controlled environment. This ensures that only needed changes are made, that each organization can understand the impact the change has to their work activities, and that the change is made at the proper, orchestrated moment in the project cycle. The goal is to maintain control throughout the product development cycle by strictly enforcing a defined change control process.

What Should Product Specifications Address?

The goal here is to define and document a reasonably complete and accurate description of the product. Emphasis is on *reasonably complete and accurate*. It will be next to impossible to describe all of a product perfectly the first time. As stated earlier, some refinement to the specifications is expected as design, coding, and testing unfold. However, there is a major difference between refining some areas of the product and making major functional changes. If the necessary time and creativeness is expended early in the product development cycle, then changes to the product specifications for the duration of the product development cycle will likely be far less serious and far more manageable.

A precise description of *what the product is* should span the full product—from installation of the product to use of the product to providing help in recovering from errors. The following topics are some guidelines for use in determining what should appear in the product specifications document. Refer to Chapter 8 for more information on references made to the product objectives.

Deviations from Objectives

If the product to be described is different in any way from the direction provided in the product objectives, list those deviations here. This will prevent the need to update, redistribute, and reapprove the product objectives document. It will also ensure that the product objectives and the product specifications properly support one another.

Functions

Describe all the functions to be provided by the product. The functions described here are also called the product's **externals**—that is, what the user of the product will see and use. Externals include commands, programming interface instructions and linking conventions, and their complete syntax and semantics. Also, include what many think of as ease-of-use considerations. These include presenting all screens and their contents, the steps that the user must take in selecting each screen, displaying all the responses from the product that the user may see, and including all messages and return codes. If the product comes with an on-line tutorial then that, too, should be documented here. This section, which describes the product functions, will be the largest section in the product specifications document.

Installation

The precise procedure and tools for installing a product should be defined in full. This should also include packaging information if it affects the installation. For example, if the product is being shipped on diskettes, you should describe the number of diskettes that make up the product, the sequence in which they are used in the installation process, and the layout of each diskette.

Resources

The system resources that the product requires should be listed. These include memory and DASD storage requirements, and buffers. Also, any related product information should be included. For example, if the product requires a specified minimum amount of memory, describe what happens if more memory is available. Will the product take advantage of the additional memory?

Compatibility/Migration

If more detail is needed than that already stated in the product objectives, document it here. Remember, test groups will rely on the detail here to plan their testing, so be precise.

Security

State what the security-related product offerings are. Whether it is password protection, an encryption provision, a function that checks the infection and spread of computer viruses, or a physical key lock, the details of its use must be stated in the product specifications.

Hardware Supported

There is no need to duplicate what is written in the product objectives. If, however, more detail about specific hardware devices must be clarified before the product can be completely built, tested, and documented, then do it here.

Performance

If there are performance requirements in addition to those already stated in the product objectives, state them here. Performance requirements typically state minimum expectations. However, given that additional system resources might be available, describe what performance benefit the user will see.

Standards

List all the standards to be followed in the development of the product. These include in-house standards to be used during the design, coding, testing, and maintenance phases of the project. It can be helpful to reference a separate document that will define the standards and methodology to be followed for the project. This will allow the approval of the product specifications to be distinct and separate from the internal development methodology that programmers will follow. Thus, the approval of one does not hinder the approval of the other.

Standards that relate to industry acceptance should also be listed. An example might be the protocol to be used for transmitting a product's data from one computer system to another. Some of these standards might already have been listed in the product objectives. Again, if the product objectives list is complete, there is no need to duplicate it here.

Publications

It is advisable to avoid discussing publications in any detail in product specifications. Instead, a publications specifications document (see Figure 9.2) should be created after the product specifications have been issued. The publications specifications, also called the *publications con-*

tent plan, describes in detail the layout of each manual to be produced, chapter by chapter. This layout cannot fully be defined until the product specifications have been completed.

Other

There are other features, some that are introduced in the product objectives, that may or may not need to be in the product specifications. You need to decide whether additional information should be provided in the product specifications. The decision you reach will depend on the product you are building and whether there is an immediate need for more information by the users of the product specifications. For example, if the product will be marketed in foreign countries, a section on "world trade features" might need to be added since this could affect the functional content.

Planning for Control

There are an abundance of challenges to face and problems to be solved throughout a product development cycle. Many of these obstacles are predictable and avoidable. As in the start-up of a small business, the failure rate of new software development projects is quite high if you define "failure" as not only the cancellation of the project, but also a project that has overrun its original cost and schedule projections.

People usually think more clearly and are thought to be wiser with hindsight than when they are deeply entrenched in the middle of a demanding project. You might have found that your most objective moments seem to occur when you are just completing a project or are contemplating beginning a new project. Moreover, the further removed you personally find yourself from a given project, the more objective your views seem to be about the solutions to the problems facing that project. At these times, you might quickly recognize what could have been done differently to improve the overall productivity, quality, and cost on a project. This is also the point when there would be little argument in insisting on well-defined and approved product specifications and a clearly defined and strictly enforced change control process. Don't ignore history and your instincts—two powerful sources of input in making decisions. Define what you will build *before* you build it.

Consider a final example to illustrate the importance of defining what you plan to build before you build it. When members of a company decide that they want some *other* company or group to build a product for them, what happens? The company looking for bidders does the obvious—it defines a *statement of work*. That is, the bidders interested in building the product need to understand what they are to build. The company that wins the bid must be certain that it fully understands what it is committed to build. Only then will the winning bidder be able to satisfactorily plan the costs, resources and schedules to be committed.

Don't treat your own project any differently. If a full description of the product to be built is important both for the company asking for bids, as well as for the bidding companies, it follows that this product description is indeed a critical exercise. It also follows that it is important to closely control changes that might be attempted throughout the product development cycle, because each change introduced into the product will likely result in an added cost to build the product. If these things are required of others, then also understand the value of imposing the same requirements upon your own project. Commit yourself to defining the product and the change control process early. Commit to this before you enter your next **thrashing zone**, where your biases, emotions, commitments, and good intentions will make it infinitely more difficult to implement a sound plan for controlling creep.

10

Product Ease of Use

Great strides have been made in recent years in understanding the importance of the term *user friendly*. The widespread popularity of personal computers has made computing available to a much wider audience and a much less computer literate audience. The success of a growing number of program products has been attributed in large part to the ease with which users can both learn and become productive with these products. Today, more thought goes into the design of the person-machine interface, called the **user interface**, than ever before.

Unfortunately, many products still come to market with obvious usability deficiencies. Many of these products are being developed with little early consideration for the user interface. If attention is invested at all in product usability, it often comes during the latter part of the product development cycle, sometimes more as an afterthought than as a significant planned activity. Not only does it cost more to make coding and documentation changes later in the cycle, there also is considerably less time to validate the acceptance of the user interface. Frequently, there is too little time.

Usability as an Afterthought

The following scenario suggests how the level of attention invested in the ease of use of a product is, all too often, an afterthought.

It is an early stage of a new product development cycle. The product is recognized as being very important to the company's business. Its sponsor has convinced the company's higher management that the product can be built on a very aggressive schedule. The product objectives state that one of the features of the new product must be its user friendliness. However, the product objectives mention no specifics that can be measured or tested.

Product specifications are in the process of being written. The technical leaders of the project are "heavy techies" and are focusing on the internal design structure of the product. They object to spending any appreciable time on "Simple and less significant stuff" like product ease-of-use features. They are staunch believers in their own ease-of-use philosophy which proclaims: "There isn't any right answer anyway, so why try?" They feel that the product's usability will evolve as the product begins to be tested. "After all," they assert, "if the product can't run, what use is a friendly interface?"

The leadership in charge of the overall project, however, recognizes the need to focus early on the usability of the product. And to prove the commitment to ease of use, a junior programmer new-hire with usability experience, Angus Gladstone, is given the task of defining the user characteristics of the product. It is learned that Gladstone's usability experience consists of three *human factors* college courses and an expressed interest in usability.

It is expected that the user interface will be defined in the product specifications. However, some significant but temporary compromises are adopted to avoid delaying the completion of the product specifications. More specifically, these compromises are judged to be necessary because, first, the schedule to complete the specifications is very tight, and second, any user interface features chosen require additional internal design to support them, and third, Gladstone is having a difficult time getting a consensus on his user interface preferences. Most of the compromises are contrary to Gladstone's desires. The guidance that the experienced programmers offer him is that "We can always change the user interface later if and when we find a better interface."

Several weeks pass. The product specifications are available on schedule. Gladstone is happy in his belief that he has bought time to study the user interface alternatives further. Since he has minimal product development experience and minimal first-hand user interface design experience, he proceeds slowly, but enthusiastically. In the meantime, much of the product is being designed and coded. The temporary user interface described in the product specifications is now being implemented, with some minor improvements.

Several more weeks pass. Gladstone is now ready to introduce his proposed usability changes into the product. To his dismay, he finds that he missed the "window" for making changes of the magnitude he is proposing. He is hopeful, however, that he can lobby the programmers to make the changes "off to the side" and stage them in during the formal test phase of the product development cycle.

Gladstone soon learns that he is going to have an uphill battle. The aggressive product schedules are proving to be too aggressive. Independent of any usability changes, the schedules have slipped. Not only is a two-week development buffer lost, two weeks of the formal test phase have also been consumed. The few programmers who were on schedule with their modules must now wait for those late modules that they are dependent on for function testing. When formal testing finally starts, it has slipped another week and is now a full three weeks late. Gladstone is told that it is now too risky to jeopardize the stability of the code going into formal testing with the major user interface changes he is proposing. Most of these changes, incidentally, have still not yet been implemented. Many of the programmers who would have to implement these usability changes in their design and code are too busy trying to recover, or at least maintain, the already slipped schedule.

Gladstone is told by some of the seasoned leadership that there is still time to ensure that the product's usability is acceptable. (Notice that "acceptable" is the term used now.) Since a plan exists to have the testers evaluate the usability of the product while they are testing it, there is still some hope for making usability changes if the testers support the need for those changes. As it turns out, some usability problems are identified by the test group as well as by a few outside people who have been tinkering with the product. Unfortunately, on closer examination, it is decided that the big-ticket, usability-related corrections must be delayed until the next release of the product. However, some minor, easy to fix, usability problems are corrected. The product publications are beefed up to compensate for usability deficiencies in the code. It is hoped, for a brief moment, that this customer set will do what most other customers of these types of products *don't* do. That is, it is hoped that the product's users will actually *read* the publications to discover how to circumvent some not-so-intuitive user interface problems.

What started at the beginning of the product cycle as good intentions, has ended the same old way. Good intentions, but little results. What can you do differently?

Objectives

A product's user interface consists of *all* aspects of a system's operation that are perceived by the user. It is much more than the *look and feel* of menus, mouse selections, and help screens. It is an understanding, an intuitive feel, that the user realizes when he or she is introduced to a product and the environment in which that product operates. Ideally, the goal is to create a product that the user will feel bears a remarkably close similarity in performance to typical noncomputer *tasks*, because these are tasks with which the user is intimately knowledgeable and comfortable. Examples of these tasks are:

- Writing a note
- Checking a note for correct spelling
- Sending a note to a friend
- Retrieving a past note for reference
- Filing a note in a cabinet
- Searching for a telephone number
- Creating a budget for next month
- Calculating interest on a loan

This ideal product is one that allows the user to, in a very short time, feel at home with the concepts, logic, and interactions provided by the product. If the product is introducing a new concept in performing some common work task (e.g., discarding old files in a cabinet), then it must take full responsibility in guiding the user through the necessary actions. The user should not be given the opportunity to stray unwittingly to a point at which problems arise (such as accidentally deleting the wrong file and being unable to recover).

Having stated these things, now is a good time to assert that: "Ease of use is basic product function."

That is, ease of use must be *planned from the beginning* if there is to be any expectation that it will happen at all. If ease of use comes about as an afterthought, the user will surely recognize the inconsistent, incomplete, and unintuitive implementation. Also, when ease of use is planned and implemented as an afterthought, schedule slippages and higher product costs result.

Planning from the beginning involves defining usability objectives in the product objectives document. As is discussed in Chapter 8, the product objectives document is the first major deliverable in the product development cycle. Figure 10.1 shows the point at which the usability objectives are addressed in the product development cycle. This figure also shows where the other major usability activities occur. This figure will be cited several more times throughout this chapter.

Many meaningful statements can be made in the product objectives document that will provide ease-of-use direction. This direction is needed not only to develop the product specifications, but also to decide usability tradeoffs that might need to be made throughout the product

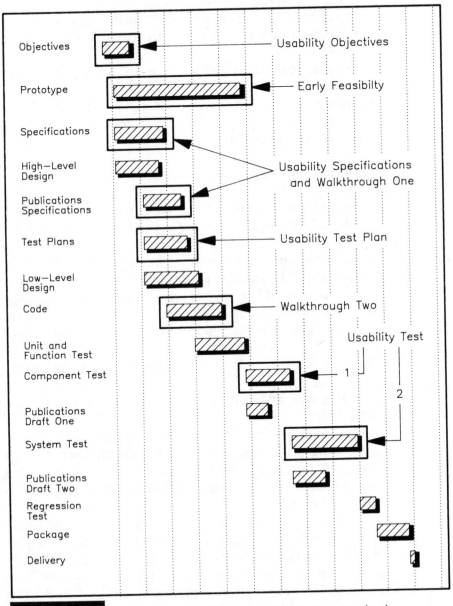

Figure 10.1. Major usability activities in the product development cycle

development cycle. Some examples of usability-related statements that could appear in the product objectives are:

- The user should not be made to respond to, or input to the program product, anything that the program could have determined itself. Examples include having to remember data that the program already is capable of recalling, or inputting information that the program could detect, such as how many disk drives are configured on the system.
- On-line help should be available for every screen and every prompt.
- All error messages should have help associated that not only explains the problem in plain English but actually suggests the responses the user should pursue.

More specific usability requirements might be:

- The user must be able to install the product within "__" minutes. The user should require no assistance beyond that provided in the final product.
- Additional information about an error message should be made available to the user by simply pressing a function key on the keyboard. The user should not have to remember the error message number and then type an operator command with that number. The user should not have to refer to the publications for at least "__" percent of the error situations.
- The basic tasks that a typical user will perform when using the product are .... (*List the tasks here*).
- The measurements to be collected for each task are .... (*List the measurements here*).
- The usability of the product is acceptable only if at least "__" percent of the tasks successfully meet their measurable criteria. (A simple pass/fail measure could also be used. For any task that fails, the problem must be corrected in the product and the task rerun until it passes.)
- The usability test results are to be evaluated against comparable test data gathered from leading competitive products. This product should be equal to or better than the competitive products in at least "__" percent of the tasks tested. The competitive products to include in the evaluation are products "ABC," "DEF," and "GHI."

- In performing usability tests, a minimum of "__" people (test subjects) must be used so that an acceptable sampling exists to support the validity of a perceived problem. The test subjects must be representative of the product's user—that is, they must have at least a "__" grade reading level, have less than "__" months experience with personal computers or equivalent, ... *(Define the audience and environment of the intended customer).*

A product that has a superior user interface must have its ease of use defined as the entire product is being defined, because the user interface is the product as perceived by the user. Delaying attention to the crucial user interface increases the separation of the user interface considerations from the rest of the product function. This all-too-typical separation makes, in fact, about as much sense as pairing a round peg with a square hole. If you are going to build a product, all aspects of that product must fit together naturally. The mutual design of different product aspects is paramount to ensure that they achieve a complementary and supportive fit with one another.

Usability Tasks

Figure 10.2 provides an example of some basic tasks that a user might perform with a new product. Notice that a task is typically a simple set of actions to be performed by the user of the product. The product chosen for this example is a word processor. These tasks will be used during the usability testing activities to ensure that the product's ease of use meets the usability objectives. The tasks should not be too complex or contain a large number of actions to perform. If a task is not defined simply, it could frustrate the test subject, not to mention the product's intended user and might also make it difficult to determine how to correct the problem.

Before going any further, this is a good point to define a frequently used term: **test subject**. A test subject is a person who helps to test a product as it is being developed. This person is expected to use the product in ways similar to those of the finished product's users. Consequently, the tasks that a test subject performs on the product are expected to be the same or similar to tasks that a user will perform. The best test subjects are actual or potential customers. This *live user* involvement is, by far, the most beneficial form of testing to employ in order to certify that a product has truly met its ease-of-use objectives.

The second-best category of test subjects includes those who appear to meet a substantial number of the characteristics that define the product's users. For example, if a product is being developed for secretaries in the insurance industry, it can be beneficial to use secretaries who have no knowledge of insurance terms and operations, yet have comparable secretarial skills. These secretaries would first be trained in insurance industry terms and operations before actually starting the tests. Choosing the right set of test subjects will greatly aid in ensuring that the right product is developed.

Measurements

> *People's minds are changed through observation and not through argument.*
> Will Rogers

The type of measurements that can be collected from running each task include:

- Recording impromptu statements made by test subjects
- Identifying the number of unrecoverable errors
- Identifying the number of assists
- Applying a user-satisfaction rating (1 through 5)
- Determining whether tasks are completed successfully

Perhaps one of the best tools for measuring a product's ease of use, a tool that is gaining acceptance in the human factors literature, is to record the spoken reactions and statements of test subjects as they proceed in performing the basic tasks of the product. These immediate verbal and facial expressions allow observers to gain insight into the journey that a user follows in exercising the product. This technique can be invaluable at discovering fundamental design problems in the product. By carefully studying the user's trail, the points in the product that caused the user to go astray can be identified easily.

Consider the next example: identifying the number of unrecoverable errors. If an unrecoverable problem occurs, it could represent a serious defect in the product. It may mean that the product user will require assistance from the manufacturer, the dealer, or from some other source. It could also mean that the user's perception is that the product's manufacturer delivered a product before it was ready.

An **assist** is help that a test subject requires in order to complete a task within a specified time limit. Identifying the number of assists is important because they indicate how long it takes a test subject to perform tasks. A product user, given enough time, might be able to accomplish a given task without assistance. However, each task should have a reasonable time limit defined. A user will not want to spend his or her limited time trying to overcome ease-of-use deficiencies in the product.

A user-satisfaction rating is a useful tool for learning how the test subject really feels about the product's functions and ease of use. Figure 10.3 illustrates some sample questions that can be asked after each task has been completed. The best results are collected when the question-

```
■    Install

■    Create a new document (Document 1)

■    Define margins and page length

■    Define heading and footing

■    Type several pages of new data

■    Save Document 1

■    Print Document 1

■    Retrieve Document 2 (already created)

■    Correct spelling errors using "spelling checker"

■    Set tabs

■    Change font of all section headings

■    Center all section headings

■    Move, copy and delete paragraphs and sentences

■    Search for and replace words and phrases

■    Left and right justify all text

■    Save Document 2 under new name

■    Delete Document 1
```

Figure 10.2. Sample tasks for a word processor product

naire is administered immediately after a task has been completed. This is when the test subject's views will be the sharpest about that task. These questions can do a lot to help pinpoint areas of annoyance to the user.

Notice that two types of questions can be asked of the test subject. One type involves questions that can be answered by choosing from a predefined set of responses. The questions listed in Figure 10.3 that fall into this category are numbers 1, 3, 6, 8, 10, and 13. A sample set of the response choices is:

1   Very satisfied
2   Satisfied
3   Neither satisfied nor dissatisfied
4   Dissatisfied
5   Very Dissatisfied

```
   1   How satisfied were you with performing this task?

   2   What would have made this task easier?

   3   How satisfied were you that the tutorial prepared
       you for performing this task?

   4   What did you especially like about the tutorial?

   5   What tutorial changes would you suggest?

   6   How satisfied were you with the terms used?

   7   List any terms that you did not understand.

   8   How satisfied were you with the on-line help?

   9   What on-line help improvements would you suggest?

  10   How satisfied were you with the documentation?

  11   What did you like about the documentation?

  12   In what areas of the documentation would you suggest
       improvements?

  13   How satisfied were you with the amount of assistance
       you required?

  14   What changes would you suggest that would reduce the
       assistance you required?
```

Figure 10.3. Sample questions to ask after each task

The other type of questions are those that require the test subject to respond by writing his or her personal comments. Figure 10.3 lists these questions as numbers 2, 4, 5, 7, 9, 11, 12, and 14.

You can also develop a special set of questions for the test subject to respond to after all tasks have been run. Examples of these questions are:

- What did you like most about the product?
- What did you like least about the product?
- What improvements overall would you suggest?

Five examples of measurements are listed earlier in this section. The first four have already been discussed. Now consider the fifth example: determining whether tasks are completed successfully. If you were to only track one measurement, this would be the one. However, the more measurements you collect, the higher your confidence will be that you can predict the user's acceptance of your product. For example, the test subject might have successfully completed a task within the allotted time, but might have had to use trial and error techniques to get a function to work correctly. In this case, the user satisfaction rating would help reveal some of the test subject's specific frustrations.

Interpreting Measurements

Once you have collected measurements from each task, what then? Must all tasks have passed in order to declare the usability of the product satisfactory? This is one approach. Another approach is to define several, measurable criteria that can collectively be used in determining whether the overall usability test was successful. For example:

- Number of assists per task <= .33
- Satisfaction rating is "2" or better for 90 percent of the tasks
- Ninety percent of the tasks are successfully completed

Notice that some assists can be considered acceptable. In the case shown, if the average assists per task is less than or equal to one assist per every three tasks, then this is within acceptable bounds. Also, note that the satisfaction rating must be a "2" or better for at least 90 percent of the tasks, while at least 90 percent of all tasks must be successfully completed.

All of these criteria are somewhat arbitrary. They should be set at levels you believe are necessary to develop a winning product for your targeted audience of users. However, the criteria must at least meet or beat predecessor products and competitive products. The levels at which you set these criteria can depend on several factors. One factor is the skill level of the audience. If first graders will be using the product without assistance, then ease of use must be superb, and you should want 100 percent of the tasks to be completed successfully. If the product is intended for an office environment in which a programmer is expected to assist in installing the product, educate users, and be on-call to assist when necessary, then development of a product with which users may require occasional assistance may be acceptable.

Other factors to consider in setting levels for measurable criteria include the type of product being developed, the number of users for the product, the availability requirements for the product, and the offerings from competitors. While many of the areas discussed in this chapter are quite subjective, it is essential that you set usability objectives very early in the development cycle so you can pace yourself against those goals.

Publications Objectives

As stated in an earlier chapter, the product objectives document should also provide direction for the publications that must be developed to accompany the product's programs. An alternative is to provide a separate publications objectives document. In either case, the statement of direction for the product publications must be defined and documented at the beginning of the product development cycle. The type of usability-related areas to be addressed might include:

- The reading grade level for the targeted audience is to be set at the "_th" grade.
- The publications will consist of four " books":
  - Installation pamphlet
  - User's guide
  - Reference manual
  - Fold-out reference card
- The introduction of every user command must also include at least one example showing how that command would typically be used.

The examples offered in this section only scratch the surface of ease-of-use direction that can be provided in the product objectives. Remember, the more vague the direction, the less likely the final product will have satisfactory ease of use. Superior ease of use must be planned.

Specifications

When the product specifications are defined in detail, all of the user interface should also be defined. This detail should be included in the product specifications (see Figure 10.1). The specifications should present the product just as the intended user will see and use it. (See Chapter 9 for general information on product specifications.)

User interface items that should be described in detail include the following:

- All screens and prompts
- All messages
- How the user will get from one screen to the next
- How the user will select options from, or input to, each screen
- How the user will select the help functions provided
- *Fast-path* functions provided for the more experienced user
- On-line tutorials
- Use of screen highlighting and colors
- The precise product installation sequence

Other areas appear in the product specifications that also relate to usability, but are better defined under a different topic. An example is the definition of the maximum time allowed for the product to respond to a user's request to switch screens. This has obvious usability impact, but can be more appropriately defined under the topic of "product performance."

Ease of use also should be addressed when the publications specifications, also referred to as the publications **content plans**, are written. The content plans will describe the user interface to be designed into the publications. Keep in mind that the product's user will judge the *friendliness* of the product from both the publications and the programs. If either fails in ease of use, the product as a whole will be perceived as failing. Some ease-of-use items to be described in detail in the content plans include:

- Definition of specific, user-oriented tasks and how they will be used in the layout of each book
- Placement, scope, and variety of examples and illustrations
- Use of colors, bold printing, and italics
- Rules to be used in developing indexes

Prototype

A prototype is defined as an early running model of the product to be built. This model may represent only a very small portion of the product, such as the interaction between several of the product's menu screens so that menu selection techniques can be studied. Or, the model may represent a substantial portion of the product so that many of the product's functions can be demonstrated. The primary purpose for building a prototype is usually to experiment with, demonstrate, or prove the feasibility of a concept, examples of which include:

- Applying new technology
- Promoting a proposed product to higher management or to customers
- Developing and fine-tuning design algorithms
- Obtaining an early start in developing a new product
- Optimizing a product's user interface

The remainder of this section will focus on the benefit of a prototype in developing a product's user interface. You should view the building of a prototype as an essential part of product development. A lot can be learned about a product very early in the product development cycle by examining and "tweaking" its prototype. This valuable information can have a positive influence on the remaining development of the product.

Building a prototype to study the user interface characteristics of the new product can begin after the product objectives are reasonably understood. (In some cases, often before a product has been approved for funding, a prototype might actually be built before the product objectives are started.) While it is possible that the development and study of a prototype will have some influence on the final product objectives, the major influence will be reflected in the product specifications and beyond.

Figure 10.1 shows the relative position of the prototype activity within the product development cycle. Notice that the prototype activity begins about the same time as the product specifications begin to be written. The benefit of prototype activity extends at least until the start of component testing. Component testing typically marks the first time that product code and documentation are available for testing. With running product code and documentation available, there is less dependency on the prototype. However, the prototype can be used throughout the product development cycle to observe the effect of potential user interface changes before the changes are adopted into the product.

The prototype code typically represents a small fraction of the total amount of code that will need to be developed for the final product. Since significantly less effort is required to build a prototype (than a complete product), prototype changes can usually be accomplished rather quickly. The ability to frequently alter various aspects of the user interface built into the prototype, and then to examine those changes for acceptance, offers a great opportunity to influence the user interface defined in product specifications. It is often observed that what looks good on paper often does not work in the "real world" with typical users. Consequently, each improvement made to the user interface early in the product development process can save a significant amount of rework later. Therefore, you want to maximize the benefit of the prototype as early in the product development cycle as possible.

As the product evolves through the development process, the prototype can continue to be used to anticipate ease-of-use problems before running product code is ready. Figure 10.1 shows the prototype activity ending at the start of component testing, the usual point at which running product code is collected in a single driver. However, the prototype can continue to be enhanced as long as it offers a quicker and less expensive way to identify user interface problems early, and to experiment in searching for the most acceptable solutions to identified problems.

It is a good idea to seek ways to port, as much as possible, the prototype code to the real product. This can especially be beneficial if you anticipate that the prototype will grow to a significant size. If a sizable amount of code is developed that works identical to the way the product's code will work, then finding a lasting use for some of that code is a great additional benefit to draw from the prototype.

Test Plan

After usability objectives are in place, some method must be followed to verify that the usability defined in the product specifications and subsequently designed into the product meets requirements. Of course, the real goal here is to ensure that the ease of use built into the product is satisfactory to the intended audience. Any use of the term "product" now refers to the entire package that the user receives at the time of purchase. The product could consist of a tutorial, several programs, and several publications.

The usability test plan defines how the product's user interface will be *certified* as having met its objectives. This test plan should address answers to the following types of questions:

- What usability tests will be conducted?
- What are the entry and exit requirements for each test?
- What are the detailed schedules supporting these tests?
- Who are the persons responsible for the various aspects of each test?
- What are the detailed scenarios that support each usability task?
- What hardware, software, and tools are required to support each test?
- When and how will the use of a prototype be employed?
- How many test subjects are to be used for each test?
- What are the experience profiles of the required test subjects?
- What process is to be used in identifying, recording and verifying the usability problems encountered?
- What training will test observers receive?
- How many test subjects per test observer?
- How will a task be recognized as passing? Failing?
- If a task has failed, how might it eventually pass?

The usability test plan is completed early in the product cycle, as shown in Figure 10.1. This ensures that each test becomes part of the official product process and is adequately planned. Tests that the usability test plan should define, at a minimum, are **usability walkthroughs** and **usability tests**. These are defined in the next sections.

Usability Walkthroughs

These tests are called walkthroughs because running product code and publications drafts are not yet available. Usually the user interface is available only on paper, such as that found in product specifications, or a portion might be available in a prototype. However, the portion of the user interface to be inspected should be completely defined at this point. The user interface is examined by "walking through" the available user interface information. A walkthrough should always include the use of a prototype, if one is available, that addresses the portion of the user interface to be inspected.

A walkthrough usually consists of several people assembled to verify the correctness and acceptability of the user interface. These people are both test subjects as well as actual developers of the programming and publications user interface functions. The test subjects are asked how they would go about performing predefined tasks based on the known detailed user interfaces of the product defined in the product specifications. As the test subjects walk through the user interface, either on paper or using a prototype, or both, any problems found are logged. Care should be taken to ensure that the *product* is being tested and *not* the test subjects themselves. The goal is to identify as many product problems as possible now so they can be addressed and the product retested at the next usability test (as defined in the product's usability test plan). The earlier that these problems are identified, the easier and less costly it is to make the necessary product changes.

Performing two walkthroughs can offer a great benefit. Although three or more walkthroughs might seem to be even better, there is a point where *more is not better*. It takes time to prepare for the tests, conduct the tests, and correct the problems discovered during each test. Figure 10.1 shows the recommended points in the product development cycle for conducting each walkthrough. If your product development cycle is longer than 18 to 24 months, you might be able to accommodate additional walkthroughs.

The first walkthrough should occur after the user interface is defined and documented, but before the final level of product specifications is completed and distributed. This process allows time for any corrections to be made before the specifications are distributed. Once distributed, the specifications are used by many groups to plan their work activities (such as designing and coding programs, writing publications, and developing test cases). The more complete and accurate the product specifications, the less rework that might be required later—rework that can impact several groups.

The second walkthrough should occur after low-level design has been completed and coding has started. This allows time for corrections to be completed for problems found during the first walkthrough. It also provides time for the developers to better understand any gray areas that surfaced either during the first walkthrough or from experience in being further along in the development of the product. The participants are the same for the second walkthrough with the exception of the test subjects. The test subjects are all new. This fresh set of views helps to ensure a more objective evaluation of the corrections made and increases the sampling size of test subjects. If the new test subjects find some of the same problems as before, and the problems were thought to have already been corrected, then careful analysis needs to be made before further product changes occur. If the test subjects find no new problems, there is a feeling of reassurance that the implementation of the user interface is on the right track. If only a small sampling of the test subjects from the first walkthrough discovered annoyances, then it might be that no corresponding corrections were made. However, if any test subjects from the second walkthrough encounter the same annoyances, then the likelihood increases that these annoyances are real problems and should be considered for fixing.

The great benefit of these walkthroughs is that problems are found early and corrected early. Notice that no running product code or publications drafts have yet been produced.

Tests

The next tests following walkthrough testing will evaluate the usability of the product with both real, running product code and complete drafts of the publications. These tests have been called by many names—customer tests, first-customer tests, user tests, user-oriented tests and user product tests. They will be called simply **usability tests** here. These tests are similar to usability walkthroughs in that new test subjects are asked to perform a series of predefined tasks with the product. A significant difference is that the test subjects do not perform the tasks in a group setting or on a prototype. Instead, the test subjects are at computer terminals and are attempting to use the product just as a first-time user would. The actions of each test subject typically are monitored for later analysis. A variety of monitoring techniques can be employed. Examples include:

- A person, called a **test observer**, sitting nearby observing and recording every action made by the test subject
- A video camera recording the actions of the test subject
- A program that records all keystrokes made at the terminal
- Various combinations of the above

If a test subject needs help, it is given only after the test subject has exhausted a search for ways to correct the problem within a reasonable time period. A time limit is usually set so the tests continue in a productive fashion. A time limit will also help to reduce the likelihood that a test subject will become seriously frustrated on any given task.

After all tasks are attempted by each test subject, the data is gathered for analysis. At this time, valuable data recorded from the monitoring process is compiled. The types of data collected and evaluated can be identified in the following questions:

- How many attempts did a test subject have to make before successfully completing a task?
- What was the precise sequence of steps taken as information was being retrieved from the publications?
- What book index entries were expected to be there but were not?

As part of the process in gathering this data, the test subjects are brought together in a room with the developers and publications writers. The test subjects then give their perceptions of the product: what was good, bad, confusing, easy, missing, and so on. The developers and publications writers are allowed to ask questions in an attempt to understand the perceived problems better. After the data is collected and analyzed, a log of the problems is prepared. Then, action plans are developed to address each problem. A prototype can be used to "correct" many of the problems and to verify resolutions before they are actually implemented in the product.

As with the usability walkthroughs, two usability tests seem to be optimum for most projects with a product development cycle of up to two years in duration (see Figure 10.1). The first usability test occurs halfway through component testing. This allows time for the code being component tested to become more stable, with the first wave of bugs identified and corrected. If the usability test starts too soon, the code might have too many defects to allow a productive usability test to occur. It is a good idea to predefine a set of test cases that must be run successfully before the usability test can begin. Once these test cases have been successfully run, the usability tests can begin. Note also that the first draft of the publications is now available to become part of the usability test. Once usability problems are identified, the goal is to have them corrected in the product before the second usability test.

The second usability test starts shortly after system testing begins. Again, there must be stable code in order for the usability test to be productive. The final draft of the publications is now available. Overall, the product is in its final stages and should be very close to what the final user will see and use. Any problems found now must be corrected before system testing ends, since system testing provides the last opportunity to make product changes. If usability design and testing have proceeded as defined in this chapter, relatively few usability problems should be discovered at this point in the product development cycle.

One more point: When product planners, designers, programmers, writers, testers, and so on, are defining and building the product, the operational aspects of the product typically seem obvious to them. Yet, to a user who has just been introduced to the product, there will likely appear a host of items that are *not* so clear. This chapter has introduced a sequence of steps that, when followed, can yield a superior ease-of-use product. However, beware of a danger that is common to many development projects: Ignoring or attempting to rationalize away the ease-of-use problems that are identified by the many test subjects participating in the planned usability tests. There are many reasons to argue about the validity of identified ease-of-use problems. The arguments include:

- The test subjects represented too small a group of users for their comments to be considered statistically valid.
- The project schedules do not allow time to make these changes.
- Ease of use is too subjective a concept for me to seriously consider these changes.
- It seems obvious to me.
- The user will only have difficulty the first time the function is attempted.
- The user will get used to it.

The fact of the matter is that test data obtained from usability tests is invaluable if you are to provide a product that will be judged to have a superior user interface. Do not ignore this data or allow it to be argued away. You might find it beneficial to have this topic discussed among the project's personnel early in the product development cycle—before potential problems can surface. Also, the project leadership must fully support the ease-of-use journey that is chosen for your project.

Working at communicating the benefits presented in this chapter to others in a project will prove beneficial, both in the short and long term. You will also be amazed at the speed with which these concepts are accepted on the next project. Most people will fairly quickly come around to understanding and supporting these benefits.

Ease of Use: The Competitive Edge

The process defined here to yield a superior user-friendly product might seem like a lot of work. But it can result in a level of success for your product that would not otherwise be achievable, a success triggered from a perception that your product is truly easy to use. You get what you plan for. If you are not willing to invest in this process, one of your competitors will. Whatever product you are building, chances are that someone has or is building a similar product. Those who offer products that are easy to use have a distinct competitive advantage.

When your product is available to customers, will it stand out as a product that is easy to learn and use? The number of users of programming products is growing rapidly. These users are increasingly less computer literate. They will purchase and stay with the products that allow them to get their work done with the least amount of effort. User-friendly products are becoming an essential customer requirement.

11

Informal Testing: Strengthening the Weak Link

Product testing falls within two categories: **informal testing** and **formal testing**. Figure 11.1 maps these two categories within the product development cycle. Informal testing is that testing typically performed by the developer of the code. Formal testing occurs after the informal testing has been completed and is best performed by programmers who have not developed the code to be tested. This chapter focuses on the informal test period.

The thoroughness with which code is tested during the informal test period has a direct impact on the quality of code that will enter the formal test period. If code is poorly tested during informal testing, formal testing will uncover many more problems than would otherwise be necessary. Furthermore, this increased volume of problems will result in longer formal test schedules. These lengthened schedules will tie up the programmers who developed the code, as well as all support personnel, causing them to remain in force on the current release of the product longer than is planned or desirable. There is yet another negative, often overlooked side effect: It has been shown that the volume of defects entering the formal test period is linked to the volume of defects that will still remain in the final code when the product is delivered to the customer. This negative relationship not only causes additional expense in making repairs to the product after it has been shipped, but also can undermine sales and, therefore, the overall success of the product.

If the formal test period is to be productive, two activities must occur:

1. Informal testing activities must be planned and anticipated.
2. A trackable process for informal testing must be defined and exercised to ensure conformance to the testing plans and to monitor schedule progress.

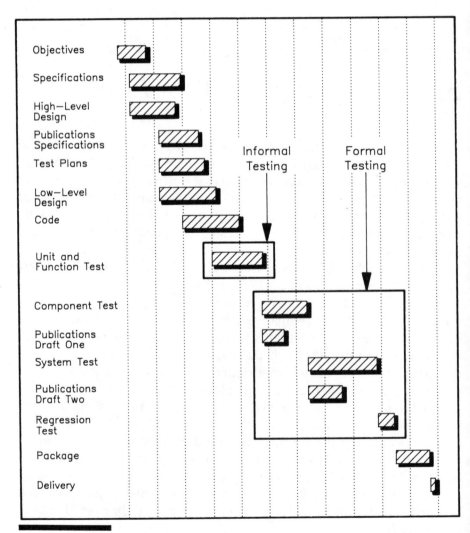

Figure 11.1. Testing in the product development cycle

Removing Defects Late

The following scenario demonstrates how a poorly managed informal test cycle can significantly disrupt the remaining product development cycle.

It is another new project. The general consensus is that the project is off to a good start. The product objectives and product specifications have been documented and approved. A control process is in place for any changes that might be made to the product objectives or the product specifications.

The schedule is in place and many of the developers feel it is reasonable. Why don't *all* the developers support the schedule? Some of the more experienced programmers feel that additional time is needed to do the right job on informal testing. The project head declares, "Additional time for informal testing would be nice, but I know you programmers. You would take all the time you could to drive your design, coding, and testing to perfection. And that time doesn't exist on any project." The project head also states that it is essential that the currently defined schedule be met if this product is to ship on time. Besides, the formal test is there to find bugs left over from the informal test period. (Isn't it?)

The general view from within the trenches is that the people calling the shots on the project have developed other products, so they qualify as being experienced. And, even though the schedules of many of these earlier products missed their original targets, the project leadership had ultimately accepted those schedule slips (what *else* could they do?). Therefore, it is rationalized, this must be the accepted way to plan and manage a product development cycle.

Two months pass. The design of the product is all but complete. Most of the coding is nearing completion. At this point, the product's work effort is defined in terms of program modules. Each module has an assigned owner, who is responsible for completing all the informal testing on his or her program modules. To perform this informal testing, two phases typically are required. The first, called the **unit test**, is the isolated testing of each logic flowpath of code through the module. The second phase, called the **function test**, checks to make sure each function executes properly through all modules that it spans. During unit testing, and sometimes function testing, artificial testing environments, also called **scaffolding**, might be necessary. This is because most other areas of the product might not be sufficiently far enough along in their development to be included in the testing of a specific module or a specific function of the product.

There are several new programmers in the group. They ask if there is any specific process they must follow during the informal test period and are told that they must have their unit and function testing completed on their modules by the start of formal testing. They also are told that, in effect,

"If you want to do any functional testing that requires modules you don't own, you must negotiate dates to do so with the owners of those modules." However, the more seasoned programmers tell the newcomers that how they choose to do the informal testing is up to them. To save time, some of the more experienced programmers say, they often bypass unit testing. Furthermore, they frequently function test only the primary paths to "spot check" their overall code quality. After all, formal testing will test error paths and most, if not all, of each function. The newcomers are relieved to hear this. They estimate that if they had to test every piece of logic in the code they would not be able to deliver their code in time to meet the schedule for the start of formal testing.

The informal testing period has started. Some of the programmers have begun to develop test plans that identify the functions they want to test and the testing process they will follow. This approach was abandoned by most since there just was not time to do a complete job of planning. Besides, some owners of modules said they could not commit to any test dates. The buzz words were, "It's available when it's available."

All are doing the best they can. When the project leadership collects status information, the answer always comes back, "We are on schedule." It was difficult not to be on schedule. Everyone knew the date when formal testing must begin. It was the same for everyone. The name of the game is to test "as much as you can" before that date.

The start date for formal testing arrives. All the product's modules are placed into a library controlled by the formal test group. This means that no developer can change any module's code without following a formal process intended to control the type and frequency of module changes. The formal test personnel do not want the modules disturbed simply to make trivial changes, like updating code commentary. Nor do they want random changes coming in at all times of the day or week. Changes must be made in stages to ensure that the more important problems are addressed and corrected first.

The modules are all linked together for what appears to be the first time. This linked set of modules, called a *driver*, is delivered to the formal test team. Formal testing begins. And immediately stops. The driver won't "come up." The developers are summoned to identify the bug. They do. The correction is patched into the driver and the updated driver is delivered to the formal test team. Testing begins again. And stops again. This series of starts and stops consumes a full week. Translated, this means that the formal testing period has lost one valuable week.

The formal test team had developed charts that projected their progress each week. They had expected to be 10 percent through their test cases at the end of the first week. They are at 1 percent. No one seems to be too nervous. There were a couple of weeks of buffer in the test schedule. One experienced tester remarked rather confidently, "This is normal. It happens this way in every product I have ever worked on."

Some testing progress is made during the second week. However, not as much as projected. Five percent of testing has been implemented. Moreover, 40 percent more problems have been found than were projected. An experienced developer of the product code stated to a newcomer developer, "See, didn't I tell you that the bugs we didn't find would be found in the formal test?"

This rather slow progress continues for several weeks. The tests are now 35 percent complete. However, they were projected to be 85 percent complete by now. Some real worry is beginning to be felt by the project leadership. Not only is the schedule end date in jeopardy, the developers are tied up fixing bugs that the testers have found. Some of those developers were scheduled to move into other projects by now. Everyone is working overtime, some an excessive amount. A work group is formed to determine what can be done to protect the schedule. Some creative ideas are found, but none that will support the existing schedule. The ideas considered include:

- Adding more developers to fix bugs
- Performing inspections of the code for the error-prone modules
- Cancelling planned vacations
- Doing more patching of code rather than fixing the source code and relinking modules
- Adding developers to the formal test team who would possess the skill to determine the cause of a problem and immediately devise a corrective patch in the failing module(s)

All of these ideas are implemented to some extent. However, the schedule slips three more weeks. If these actions had not been taken, it is believed that the schedule would have slipped six weeks.

Better progress is now being made, but still not at the rate originally projected. One major obstacle is the numerous bugs being found in the interfaces between modules. These problems are surfacing in large number now because modules from different owners were not sufficiently integrated during the informal test so that their interfaces could be tested.

The scenario could continue, but you probably get the picture. In this scenario, before the product is ready for delivery to a customer, it encounters several more delays in the overall schedule. Especially painful was the need to pull the product out of packaging several times so that newly discovered bugs could be fixed and the code regression tested again. This is a sign that the product entered packaging before it was ready. It is probably the result of someone making a schedule-related decision rather than a quality-related decision. Had more time been provided to complete the unit and function tests properly, the overall schedule might have only slipped a little, or maybe not at all, thus allowing formal testing to be more productive.

Unit Test

Recall the definition of unit testing presented in the preceding scenario: It is the isolated testing of each flowpath of code within each module. All code should be executed. Also, all primary logic path combinations should be verified for correct design and coding. Figure 11.2 can be used to illustrate this point. Assume the flowchart shown represents the flowpaths within module ABC. Seven distinct flowpaths are identified and are labeled one through seven.

However, as many as twelve flowpath combinations could conceivably be executed:

1 and 5, 1 and 6, 1 and 7
2 and 5, 2 and 6, 2 and 7
3 and 5, 3 and 6, 3 and 7
4 and 5, 4 and 6, 4 and 7

Unit testing of module ABC should result in, at a minimum, execution of *all* code. This requirement would be satisfied if the seven distinct

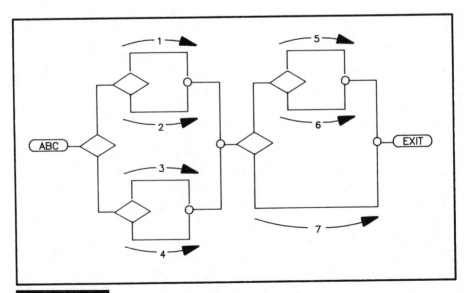

Figure 11.2. Flowpaths for module ABC

flowpaths are executed. However, another factor must be satisfied: All *primary logic path combinations* must also be executed. A primary logic path combination is defined as a commonly used sequence of flowpaths that a module will be instructed to execute. Without knowing precisely what functions module ABC performs, one cannot know what the primary logic path combinations are for this particular example. The flowpaths that make up a primary logic path combination demonstrate a relationship to one another. This is not to say that the remaining logic path combinations, referred to as *secondary logic path combinations*, can be ignored. However, many flowpath combinations in a real module will never occur. The secondary combinations that are possible stand a good chance of having been tested if both of these required conditions are satisfied:

- All code (therefore, all flowpaths) is executed.
- All primary logic path combinations are executed.

For almost any module, it is impossible to test every mathematical combination of flowpaths. This is because not all flowpaths bear a logical relationship to all other flowpaths. By definition, if there is no logic relationship between two or more flowpaths, they will never be executed together.

Unit Test Plan

Having defined unit testing, the next logical question to ask is: "What should a unit test plan talk about?"

A unit test plan should provide the following:

1. For each module, identify the set of flowpaths that will be tested to satisfy the two required conditions presented in the preceding section:
   - All code (therefore, all flowpaths) is executed.
   - All primary logic path combinations are executed.
2. State the procedures to be used to create the test environment that will allow all these flowpaths to be executed.
3. List the entry and exit criteria for starting and ending the unit test period. Include dependencies on people and equipment.
4. State the schedule to be followed for starting and ending the unit test for each module.

Item 1 has already been discussed in the preceding section. Notice that if you follow these recommendations you should find that all error conditions within a unit will also be tested.

Item 2, which states the procedures to be followed, primarily refers to the manner in which the unit testing on a given module will be conducted. Since other interface-related modules will probably *not* be available for the module's unit test, the environment on entry to the module (data areas, registers, and buffers) must be artificially generated to simulate the conditions necessary to test against. To prevent unpleasant surprises later, this temporary testing environment should be carefully and rigorously planned. Also, the expected output from the execution of each logic path should be identified so you can compare actual output against planned output. Care should also be taken to ensure that a comprehensive range of possible data values is tested. For example, if the valid range of values for an input field is 1 through 10, it is advisable to test at least the outside values of 0 and 11, as well as 1, 10, and some value in between. The point here is to include range-testing where appropriate.

Item 3 simply says to define what must be in place before the unit test can begin. One obvious example is to specify that each module's code has been completely written and compiled error-free. Another example is to have a completed unit test plan in place. Also list dependencies that must be satisfied in order to start unit testing, such as the necessary hardware or software that must be available. This hardware/software list should include any testing and debugging tools that are needed. Item 3 also requires that the exit criteria be defined. In other words, how does the programmer know when testing has been completed? Having specific exit criteria identified helps to keep one honest and better able to keep the testing progress in the proper perspective. One example of unit test exit criteria: All unit test flowpaths and combinations of flowpaths must have been run and have produced expected results, with any problems corrected in the source code and verified.

For Item 4, if a module is very large and its unit testing will spread across many days, then more than just starting and ending test dates are required. Milestone dates that fall between the start and end dates should be identified for the module. These milestones could signify when certain percentages of code and/or flowpaths have been tested. This tracking approach helps the module owner to compare actual progress with his or her plan. It also provides the project leadership with a method to routinely track the progress of unit testing.

The test plans should be written sufficiently in advance of the actual unit testing to ensure enough time to prepare for the unit test. If code reviews are performed on the module's code, this is also a good time to have the unit test plan for that module ready. It is strongly recommended to have at least one peer or the team leader review the unit test plan. This offers a good check and balance to ensure completeness and accuracy of the plan.

Function Test

Function testing is the testing of each product function through one or more modules, but more typically across two or more modules. This is the first time that modules are linked together and the interfaces across modules are verified. In fact, testing the interfaces across modules is a primary objective of function testing.

Another objective is to do as little "jury rigging" as possible. That is, you want to minimize the need to construct artificial testing environments. All modules of the product do not have to be available and linked together at the same time. However, it is strongly recommended that those modules related through functional dependence with one another be available at the time of testing for that function.

Figure 11.3 illustrates this point. The product shown is a text editor. The GET command can be used as an example of a function to be tested. Assume, for purposes of illustration, that every text editor command must first be *parsed* and *syntax checked* before it can be processed by its corresponding *command module* (in this case, the GET command). To test the GET command, the following modules must be available and linked to avoid creating an artificial test environment:

EDITOR, PARSE, SYNTAX, MESSAGES, GET, READ, ERRORS

Figure 11.4 is a matrix that shows the modules that are executed depending on the function being tested. This example lists seven functions: invalid command, three variations of the GET command, and three variations of the SAVE command. Take a closer look at the GET command. Since the other modules (such as SAVE and EDIT) are not necessary to test the GET <file> functions, they do not have to be linked with the needed modules. Notice that if only the error-free paths of the GET command are to be tested, then the modules MESSAGES and ERRORS would not be necessary. Figure 11.4 is grossly simplified to illustrate the basic concept of a "function versus module" test matrix. This matrix is a useful tool to ensure that all modules required to test a function have been identified and planned for accordingly. This example has assumed only one parameter (<file>) on the GET and SAVE commands. If you were applying this example to your modules, you would not only need to test every parameter of each command, but you would want to test the ranges for each parameter that allows a value to be specified. Although much of this range checking can be tested during unit testing, it is wise to include some range checking during the function test.

Function Test Plan

The function test plan is created by the developer of the code to be function tested. This plan should address the following items:

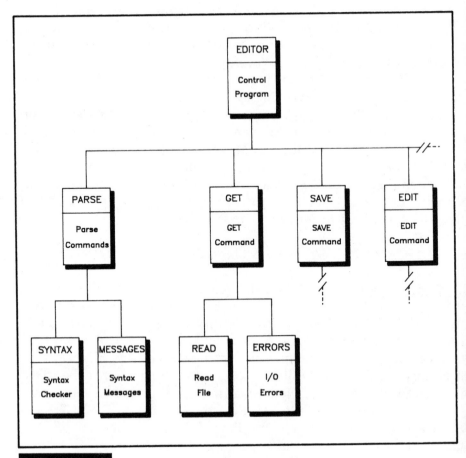

Figure 11.3. Module linkages for a text editor

1. Identify a "function test case" matrix of function versus test cases.
2. State the procedures to be used in creating an environment that will allow all functions to be executed.
3. List the entry and exit criteria for starting and ending the function test period. Include dependencies on people and equipment.
4. State the schedule to be followed for starting and ending each test identified in the function test matrix.
5. Define the problem-tracking process.

Figure 11.5 shows an example of a simplified "function test case" matrix that item 1 references. Item 1 requires that all the functions to be tested are listed, say, along the left margin of a matrix. The product specifications document should be used to identify *all* functions of the product (see Chapter 9). Listed along the top of the matrix are the *names* that identify the test cases to be written. An X is marked for each function that a given test case will test. Ideally, you want to avoid testing a given

FUNCTION TO TEST	MODULES								
	EDITOR	PARSE	SYNTAX	MESSAGES	GET	READ	ERRORS	SAVE	EDIT
INVALID CMD	X	X		X					
GET <FILE>									
NO ERRORS	X	X	X		X	X			
SYNTAX ERROR	X	X	X	X					
READ ERROR	X	X	X		X	X	X		
SAVE <FILE>									
NO ERRORS	X	X	X					X	
SYNTAX ERROR	X	X	X	X					
WRITE ERROR	X	X	X					X	

Figure 11.4. "Function versus module" test matrix

function with more than one test case. However, this situation might be unavoidable for some products since the testing of different functions can actually invoke common modules as part of the execution process. For example, Figure 11.5 shows that test cases TEST02 and TEST03 both test for a syntax error in the GET and SAVE commands. This would signify that the same syntax-checking function in the SYNTAX module would be invoked for both the GET and SAVE commands.

Figure 11.5 implies a matrix of 25 test cases. The actual number of test cases required is largely dependent on the amount of function that each test case has been designed to test. It is more productive, in the long run, to develop many simple test cases than to develop only a few complex test cases. Once this matrix is completed and approved, the corresponding test procedures can be written.

Now look again at Item 2 (of function test plan contents presented earlier). Item 2 addresses the procedures required to perform function

FUNCTION TO TEST	TEST CASES					
	Test01	Test02	Test03	Test04	···	Test25
Invalid cmd	X					
GET <file>						
No errors		X				
Syntax error		X	X			
Read error		X				
SAVE <file>						
No errors			X			
Syntax error		X	X			
Write error			X			

Figure 11.5. "Function test case" matrix

testing. Since a goal of function testing is to minimize the creation of artificial testing environments, little may be necessary in this regard. However, if some scaffolding (temporary code that will eventually be discarded) will be necessary, then it should be included as part of the plan.

As with unit testing, Item 3 defines what must be in place before the function test can begin. Unit testing should have already been completed on all modules to be included in a function test. Also, an approved function test plan should be in place. Unlike unit testing, the function test procedures, also called **test cases**, are probably not trivial. In fact, they could even require several weeks to prepare. These test procedures should also be complete and as bug-free as possible before function testing begins. Also, as with unit testing, the dependencies that must be in place should be listed in full. These dependencies may span the range of hardware, software, special tools, and people required to help run the test procedures. Do not overlook the exit criteria, which are especially important here since the next phase of testing—formal testing—will likely be performed by an independent test organization. Therefore, the function test exit criteria will be highly visible. One example of exit criteria: All function test procedures must have been run and all *major* problems corrected and verified in the source code. Another exit criterion might be that minor problems must be negotiated with the formal test group before the testers will accept the code into the formal test phase. The formal test group may require a *resolution plan*, which identifies all minor problems and committed dates by which each problem will be resolved.

The schedules (Item 4) should show when each function will be tested. In developing these schedules, one must factor in when various module groups will be available. For example, in illustration Figure 11.3, the MESSAGES and ERRORS modules can be among the last modules to be made available. Therefore, the function testing of the message and I/O error handling facilities may be performed later in the function testing period. Putting the schedules in place requires the developer to think through the way in which modules will be integrated. It also requires one to focus on the dependencies for modules that are owned by others. These dependencies obviously need to be negotiated and committed in advance if they are expected to happen according to schedule.

The problem-tracking process (Item 5) should define the process by which a discovered problem is logged, corrected, and then verified. There are several reasons why a clearly defined problem-tracking process must be in place to support the function test. Since function testing requires multiple modules to be tested together, whenever an interface-related problem is found there needs to be some orchestrated method for the module changes to be simultaneously made across all affected modules. The fact that the modules in question are often owned by more than one person magnifies the need to coordinate these changes.

Another need for a problem-tracking process is to provide a careful accounting of all problems found, both major and minor. It is this list of discovered problems that the formal test group will have a great interest in assessing. Negotiations to enter the formal test phase will rely on the disposition of the problems comprising this list. The list will also be valuable for the function test personnel to help them decide the most important problems to correct first. The problem-tracking process, of course, provides yet another benefit—it allows the project leadership to better follow the progress being made in the function test.

As with unit test plans, it is strongly recommended that the function test plan be reviewed by a peer or team leader. It is also useful for the formal test group to review the plan. Not only can the group members add value from a functional test coverage point of view, they also have a vested interest in receiving quality tested code when their own tests begin. The quality of the code they receive will obviously have an impact, one way or another, on their ability to meet their schedule commitments. Once again, it is easier and cheaper to find bugs earlier in the product development cycle rather than later.

Anticipating Quality's Weak Link

A decision to leave informal testing to the whim of each developer to manage as he or she chooses will usually be regretted later. And the problems that result are usually not intentional or the result of recklessness. The informal test period is simply often used as a scapegoat for maintaining schedules. Because tracking is usually very informal and has low visibility, the informal test period often appears to be unproductive and of little use. The project leadership is anxious to get the code into formal testing where visibility, control, and tracking progress are high.

Anytime you hear, "But we don't have time to write the unit and function test plans," beware. It is a sure sign of impending disaster. Programmers are human, too. (You heard it here!) When no formal plan exists for some activity, each programmer will implement a discipline that suits his or her skills, perceptions, or desires. Very experienced programmers may do a top-notch informal test. Inexperienced programmers will do what they naively believe to be a thorough and conscientious effort. All others may do whatever the schedule or their other activities allow. Informal testing should not be left to chance. If you gamble on the outcome, the odds favor failure.

Ensuring that unit test plans and function test plans are written, reviewed, and followed will significantly help to ensure that quality code enters formal testing. Whenever you have a plan, there then exists a vehicle to track against. The unit test and function test plans are a great tool for programmers to use in planning pacing activities. They are also great tools for the project leadership to use to track the progress being made during this informal test period. This tracking is very important if the full benefit of these plans is to be derived. Quality's weakest link in the product development cycle is the period defined as **informal test**. This chapter demonstrates how the "dark cloud" surrounding this activity can be removed. There is absolutely no reason why the informal test period cannot be planned, anticipated, and tracked in an open and objective fashion.

With unit and function test plans in place, programmers will also feel better about their contributions during this phase of the cycle. They will understand what, specifically, is expected of them and will have visible plans to follow to demonstrate their compliance and progress. If it sounds like an investment that results in a win-win situation, you are right!

12

Post-Project Review: Understanding the Past to Improve the Future

Optimism is eternal. We are forever hopeful that the next software project will proceed infinitely smoother than the last. We know that we wouldn't be so *dumb* as to make the same mistakes again. But history has shown that we will make many of the same mistakes that were made last time and the time before that and before that. We will do this knowing full well that *mistakes cost money, time,* and *resources*. These mistakes could cause the cancellation of a project or even our jobs. Yet, most projects continually replay many of the same problems.

History repeats itself in war, economics, love, and software development projects. This recurrence of history is not for lack of recorded information or good intentions. It is a lack of balance in *understanding* what went wrong on past projects, applying the *experience* of past campaigns, and exhibiting the *discipline* to apply this knowledge and experience.

This chapter can show you how to learn from your past mistakes. It also demonstrates how to apply this new knowledge to your current or next project.

Hang On! Here We Go Again!

As the lessons of past mistakes are ignored and the project continues daily to sink deeper into a quagmire, warning signals *can* be heard. These signals come from both the lack of clear progress within the project and from the project participants themselves. The following collection of short scenarios reveals sample problems that are historically common across software development projects. Although costly to the overall well-being of a project, these representative problems are among a multitude that have a penchant for recurring.

> The project is young, but already the frustrations of a new battlefront are surfacing. A team leader responsible for a small programming team feels a sense of helplessness and abandonment. When he committed his team to develop a 10,000 lines-of-code program, he also had stated requirements that his team be comprised of seven programmers with specific skills. Also he expressed the requirement that the team be fully staffed within two months of his commitment. Four months later, four semi-skilled members are on his team, and their product is six weeks behind schedule. He had feared this would happen, but gave way to his own optimism and his project leader's good intentions. The really distressing part is that his project leader still holds him and his team accountable for the original commitment. Because the team was short-handed, his project leader had personally dedicated most of the past four months in assisting the team with its design and coding. Somehow, the project leader has not gotten the message that his time would best serve the department if he was actively supporting the needs of the team and department rather than doing the work of a team member.

*   *   *

> The project is in the midst of its numerous design inspection meetings. These meetings are intended to discover defects early rather than during the coding and testing phases. Unfortunately, all the inspection meetings are not being conducted in the same manner. Some of the moderators have had prior training or coaching, while others appear to be totally new to the inspection process. Some moderators are failing an inspection that has revealed *one* major problem, while other moderators are passing inspections that uncover *several* major problems. Some moderators document their meeting's results and then track the open problems to ensure their timely closure, while other moderators are not documenting any results from their meetings. Some inspections have all the required inspectors and organizations represented, while other inspections have poor attendance and often overlook inviting certain key inspectors. Two participants who

have attended several different inspection meetings look at one another and agree, "We've seen this 'movie' before. I thought 'John' was supposed to fix this after the chaos from the last project. Oh well, at least we're getting paid for all this nonsense and rework." (Paid, yes. But for how long?)

* * *

It is a new project. The design phase has been completed and the coding phase is just starting. In another three months, lab hardware will be required to implement various test phases. There never seems to be enough hardware for everyone to use, even when multiple shifts of 6 to 7 days a week are employed. This situation existed on the past three projects. However, due to the griping and apparent awareness on the last project, the view is that this probably won't be as great a concern this time around. After all, it seems everyone had an opinion on how to correct the problem, and it seemed as though it would have been an easy problem to fix if only a little advanced planning would have been done.

Three months pass. Several groups converge on the available hardware almost simultaneously. It's *déjà vu*. Not only has the problem not been sufficiently corrected, there still appears to be no one who will take ownership to understand everyone's requirements and to put a mutually agreeable solution in place. "I can't believe this was allowed to happen again! This place is unreal! Won't we ever learn!" is heard—again.

* * *

Formal testing is finally ready to begin. The code has been delivered to the module build group and, after much pain, has been successfully linked together. But alas! The program won't run! Several developers swarm over the listings and the machines in an attempt to locate the problem. It is suspected to be in the piece of code that was delivered by a vendor. After two days of concentrated effort, it is discovered that the problem was not in vendored code, but within the in-house code. The problem is corrected and another attempt at running the program is made. It is unsuccessful. This time, after a full day of debugging, the problem is isolated to modules provided by a vendor. Complaints abound: "Why aren't people from the vendor here to debug their own code? Why aren't people here representing all the major departments?" It seems no one has put together a comprehensive plan to support the formal testing. Although the development groups have agreed to fix their problems, no one has agreed to spend the needed time isolating a suspected problem to the failing module. What if a programmer spends all day isolating the problem down to someone else's code? No one has time for that. Said more accurately, no one has *planned* time for that. No one has planned to allocate any time or staff in performing this essential role. Someone quips, "Will we ever learn? This same thing happened last time! You would think a different project leader would be wiser than the last one."

* * *

The project is two-thirds complete. The performance test group members are swinging into full gear. They immediately discover performance problems that, after careful analysis by the development team, will cause up to one month in schedule slippage to correct. The performance team is proud that it was able to discover these problems so quickly. The development group is furious that the performance people had not identified these problems earlier. "Why didn't those performance guys participate in our design and code inspection meetings months ago? They could have gotten all the insight they needed to conclude that these performance problems would have resulted. It would have been a whole lot easier and less costly to have discovered these problems back then," says a frustrated developer to another developer.

This opinion trickles into the performance department, whose response is, "We could have discovered these performance problems earlier if development would have invited us to all their inspection meetings. Also, why are we always the last to know when the function or design is changed? It seems the developers never learn!" In a developer's office down the hallway can be heard, "It seems those performance guys never learn!"

* * *

The publications work is already considerably behind the latest adjusted schedule. The first draft was nearly six weeks late. Even then, the magnitude and type of comments caused several chapters to go through major revisions. The next draft was a full two months late. The primary problem was that the product's functions continued to change drastically between drafts. Compounding the problem was the limited availability of programmers to review early chapters and to provide needed source material to the writers. Acknowledges a publications writer, "The programmers do this to us every time! I sometimes wonder how committed they are to putting out a quality product. Particularly an on-time quality product."

* * *

The product is nearing completion. The publications are almost finished. Suddenly, the quality assurance group realizes that the product manuals have too few examples. Unless more examples are added, it is viewed that the product will not be user friendly enough for the targeted audience. Someone comes up with the idea that the examples can be taken from some of the system test scenarios and test cases. Someone else chimes in, "That's a good idea! I wish we would have thought of that before." The idea originator responds, "It's not a new idea. On the last two projects I worked on, that was also a shortcoming in planning for the manuals."

＊　　＊　　＊

A request for a plan is made to the product packaging and distribution (P and D) department. A plan is needed that defines precisely how and when the new product will be readied for customer delivery. The product is currently in the early stages of its development. Legal and other concerns from within P and D delayed the last product's announcement and delivery. The product leader hopes to avoid these delays on this product. The P and D leader insists that this won't happen again. She only needs six months lead time, and there are ten months from today. However, she also states that her department is tied up on other matters, but will shortly begin to work on the request. The product leader, feeling his job of formalizing the request is complete, continues about his own business. Four months before the product is scheduled for delivery, someone realizes that P and D has not been included in weekly status meetings. Once again, P and D's activities are holding up the announcement and delivery. Someone comments wearily, "This is exactly what happened last time."

＊　　＊　　＊

As you read through the above scenarios, some might have struck very close to home. Perhaps you were reminded of similar or even additional examples from your own pool of experiences. The remainder of this chapter will present an effective method that you can follow to avoid repeating these types of mistakes. You can use this method to better learn from your own wealth of experiences and from the knowledge and experiences around you.

Project Review

> *Those who cannot remember the past are condemned to repeat it.*
> *George Santayana*
> *Spanish-born American philosopher, poet, humorist*

The objective of this chapter is to explain how to learn from past mistakes. Mistakes are things that happen accidentally. They are blunders that result from misunderstandings. They are things that are done through ignorance, inattention, failure to think. If you accept any of these definitions, then you might conclude that using "mistake" as a reason for repeating the same errors from project to project is a misuse of the word. Don't people *consciously* repeat the same problems? The first time a problem situation occurs, then the word "mistake" might apply. But successive recurrences of that same situation is hardly a mistake. It is called **neglect**.

> Neglect is the act of ignoring, disregarding, or failing to care for or give proper attention to something of notable importance. Said another way, neglect is the failure, either through oversight or desire, to fully utilize knowledge and experiences.

No one is infallible—we all make mistakes. So, this chapter addresses neglect, that is, making the same mistakes more than once. This involves conditions that are not only often preventable but can be downright nasty if not attended to early. These are conditions which, if left unchecked, can destroy a project and the spirit of its people.

The primary tool to counter neglect is the project review. The project review provides an opportunity to learn from past experiences. It is a sequence of activities that, when followed, will result in a conscious and planned attempt to prevent the next project from having to repeat the same neglects of its predecessors.

Project reviews have been called by many different names. Some of these names are *post-project review, post mortem, autopsy review, project analysis review, quality improvement review,* and *quality improvement team*. This last term is my favorite because of its positive statement and because the underlying objective is carried in the name:

> *Work as a team to improve the quality of the next process and the next product.*

A project review is scheduled to occur at the end of a project. (There are exceptions. See the final section, "Some Added Benefits.") Figure 12.1 shows the sequence of steps to follow to yield a successful project review. Each of these steps is explained in the sections that follow. However, a simple overview of a project review is presented here:

> A project review begins with the selection of people who represent all the major organizations within the project. These people then independently identify the elements that went right and those that went wrong. Then, each representative attends a group meeting to share his or her findings. The group then creates two lists: a *good list* of those things that went right, and a *problem list* of those things that went wrong. The items in both lists are

independently sorted in order of importance. A recommended solution is developed for each of the more important problems stated in the problem list. Then presentations are made to both the project leadership and the project members. At this time the project leaders declare their level of support to ensure that both the good list and the list of identified solutions are implemented in upcoming projects.

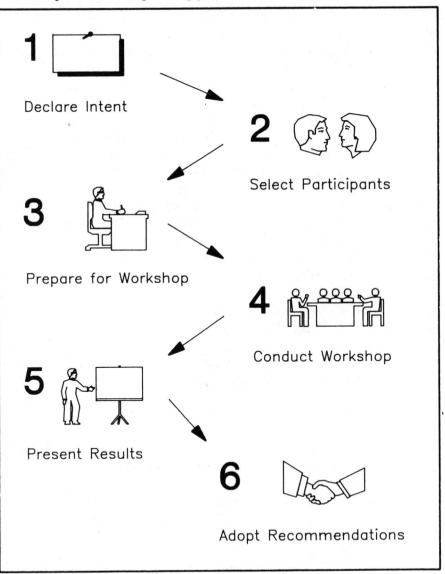

Figure 12.1. Steps in a successful project review

Step 1: Declare Intent

Early in a project, the project head should state his or her intention to have a project review at the completion of the project. This intention is best communicated verbally at an organizational meeting, then followed-up with a letter to all the project participants. The letter should state the goals of the project review. Everyone must understand that, not only do the project leaders want to do things the best way, but they are also receptive to having their decisions reviewed in retrospect. The clear goal is to learn from both the errors of the past as well as from those things that went right, and to apply these lessons to future projects. For maximum effect, the letter should include an attachment that describes the project review process. Included in this attachment should be the identification of a minimum set of organizations that will be expected to participate, leaving open the option that more may be added by the time the project is completed. The attachment should also identify the questions or topics to which each organization will be responding. (More on this in the upcoming section, "Step 3: Prepare for Workshop.") This will result in some organizations paying closer attention to these areas of their processes throughout the product development cycle.

If this is the first time this approach will be followed in your organization, then it will be met with mixed emotions. Most will view it with some skepticism, but everyone will hope it will come true. Take a risk and declare early your commitment to a project review. Make certain, however, that you follow up at the end of the project and make this project review happen. As a planning technique, add this event to the checklist of project activities that you track. There is much to gain from declaring these expectations early in the product development cycle.

Step 2: Select Participants

Once the project has been completed, it is then time to start the project review. The first act is to select the participants. At least one person should be selected from each major organization. Examples of major organizations are planning, development, test, publications, performance, usability, module build group, quality assurance, and any others that you feel are appropriate.

The people selected should have a strong knowledge of the processes that were used in the project. They should also be people who interfaced with groups outside of their own immediate areas. The best candidates are team leaders. The experiences that they originally brought to the project as well as their lead roles within the project make them the favored choices. The goal is to select people who will offer the breadth and depth of perception required for a comprehensive project review.

Managers, those project leaders in a position of evaluating the performance of people, should not participate on the review team. This is a time for the nonmanagers to use their hindsight to evaluate the process that they spent many months or even years developing. Nonmanagers are in the best position to offer both praise for the things that went well and criticism for those things that need improvement. Managers on the team can inhibit the candidness of the group and the free flow of ideas. The project leadership need not feel left out, though. The recommendations by the review team must have support and commitment from the project leadership before being implemented.

The chairperson should be chosen by the project leadership and can be anyone in the review team. However, the person leading the team should be someone who is well respected by the members of the team. The team leader should be someone who can lead as well as be a good listener and facilitate discussion among the members. If the development representative is qualified to lead the team, then this person is recommended as the first choice. Since development is often the largest organizational group and often the group with the greatest impact throughout the project, there is a special benefit to be gained if development takes the team leader role. This may influence development to feel a stronger ownership for the team's final recommendations.

The participation of each representative in the review team must be mandatory. All organizations must be heard and must feel that the final results have their commitment. If the project leadership is truly supportive, participation on this review team will be viewed as a positive form of recognition. People want to be heard and they also want to be members of a progressive organization.

Step 3: Prepare For Workshop

After workshop participants have been selected, the next step is to define the homework to be completed prior to the workshop meeting. Each participant is asked to respond to a set of topics. The responses should primarily relate to each respondent's mission in the project.

These topics can be generalized as shown in Figure 12.2. This way, each participant responds to the same general areas of interest. These subjects are somewhat broad and can be stated, if desired, more pointedly. For example, the topic "productivity" could be more finely addressed with these additional questions:

- What level of productivity was achieved for your tasks? How did it compare with what you expected?
- What could have changed to improve your productivity? How much would each change improve your productivity?

Another approach is to customize a subset of topics that would be unique for each organization. Figure 12.3 provides an example of customized topics that would be addressed by the component test group. This approach can ensure that very specific topics will be

```
    ■   Staffing

    ■   Mission objectives

    ■   Schedules

    ■   Processes that worked well

    ■   Processes that did not work well

    ■   Productivity

    ■   Tools

    ■   Quality

    ■   People communications within your shop

    ■   People communications from outside your shop

    ■   Support from other shops

    ■   Product development cycle improvements

    ■   Other problems and/or suggestions
```

Figure 12.2. General topics for each organization to address

addressed. These topics can also be refined to another layer of detail. As an example, the topic "problems discovered in product code" could be supported by the following questions:

- How many problems were reported found per every 1000 lines-of-code? Of these problems reported, how many were found to be true defects? Testers' errors? Not reproducible?
- How did the actual number of problems reported compare to what you expected?
- What was the severity of the problems found? What was the average response time (in days) required to fix each category of severity assigned? Was the response time within the expected range? Was this acceptable?

Either of these approaches, generalized or customized, can be effective. Whichever method is used, do not overlook asking each organization to identify those things that went particularly well. A single focus on bad news can be depressing. In fact, in every organization, there are

- Availability of needed product information
- Test plan
- Functional coverage of test procedures
- Developing the test procedures
- Test procedure inspections
- Running the test procedures
- Automation of test procedures
- Problems discovered in product code
- Self-documentation of test procedures
- Tools required and/or used
- Hardware availability

Figure 12.3. Topics for component test organization

always activities that "went right." Make sure these positive areas are consciously carried forward to future projects.

Step 4: Conduct Workshop

The duration of the workshop meeting can be expected to run anywhere from one-half day to two days, depending on the size of the project and the number of workshop participants. One day might be a reasonable time for most projects. Every attempt should be made to prevent the meeting or anyone in the meeting from being disrupted by outside business. The meeting participants should be free to concentrate their attention on this valuable exercise.

The workshop is a working meeting. The first portion of the workshop should be allocated to listening to each representative present his or her responses to the topics that were distributed earlier. It is helpful if the order of presenters matches the general sequence of phases in the product development cycle. For example, the planning representative would present before the development representative, who would present before the test group representative, and so on. It is also beneficial to set a time limit for each representative—somewhere in the range of 10 to 30 minutes is sufficient for most workshops, but you may choose a more specific range that best suits your project. For example, allow 10 minutes for representatives of small organizations and 30 minutes for representatives of larger organizations.

Questions should be encouraged from the participating audience. It is vitally important that the attendees share their views among one another. You should expect to have differing views surface on many topics. This is healthy for the meeting atmosphere and provides a great opportunity for each group to understand the views of other groups. This insight and growing camaraderie is a wonderful side benefit of the meeting. Criticism of the process should be encouraged. However, criticism of people should be prohibited, regardless of whether it is directed at people in the meeting or people elsewhere in the organization.

Once all responses have been presented and shared within the workshop team, the next step is to create two lists. The first list is of the things that "went right." These are things that you want to carry forward to future projects. It is helpful to order the list, with the most beneficial items placed at the top. These top items will later be shown to the project leadership and project members.

The second list is of the things that "went wrong" with the project (not defects in the product). This problem list must be sorted in priority order, with the most important problems listed first. What you are really interested in is focusing on the top 5 to 10 problems. Problems that do not make the significant list should not be ignored. Members of each organization that has these problems should independently resolve them to their own satisfaction.

Once the more important problems have been identified, the next task is to develop proposals—to be submitted to the project leadership—that address these problems. You can break into smaller teams or work collectively on these problem solutions. In either approach, the entire team should reach a consensus on each recommendation before it is presented to the project leadership. These recommendations should address or answer the following questions:

- Who has the ownership to ensure closure of each problem?
- What constitutes closure of each problem?
- How will the solution be tracked? What should be the frequency of tracking?

Note that it is unlikely that all these problems can be resolved in a single meeting. Some problems might require considerable research with data and skills not readily available at the workshop. In these cases, it is acceptable not to have a final solution. Instead, a plan can be drawn up recommending that a group be assembled to further study a given problem, with the goal of proposing one or more solutions. However, remember to ensure that an owner is assigned to work on each unresolved problem. This will better ensure that each problem is successfully addressed by focusing the responsibility on a single, accountable individual. Also, ensure that target dates are set so that progress can be tracked properly.

At this point, it is time to get the final charts together that will be reviewed by the project leadership. These charts will also become part of the Project Review Report for follow-up and historical purposes. It is suggested that a good news chart be presented first. This chart lists the things that "went right"—to the extent that these items are noteworthy.

The remaining set of charts lists the problems that the review team felt were significant enough to receive special visibility. Each problem should be followed by a recommended solution or a plan that will yield a solution. Where appropriate, you may want to provide the project leadership with more than one solution from which to choose. Not only does this give the project leaders flexibility, it also gives them a greater feeling of ownership of and commitment on the final solutions *they* choose.

Step 5: Present Results

Two meetings are recommended at this point. The first meeting is used to present the workshop's results to the project leadership. The second meeting is called to present the final results from the project leadership meeting to all the other project members.

The attendance at the project leaders' meeting should be, at a very minimum, the first and second levels of the project leadership. These levels are typically those defined in Figure 6.1 as leaders of teams (first level) and of departments (second level). (On some projects, the leaders might all be defined as one "notch" higher: The first level leader is defined as the department leader, and his or her leader is the second level leader.)

The first level typically encompasses project leaders who are responsible for addressing the problems and their recommended solutions. The next level of project leaders is in attendance since they will need to know what resources are being committed and what the impact of these commitments will be. These leaders will also need to provide support to their subordinate project leaders as well as to measure the commitment of their project leaders in following through on plans.

You will also find it beneficial to include levels of project leadership higher than the second level. It is helpful for higher levels of project leadership to understand, first-hand, the problems experienced within projects. Often, their support will be required to address some project problems. Also, their insistence on tracking the action taken by the first and second levels of project leadership can have a profound, positive effect on resolving the problems.

The goal of the project leadership meeting should be for the project review team to get the full support of project leadership to implement recommendations. This means an attempt should be made to get acceptance of the recommendations. Note, however, that some solutions might not lend themselves to quick decisions and might instead require further analysis by the project leadership.

For the project members' meeting, the project leaders have an opportunity to express their commitment to the quality of the product, the processes, and the overall work environment. This event can show that the project leadership is listening and responding with positive action.

The recommended presenter for the project leadership meeting is the workshop chairperson. The presenter at the project member meeting can be either a project leader or the chairperson, depending on organizational structure and preferences.

Step 6: Adopt Recommendations

The art of life lies in a constant readjustment to our surroundings.
Kakuzo Okakura
Japanese art critic

The benefit of the project review does not end after the results have been presented to the project leadership and to the project members. Quite the contrary. The real benefit of the project review is to learn from past errors and from those things that went according to plan, and to apply these lessons to future projects. The first order of business is to complete the Project Review Report. This report, at a minimum, should contain the charts that were presented to the project leadership. The final recommendations that were adopted by the project leadership also should be included. Optionally, include the original charts that each representative presented at the workshop.

After the report is completed, a copy should be sent to each project leader. In turn, each project leader should make the copy available to his or her employees. Another option is for the project head to distribute the report to all project personnel—both project leaders and project members. When new projects are started, a checklist or some list of activities should be in place to measure the project against. An activity should be added to this list that requires past Project Review Reports to be reviewed for possible action to be taken on the new project. This must be tracked as a required activity before the new project's schedules and activities can be approved. Not only does this technique make it difficult to forget or overlook the results of a past project review, it is also insurance when major project players from past projects have left the organization. In this way, the valuable experiences of the past can continue to influence the future.

The project leadership is responsible for acting on these committed recommendations. If checks and balances, additional to those just described, are required in any particular organization, this is the time to put those checks in place. All eyes will be on the project leadership to see whether the promised support occurs. This is not a time for rhetoric, but a time for support and action.

Some Added Benefits

Previous sections in this chapter treat project reviews as events that happen at the end of a project. Earlier sections also indicate that project reviews are implemented so that subsequent projects can avoid repeating the same errors. However, all the steps that have been defined for a successful project review can just as effectively apply to two other interesting and beneficial activities: **phase reviews** and **product certification reviews**.

Phase Reviews

For a project with a duration of 6 to 12 months, placing a project review at the end of the project has been shown to be constructive and productive. However, for projects that have a duration of more than one year, waiting until the end of the project to implement an overall review can result in the loss of valuable data, or at least will result in less objective and therefore less meaningful data. Not only do project members forget some useful pieces of information, the movement of project members to new assignments has a much higher chance of occurring. So, what do you do in a case where a project exceeds one year in duration? You conduct phase reviews along the way.

The phases in a product development cycle can be defined in a number of ways. Figure 5.2 suggests these typical phases:

- Product definition
- Product design
- Code
- Informal test
- Formal test

However, some projects may define phases as specific activities. Again, Figure 5.2 lists activities that could also be treated as phases. For example, the part of the product development cycle that was referred to as "formal test" could be viewed, instead, as six phases:

- Component test plan
- Component test
- System test plan
- System test
- Regression test plan
- Regression test

Once you have defined the key activities or phases that you view represent significant milestones, then planning for phase reviews can occur. The steps to follow in a phase review are identical to the steps described earlier for a product review, with two exceptions: the scope of the review and the impact on the next set of activities.

The scope of a phase review is, of course, much narrower than it is for project reviews. Attention is focused on a single activity or a small set of activities. Also, there may be fewer organizations participating, depending on their involvement in the activities being reviewed. Recommendations made by the phase review team will not only address ways to avoid making similar errors on the next project, but will also address recovery plans that can be applied to upcoming activities. These recovery plans would address shortcomings in the quality of the product at this point in the product development cycle (such as, "The code has more defects than expected") and would describe ways to compensate for those deficiencies.

Product Certification Reviews

A product certification review is conducted immediately before a product is to be approved for announcement, and again before the product is to be approved for delivery to the first customer. The steps to follow in a product certification review are also identical to the steps discussed earlier for project reviews, with one major difference: The analysis of the product certification review is primarily directed toward the product rather than the process. More specifically, the focus of the review is on determining the readiness of the product. This analysis culminates with a "Go" or "No go" signal for announcing or delivering the product. The final decision is made by the project leadership, but the recommendation is presented by the product certification review team.

Summary

I hope you will agree that the concept of reviews, whether they are project, phase, or product certification, has great value to an organization and ultimately to the acceptance of the product by its customer(s). Organizations that demonstrate the foresight to plan for these reviews are also those organizations that are likely to report fewer problems during the actual reviews.

Neglect always carries a high cost. By understanding past projects—that is, what went right and what went wrong—an organization can realize big savings. Applying this knowledge to future projects can mean taking greater profits to the bank.

Bibliography

This bibliography provides additional reading material for many of the subjects presented in this book. Bracketed numbers at the end of each entry correspond with the chapter numbers of *Managing Software Development Projects: Formula for Success* in which material applies.

Aron, J. D., "The Program Development Process: The Programming Team, Part II," Addison-Wesley Publishing Company, Inc., 1983 [4,5,6,7,9,11]

Bennett, John, Donald Case, Jon Sandelin, and Michael Smith, "Visual Display Terminals: Usability Issues and Health Concerns," Prentice-Hall, Inc., 1984 [10]

Blanchard, Ken, Spencer Johnson, "The One Minute Manager," William Morrow and Company, Inc., 1982 [2,3]

Branscomb, L. M., J. C. Thomas, "Ease of Use: A System Design Challenge," IBM Systems Journal, Volume 23, No. 3, pp. 224-235, 1985 [10]

Brooks Jr., Frederick P., "The Mythical Man-Month: Essays on Software Engineering," Addison-Wesley Publishing Company, Inc., 1975 [4,5,6,8,9]

Burrill, Claude W., Leon W. Ellsworth, "Modern Project Management: Foundation for Quality and Productivity," Burrill-Ellsworth Associates, Inc., 1980 [4,5,6]

Crosby, Philip B., "Quality Is Free: The Art of Making Quality Certain," McGraw-Hill Book Company, 1979 [5]

Crosby, Philip B., "Quality Without Tears: The Art of Hassle-Free Management," McGraw-Hill Book Company, 1984 [5]

DeMarco, Tom, "Controlling Software Projects: Management, Measurement, and Estimation," Yourdon Press, 1982 [4,5,9]

DeMille, Richard A., W. Michael McCracken, R. J. Martin, John F. Passafiume, "Software Testing and Evaluation," The Benjamin/Cummings Publishing Company, Inc., 1987 [11]

Deming, W. Edwards, "Quality, Productivity, and Competitive Position," Massachusetts Institute of Technology, Center for Advanced Engineering Study, 1982 [2,5]

Dyer, Wayne W., "The Sky's the Limit," Pocket Books, Division of Simon W. Schuster, Inc., 1980 [2]

Dyer, Wayne W., "Your Erroneous Zones," Funk and Wagnalls, 1976 [2]

Fagan, M. E., "Design and Code Inspections to Reduce Errors in Program Development," IBM Systems Journal, Vol. 15, No. 3, pp. 182-211, 1976 [5]

Gaffney Jr., John E., "On Predicting Software Related Performance of Large-Scale Systems," Presented at CMG XV, December 1984, San Francisco [5]

Gardiner, Margaret M. (ed.), Bruce Christie (ed.), "Applying Cognitive Psychology to User Interface Design," John Wiley and Sons, Inc., 1987 [10]

Gilbreath, Robert D., "Winning at Project Management: What Works, What Fails and Why," John Wiley and Sons, Inc., 1986 [2,4,6]

Gitlow, Howard S., Shelley J. Gitlow, "The Deming Guide to Quality and Competitive Position," Prentice-Hall, Inc., 1987 [2]

Guaspari, John, "I Know It When I See It: A Modern Fable About Quality," AMACOM, 1985 [5]

Harrison, F. L., "Advanced Project Management," Gower Publishing Company Limited, 1985 (Second Edition) [4,6]

Humphrey, Watts S., "Managing for Innovation: Leading Technical people," Prentice-Hall, Inc., 1987 [2,3]

Humphrey, Watts S., "Managing the Software Process," Addison-Wesley Publishing Company, Inc., 1989 [2,4,5,6,11,12]

Jones, C. J., "A Process-Integrated Approach to Defect Prevention," IBM Systems Journal, Volume 24, No. 2, pp. 150-167, 1985 [4,5,11]

Levine, Harvey A., "Project Management Using Microcomputers," Osborne McGraw-Hill, 1986 [4,6]

Miller, William C., "The Creative Edge: Fostering Innovation Where You Work," Addison-Wesley Publishing Company, Inc., 1987 [2,3]

Moder, Joseph J.,Cecil R. Phillips, Edward W. Davis, "Project Management with CPM, PERT, and Precedence Diagramming," Van Nostrand Reinhold, 1983 [4,6]

Myers, Glenford J., "The Art of Software Testing," John Wiley and Sons, Inc., 1979 [11]

Myers, Glenford J., "Software Reliability: Principles and Practices," John Wiley and Sons, Inc., 1976 [8,9,11]

Norman, Donald A., "The Psychology of Everyday Things," Basic Books, Inc., 1988 [10]

Norman, Donald A. (ed.), Stephen W. Draper (ed.), "User Centered System Design: New Perspectives on Human-Computer Interaction," Lawrence Erlbaum Associates, Inc., 1986 [10]

Page-Jones, Meilir, "Practical Project Management," Dorset House Publishing Company, Inc., 1985 [2,4,6]

Peters, Thomas J., Robert H. Waterman Jr., "In Search of Excellence: Lessons From America's Best-Run Companies," Harper & Row, Publishers, Inc., 1982 [2,3]

Peters, Tom, Nancy Austin, "A Passion for Excellence: The Leadership Difference," Random House, Inc., 1985 [2,3]

Peters, Tom, "Thriving on Chaos: Handbook for a Management Revolution," Alfred A. Knopf, Inc., 1987 [2,3]

Radice, R. A., N. K. Roth, A. C. O'Hara Jr., W. A. Ciarfella, "A Programming Process Architecture," IBM Systems Journal, Volume 24, No. 2, pp. 79-90, 1985 [4]

Radice, R. A., J. T. Harding, P. E. Munnis, R. W. Phillips, "A Programming Process Study," IBM Systems Journal, Volume 24, No. 2, pp. 91-101, 1985 [12]

Radice, Ronald A., Richard W. Phillips, "Software Engineering: An Industrial Approach, Volume 1," Prentice-Hall, 1988 [4,5,10]

Roman, Daniel D., "Managing Projects: A Systems Approach," Elsevier Science Publishing Co., Inc., 1986 [2,4,6]

Ross, Joel E., William C. Ross, "Japanese Quality Circles and Productivity," Reston Publishing, 1982 [2,5]

Shneiderman, Ben, "Designing the User Interface: Strategies for Effective Human-Computer Interaction," Addison-Wesley Publishing Company, 1987 [10]

Simpson, W. Dwain, "New Techniques in Software Project Management," John Wiley and Sons, Inc., 1987 [4,12]

Spencer, Richard H., "Computer Usability Testing and Evaluation," Prentice-Hall, Inc., 1985 [10]

Spencer, Richard H., "Planning, Implementation, and Control in Product Test and Assurance," Prentice-Hall, Inc., 1983 [4,8,9,10,11]

Thayer, Richard H. (ed.), "Tutorial: Software Engineering Project Management," Computer Society Press of the IEEE, 1988 [2,4,5,6,8,9,11]

"Thirty Years of Management Briefings, 1958 to 1988," published by IBM Corporate Communications, 1988, Mechanicsburg order number: ZZ04-1201 [2,3]

Walton, Mary, "The Deming Management Method," Dodd, Mead, 1986 [2,5]

Watson Jr., Thomas J., "A Business and Its Beliefs, The Ideas that Helped Build IBM," McGraw-Hill Book Company, Inc., 1963 [2,3]

Westney, Richard E., "Managing the Engineering and Construction of Small Projects," Marcel Dekker, 1985 [4,5,6]

Glossary

NOTE: Highlighted terms within a definition are also defined within this glossary.

activity. A defined portion of work within a **project** that typically has a designated owner, **entry requirements, implementation requirements, exit requirements**, duration, and schedules. Examples: developing the **product specifications document**, creating the **high-level design, coding**, and performing the **system test.**

artificial test environment. *See* **scaffolding.**

bottom-up schedule. A schedule that has been developed with participation from the actual owners of the **activities** that make up the total schedule. Data collected from each activity owner includes the activity duration and the dependencies on other people, resources, or activities.

buffer. A designated period that is built into a schedule to serve as extra time, or a contingency, to help absorb delays that might unexpectedly occur.

burnout. A condition experienced by a person that typically results from working excessive hours across many days and taking an insufficient amount of time away from the workplace for rest and relaxation. Burnout results in a person making more mistakes, being less productive, and frequently being more irritable to coworkers.

CASE. Computer-Aided Software Engineering is the automation of well-defined methodologies that are used in the development and maintenance of software **products.** These methodologies apply to nearly every **process** or **activity** of a **product development cycle,** examples of which include **project** planning and tracking, product designing, **coding,** and testing.

change bars. A notation made in the margins of an updated document to highlight where changes have been made. These notations allow users of a document to more quickly locate the most recent changes to the document.

change control process. A defined **process** to be followed when a change to a controlled document or procedure is proposed. A typical use is to control changes proposed to **product objectives** or **product specifications** once these documents have been approved.

coding. The act of writing instructions that are immediately computer recognizable, or can be assembled or compiled to form computer-recognizable instructions. Within a **product development cycle,** this **activity** follows the **low-level design** activity and precedes the **unit testing** and **function testing** activities.

component. A major design piece of a **product.** It is the collection of components that comprises the **programming** portion of a product. A component is usually comprised of one or more **modules.**

component test. The first independent test of a **product,** whereby the **components** are tested together. This test typically includes the testing of all the product's **externals.**

content plan. *See* **publications specifications.**

critical path. The collection of work **activities** in a **product development cycle** that are neck-to-neck with one another and define the longest duration for a **project.**

defect. A deviation from the requirements of a **product** or **process.**

deliver product. The distribution of the final, **packaged product** to a customer.

department. A group of people typically comprised of two or more **teams,** having a distinct mission and headed by a **manager.**

discipline. The act of encouraging a desired pattern of behavior.

document review cycle. *See* **project document review cycle.**

drift. A condition that applies to a **project** and its participants when the project's resources are not properly focused on solving the most important problems first. Drift can have a serious negative effect on a project by increasing rework, decreasing **productivity,** lengthening schedules, weakening morale, and reducing **quality.**

driver. In a **product development cycle,** a collection of **modules** that are linked together to make a workable **product** that can be tested and evaluated.

ease of use. A basic **function** of a product that simplifies operation of the product for users and aids users in understanding other product functions. This user-friendly condition is typically attributed to the ease with which users can both learn and become productive with a product.

entry requirements. Resources, actions, or **activities** that are required to have been started, completed, or be in place before a designated activity can begin.

escalate. The act of calling upon higher levels of **project leadership** to resolve an **issue**. When two parties cannot agree on the solution to an issue, and an earnest attempt to negotiate a resolution has occurred, then an escalation is pursued to resolve the issue.

exit requirements. Resources, actions, or **activities** that are required to have been started, completed, or be in place before a designated activity can be completed.

externals. The portions of a **product** that are directly visible and assessable to the product's user. Externals are documented in **product specifications**.

formal test. The testing performed on a **product** that occurs in a controlled environment and is best performed by programmers who have not developed the **code** to be tested.

function. An action that a **product** is capable of performing. For example, actions for a word processor might be: define margins, define page length, set tabs, change font for all section headings, search for words and phrases, and automatic document save.

function test. The testing of each **product function** across one or more **modules**. Some amount of **scaffolding** is typically required to perform this test.

high-level design. The level of design required to understand how the **components** of a **product** will technically work with one another and with the surrounding hardware and software environment in which the components must operate. This design identifies the components that make up the product, defines the **functional** mission for each component, and defines the interface across these components and externally to the operating environment. (In some development shops, high-level design is called *architecture*.)

hit list. An up-to-date list of the most important problems to be solved within a **project**.

implementation requirements. **Process**-oriented requirements that define how a designated **activity** will be implemented.

informal test. The testing performed on a **product** that is typically conducted in a loosely controlled environment and is performed by the programmers who developed the **code** to be tested. Both the **unit test** and **function test** are considered informal test activities. Some amount of **scaffolding** is typically required during the informal test period.

inspection. A group of people, typically peers, who meet with the goal of examining an **activity** to identify and remove **defects** and problems.

low-level design. This term represents two levels of design: The first level is the design required to understand how the **modules** within each **component** will technically work with one another. This design identifies the modules that make up each component, the **functional** mission of each module, and the interface across these modules. (In some development shops, this level of design is called *high-level design*, not to be confused with the use of this term in this book.) The second level of design is required to define the design within each of the many modules that may comprise each component. This design level identifies each programming decision path within each module and is the lowest level of design prior to **coding.**

management. A collection of **managers**, from across one or more **projects**, who are viewed as responsible for the efficiency of the work environment and for the morale of the people involved.

manager. A person responsible and accountable for both employees and one or more work **activities.** This person is usually the head of a **department.**

milestone. An important event, accomplishment or turning point.

moderator. A person leading and controlling an **inspection.** This person is also responsible for ensuring that all problems discovered at an inspection are properly recorded and tracked to their satisfactory resolution.

module. Code that represents part of a function, a single function, or more than one function. A module is code that can be independently compiled. One or more modules usually makes up a **component.**

objectives. *See* **product objectives.**

observer. *See* **test observer.**

organization. A group of people, divided into two or more **departments**, who typically share a common mission (such as everyone working on the same **product release**) or a common skill group (such as all **publications** writers or programmer/testers).

packaging. Collecting the pieces of a **product** together (e.g., code and **publications**) for **delivery** to a customer.

phase. A defined portion of a **product development cycle** (i.e., **product definition, product design, coding, informal test,** and so on). The portions defined as phases are arbitrary and are usually determined by the group that plans the **project.** Also, a subset of **activities** that make up a major activity. For example, a **project document review cycle** is comprised of five phases: preparation, review, update, approval, and information.

phase review. The review of a completed portion of a **product development cycle** (e.g., **product design, coding, informal test,** and so on) by a selected group of people charged with independently identifying areas that did and did not go according to plan. Objectives are to learn from the past to prevent similar errors on the next **project** and to develop recovery plans that can be applied to upcoming, related **activities** of the current project.

process. The manner in which a **software development project,** or any of its many integral parts, is planned, developed, or tracked. For example, the method of logging a problem, and tracking that problem to a satisfactory closure, is defined as a process.

product. A **software package,** consisting of **code** and **publications,** that is eventually **delivered** to a customer. In a more global sense, the definition of *product* also includes the product support materials that are related to such **activities** as marketing and maintenance.

product certification review. The review of a **product** by a selected group of people charged with independently assessing the product's readiness to be announced or **delivered.**

product definition. A phase of the **product development cycle** that focuses on what the **product** will be. The completion of the **product objectives** and the **product specifications** are the major **milestones** for this phase.

product design. A **phase** of the **product development cycle** that focuses on how the **product** will be designed. Completion of the **high-level design** and the **low-level design** are the major **milestones** for this phase.

product delivery. *See* **deliver product.**

product development cycle. A sequence of **activities** that is followed in developing a **product.** A product development cycle covers a wide range of activities that typically include creating the **product objectives** and the **product specifications,** designing, **coding,** testing and **packaging** the final product for **delivery** to customers.

product function. *See* **function.**

productivity. A measure of accomplished work over a designated period of time (for instance, lines of code per person-month).

product objectives. A document that defines the requirements and operational need that must be satisfied for a **product.** This document also provides direction for **functional** and design trade-offs that may be necessary throughout the **product development cycle.**

product specifications. A document that describes, in detail, precisely what the user will receive and use when the completed **product** is made available. Also, every **function,** command, screen, prompt, and so on is documented here so that all participants involved in the **product development cycle** know the product they are to build, test, document, and support.

program. The **code** portion of a **product** or **test case** or a collection of **components** linked together. *See also* **module.**

project. The combined resources (i.e., people, machines, materials), **processes** and **activities** that are dedicated to building and **delivering a product.** Also, a group of people, typically comprised of two or more **organizations,** working on the same product.

project document. A document that is generated within a **project** for use by that project (e.g., **product objectives, product specifications, system test** plan). Also, a document that is created outside the project but is adopted for project use (e.g., programming standards document).

project document review cycle. The **phases** that a **project document** typically passes through on its journey to being approved. The phases are preparation, review, update, approval, and information.

project head. The person responsible for an entire **project;** the top **project leader** within a project.

project leader. A person responsible for one or more work **activities** who provides direction to the employees assigned to these work activities. This term is sometimes used synonymously with the term **manager.**

project leadership. A collection of **project leaders** and **managers** from across a **project** who are viewed as responsible for the efficiency of the work environment and for the morale of the people.

project review. The review of a completed **project** by a selected group of people charged with independently identifying those activities that did and did not go according to plan. The objective is to learn from the past so that future projects can benefit from the lessons of past projects.

project schedule model. A method used to help understand the relationships between a **project's activities** and the ways these relationships impact the duration of the total project.

prototype. An early-running model of a **product** whose primary purpose is usually to experiment with, demonstrate, or prove the feasibility of a concept.

publications. The manuals or books, also called user manuals or user publications, that are included in the **delivery** of the **product** to the customer. Also, the manuals or books that are created to support the maintenance of the delivered product.

publications drafts. Preliminary copies of the **publications** that are in the process of being reviewed and updated.

publications specifications. A document that describes the content and layout of each of the **publications**. Also called **content plan**.

quality. Conformance to requirements. Once the **product** and **process** requirements have been defined, the quality can be measured for compliance.

quality assurance group. People assigned to perform an "outside check-and-balance" role of ensuring that a **product** is being developed according to an acceptable **process**.

quality improvement team. A group of people who meet to solve one or more problems.

quality plan. A document that can be used to define, track, and measure both **product** and **process quality** goals throughout the **product development cycle**.

regression test. The final test for a **product**. This test is comprised of a selected set of **component test** cases and **system test** cases that is run as a final verification that the product **code** is operating as intended. Also, a verification test that is run at various points throughout the development of the code and throughout testing. This test typically verifies that the **function** that used to work still does.

release. A fully functioning **product** to be distributed to a customer.

risk list. A list containing the more significant risk areas of a **project**.

scaffolding. Temporary **code** that has been developed to interface with one or more **modules**. This temporary code allows modules to be independently tested while waiting for the permanent interfacing modules to be developed and readied for use. This term is often used synonymously with the term **artificial test environment**.

software development cycle. *See* **product development cycle**.

specifications. *See* **product specifications**.

system test. A test of a **product** in a total systems environment with other software and hardware product combinations.

task. *See* **usability task**.

team. A group of typically 2 to 10 people that has a specific **functional** mission.

test cases. Programs and procedures that are written to test specific elements of a **product**. Examples: Installation process, **product functions**, messages, and examples defined in the product **publications**.

test observer. A person who watches, or observes, a **test subject** and records that subject's actions.

test plan. A document that describes the who, what, when, where and how for a designated test. Test plans are completed before the corresponding test is conducted to allow for the satisfactory preparation of the test. Examples: **function test** plan, **usability test** plan, **component test** plan, and **system test** plan.

test subject. A person who helps to test a **product** as it is being developed. This person is expected to use the product in ways that are similar to customers of the finished product.

thrashing zone. A period of time in a **product development cycle** when a person is so deeply entangled in daily problems that his or her biases, emotions, and commitments can interfere with making optimum decisions.

top-down schedule. A schedule, usually preliminary, that has been developed by a single person or a small group of people. The development of the schedule has little or no participation from the actual owners of the **activities** that make up the total schedule.

unit test. The isolated testing of each flowpath of **code** within each **module**. Some amount of **scaffolding** is typically required to perform this test.

usability. *See* **ease of use.**

usability task. An activity, typically comprised of a simple set of actions, that a user might perform with a **product**. These tasks are identified and then their **ease of use** is tested as the product is being developed. For example, tasks for a word processor product might include: installing the product, creating a new document, and printing a document. Problems discovered are then corrected prior to the **delivery** of the product.

usability test. A test to evaluate the **ease of use** of a portion or all of a **product**.

user interface. The **functions** of a **product** that allow a user to interact with that product; also called *man-machine interface*. Examples: operator commands, user screens, and messages.

vacation factor. A useful planning tool that encourages **project** personnel to plan some, or all, of their vacation during the least busy periods of a project.

variable productivity potential. The flexibility a person has to vary his or her **productivity** to better match the needs of the task at hand.

walkthrough. A group of people who meet to verify the correctness and acceptability of a **product's user interface**. The people in the group include the product developers and test subjects. Since running **code** and product **publications drafts** are not yet available, the user interface is examined by "walking through" the available user interface documentation. This documentation typically includes the **product specifications.**

work activity. *See* **activity.**

Index